W9-BQS-022

Women of the Forest

Columbia Classics in Anthropology

Columbia Classics in Anthropology

This series celebrates the longstanding tradition of influential works in anthropology from Columbia University Press.

Women

∧∧∧∧∧∧∧∧∧∧∧∧∧∧∧∧∧∧ of the
Forest

Thirtieth Anniversary Edition

*Yolanda Murphy
and Robert F. Murphy*

With a new foreword
edited by R. Brian Ferguson

Columbia University Press
New York

Columbia University Press
Publishers Since 1893
New York   Chichester, West Sussex
Second edition © 1985 Columbia University Press
Foreword to the thirtieth anniversary edition copyright
© 2004 Columbia University Press
All rights reserved

Library of Congress Cataloging-in-Publication Data
Murphy, Yolanda.
    Women of the forest / Yolanda Murphy and Robert F. Murphy ; with a new foreword
edited by R. Brian Ferguson.—30th anniversary ed.
        p. cm.—(Columbia classics in anthropology)
    Includes bibliographical references and index.
    ISBN 0–231–13232–8 (cloth : alk. paper)—ISBN 0–231–13233–6 (paper : alk. paper)
    1. Munduruku women. 2. Munduruku Indians—Social life and customs. I. Murphy,
Robert Francis, 1924– II. Title. III. Series.

F2520.1.M8M83 2004
305.8′0049838—dc22

                                                                    2004051849

Columbia University Press books are printed on
permanent and durable acid-free paper.

Printed in the United States of America

p   10 9 8 7 6 5 4 3 2 1
c   10 9 8 7 6 5 4 3 2 1

FOR PAMELA
AND ROBERT

*who will find
a portion of
their parents'
lives woven
into these pages*

Contents

Contributors to the Foreword

Edited by R. Brian Ferguson

R. Brian Ferguson, Department of Sociology and Anthropology, Rutgers University—Newark

William Balée, Department of Anthropology, Tulane University

Janet M. Chernela, Department of Anthropology and Latin American Studies Center, University of Maryland

Judith Shapiro, president, and Department of Anthropology, Barnard College

Orna Johnson, Department of Anthropology, UCLA

Thomas A. Gregor, Department of Anthropology, Vanderbilt University

Foreword to the Thirtieth Anniversary Edition

Women and Men in the Dark Forests of Culture

R. Brian Ferguson

Why mess with a classic? One colleague contacted for this project demurred for just that reason. Yet the appearance of a new printing of *Women of the Forest*, three decades after it first appeared, is an occasion worth marking, even celebrating. So, for better or worse, six students of Yolanda and Robert Murphy, all of whom have studied Amazonian peoples, take this moment to look back on (and up to) a work that shaped our own perspectives—and the discipline of anthropology. The Murphys are a tough act to precede, and reasonable advice to the reader might be to skip us and go right to them. But a masterpiece deserves to be acknowledged, and so we do.

Research on the Mundurucú was a joint project for the Murphys from the very start. Yolanda and Bob were a team in the field, although for years it was Bob who did the publishing. The reader should know that in many ways their fieldwork, and the Mundurucú they encountered, were outstanding. In 1952, the Murphys were pioneers in the ethnography of South America, which as late as 1974 was still being called "the least known continent" (Lyons 1985). Comparing what they found to the patchy earlier reports about the Mundurucú produced documentation of something that was then quite rare: a clear case of social change within a "primitive" culture, specifically, a shift from patrilocal to matrilocal (or uxorilocal) postmarital residence, where households were organized around mothers, sisters, and daughters. Showing that this kind of household coexisted with patrilineal descent—where membership in lineages is passed through the male line—came as an anthropological shock, since patrilineality and matrilocality were at that time thought to be incompatible (we know of many cases now). This combination of structural features was related to the Mundurucú's nineteenth-century career as "the fiercest headhunters in the Amazon" in a hypothesis about social structure and external violence that helped to launch the anthropology of war (R. Murphy 1957). Within that field of study, the Mundurucú are also famous as a striking example of the cultural construction of aggression, which in their case was suppressed internally (except toward witches) and directed outward to non-Mundurucú enemies. In also emphasizing the role of Western contact in transforming Mundurucú warfare (R. Murphy 1960), this research foreshadowed a much later interest in how the European intrusion transformed indigenous war patterns.

This book, of course, focuses on Mundurucú women and their relationships to other women and to men, and the five commentaries that follow concentrate on gender relationships. William Balée will bring you to the looking glass through which Yolanda and Bob stepped. He and others situate the Murphys' work within the traditions of Columbia anthropology, transmuted by the Murphys' own "dialectical attitude" (R. Murphy 1971)—where nothing is as it seems, where conflict and ignorance generate the misunderstandings that make up daily life, and where ambiguous and tense relationships and interactions replace the illusory certainty of fixed realities. Balée notes the importance of local ecology and stresses the interactions of culture and history, of structure and change. Janet Chernela develops these points and emphasizes the dialectic between collective norms and the day-to-day practicalities of individuals. She shows how what the Murphys called "the negative attitude"—in a positive sense of critical doubt—exposes basic flaws in our professional image of culture.

Chernela raises the central point of this book and the other commentaries that follow: in a culture where men seem so obviously dominant over women, their superiority is fragile enough to need constant reinforcement, and its exercise produces a solidarity among women who refuse to be impressed by the masculine mythtique. Judith Shapiro and Balée add another dialectical axis: women, as agents of change (rather than of conservatism as usually imagined), may encourage actions that look good in the short term but that in the long term reduce their freedom. *Women of the Forest* was written in a time when most anthropologists pessimistically concluded that indigenous peoples of Amazonia, like those elsewhere, were headed for cultural extinction as their ways were bulldozed by ever expanding global "civilization." Unexpectedly, happily, many indigenous peoples have organized and found ways of preserving the traditions they value, even while coping with an insistent outside. The Mundurucú span both possibilities. As Balée notes, when their student Brian Burkhalter arrived to do fieldwork in 1979, much of what the Murphys describe here continued, in attenuated form, in some villages (Burkhalter 1988), but many Mundurucú had learned to put a price tag on just about everything.

All these commentaries note yet another dialectic—looking at "others" to scrutinize ourselves. This comes in surprising ways, for example in their comparison of Mundurucú and California houses (this volume, 138); or the way Mundurucú parents see the younger generation as what we would today call "slackers"—as epitomized by their *rejection* of tattooing (79). Again and again, the Murphys draw illuminating and sometimes disturbing parallels between gender among the Mundurucú and in our own culture. Shapiro runs with this one, framing observations from her years of experience in women's colleges in terms of what Mundurucú women achieve through separation.

These brief appreciations cannot begin to describe the scholarly influence this book has had, but they do give you a taste of it. They describe it as a critical piece in the birthing of gender studies, now a virtual industry in anthropology but then just beginning. *Women* showed ways of exploring intra- and intergender relationships that went beyond simply who was on top (so to speak). Chernela describes more particular applications for Amazon specialists, dealing with topics such as men's houses, women's solidarity, and the gendered interpretation of myth. One of my first publications on war (Ferguson 1988) was a test of Bob Murphy's hypotheses. A broader selection of Murphyesque ideas can be found in a book in their honor, *Dialectics and Gender* (Randolph, Schneider, and Diaz 1988).

Orna Johnson, one of the first people to read *Women* in manuscript form, here discusses how it shaped her later perspective on why it is that men seem to be in need of ideological props and on how war fits into the complex of male supremacy. Johnson makes another, most important point, that the Murphys' emphasis on ecology and labor provided an important guide on how to explain cross-cultural variation in gender relations. Thomas Gregor fills out these ideas. Gregor was guided by the Murphys when he went to work among the Mehinaku, where he also found gender antagonism, though in a different form. He describes some of his recent work on the cross-cultural significance of men's houses—the separate dwelling structures so prominent among traditional Mundurucú and the institutional bulwark of their masculine domination—and contrasts these cases to societies where gender issues are organized around individual, rather than collective, oppositions. Gregor also emphasizes the important point that even though Mundurucú women demonstrate solidarity, independence, and resistance, we should not overlook that they still are often treated badly by men.

Having briefly introduced the introductions, the rest of this short piece will add a few of my own observations about *Women of the Forest.* Contemporary theory of the origins of sex differences in behavior draws on a vast amount of literature and statistics (e.g., Eagly and Wood 2003). It begins with a division of labor built upon differences in strength and the exigencies of pregnancy and child rearing and sees these as built into and reinforced by social structures and acquired psychological accommodations. *Women of the Forest* is a perfect companion for these theories because, although published much earlier, it follows the outline of that argument though one cultural case, bringing the statistics to vibrant life.

The Murphys' work unifies that theory because of the remarkable scope of their own analysis. They start with the body as a situation, an idea Bob later explored so eloquently regarding his own decline into quadriplegia (R. Murphy 1987; Bob died in 1990). Here the body situation is first and foremost one of *work.* They then tour all around the complicated social organizations of matrilocality, patrilineality, an elaborate clan system, and a men's house with all the precision and enthusiasm of old-time British social anthropologists—though, as Shapiro notes, Bob turned this around to make it "Irish" ("All things real are ephemeral; all things enduring are false"—R. Murphy 1975:15). They top this off with a penetrating psychoanalytic analysis of child rearing, ideology, and myth. Freud may be in retreat within Western civilization, but Oedipus lives among the Mundurucú.

What we see is that much of what is taken as male domination is more basically a division of labor. Women and men do different things, and each gender controls what it does without interference from the other. But what men do tends to be what we call "politics"—public activities involving travel and sometimes danger. Still, women could control the village ritual cult, as they once did in the central myth of the sacred trumpets—except for being able to provide game meat to the ancestral spirits in the instruments (this volume, 114–17). Why do men so jealously guard that formal superiority? They do so certainly because it is always in jeopardy but also, I would add, because in their dominance, men exploit women, both sexually and in terms of labor. Their public efforts at a separate superiority are to keep women in their place, and men as well. As Bob once said to me, "macho" is directed as much to other males as to females. We see that when, in an impromptu challenge, women call on men to share the laborious task of bitter-manioc processing. A few men sheepishly do, to the loud derision of their fellows who made them get back in line (this volume, 164).

The general theory of gender differences just noted has been argued in opposition to origin theories from sociobiology and evolutionary psychology. Although *Women of the Forest* was published a year before E. O. Wilson's big splash, *Sociobiology*, one can read this book with that approach in mind. Certainly, evolutionary psychologists could comb through it and find a lot to support their views. But more broadly, the Mundurucú show just how limited is any evolutionary explanation of the lived experience of difference, and much about the Mundurucú flatly contradicts evolutionary interpretations. For instance, evolutionary psychologists emphasize the importance of paternity guarding. Mundurucú men may fume if their wives are carrying on affairs, but within the constraints of local culture they can do little more than that—except leave. Yet a Mundurucú man does not make much of a fuss if another man has sex with his wife because they do not believe pregnancy is possible from one copulation. ("Faulty embryology and ideology are one among the Mundurucú, just as ideology often unites with bad genetics in our own society.") They are extremely concerned, however, that *some* man be identified as the father of a child—the husband of the mother—because without a father it is impossible to assign a child to a clan, and thus those offspring are outside the system of social classification (this volume, 127–28, 135, 184). Or another example: evolutionary psychologists emphasize the supposed cross-cultural universality of romantic love as the evolved human basis of creating enduring female-male bonds, and so family units. The reader is invited to try to find that complex among the Mundurucú (see this volume, 172–86)

This book and these introductions also conjure up a strong sense of time and place—not just the Mundurucú villages of 1952 but the academic world around Columbia University in that year and the years just before and after the great wave of feminism. Yolanda today says she can still hear Gene Weltfish telling her, "you do something on the women, because the anthropology that is being done is only about men." That situation did not improve much in anthropology for over a decade. As Shapiro writes here, "sex roles" were still of marginal interest in 1967. That would change with the times, and a pioneering edited volume appeared (Rosaldo and Lamphere 1974) in the same year as *Women of the Forest*. We know that such coincidences are hardly coincidental.

As Yolanda explained it to me, their book began with their prosaic desire to "get more of the Mundurucú material out." Bob suggested focusing on her field research on child rearing. But Yolanda had just completed her thesis on women, as Chernela discusses, and when she turned to child rearing, the women "just kept coming in." So women became the focus. In retrospect, how could they not? When I arrived as a freshman at Columbia College in 1969, I wandered into an open meeting of two factions of SDS, including the very macho Weatherman. At one point, some disappeared into a corridor and came back asking for "some good men" to help repel an expected invasion by Lyndon LaRouche's Labor Committee (as I recall). Yet within months, the Weather women had overthrown the male chauvinist leadership, transforming their group into the Weather Underground. All of this was very public news on Columbia campus. The women had overthrown the men, and male dominance was being challenged everywhere. The Mundurucú might have understood this as realization of men's fears in their myth of the sacred trumpets.

Then there was the place. Although Yolanda taught at Empire State College, she was very much a part of the community of Columbia University anthropologists, where both she and Bob were graduate students and where Bob had taught since 1963. True to its New York sensibilities, Columbia anthropology seemed to be the center of its own universe. The important issues were not necessarily what other anthropologists were debating but what Columbia anthropologists argued among themselves, in the classrooms, barrooms, and greasy spoons of Morningside Heights. This attitude appeared in crystalline form one day in the late 1970s while I was working as Bob's assistant. David Schneider, an anthropologist for whom Bob had the greatest respect, was visiting. Sitting on Bob's couch, he ticked off a list of the failings of Columbia anthropology as they were discussed at the University of Chicago. Bob listened attentively, thought a second, and replied, "That's funny David, at Columbia we never talk about Chicago."

That attitude is implicit in this book. "So what if many other anthropologists are not talking about women—we think its important to do so." Now of course, all anthropologists would agree. And although an entire field of study on gender has emerged in the intervening three decades, it would be hard to name any subsequent publication that combines the scope, insight, elegance, relevance, and humor of *Women of the Forest*. Books like this one do not come along very often.

Reflections on the Looking Glass

William Balée

In the microcosm of a day, from sunrise to sunset, in the life of a woman in a village in a forest, Yolanda and Robert Murphy begin a rich and compelling tour of Mundurucú women, society, and culture as once they knew them. *Women of the Forest* provides a window onto a lost world, indigenous Amazonia in the ethnographic present of half a century ago.

The first edition of 1974 described this world, but the Murphys found that the first version needed a bridge, to bring readers from their own world to that of the Mundurucú. The revised edition of

1984 made that connection with the addition of chapter three. The new material offers detailed incidents and encounters that give the reader an almost tangible sense of the people and place, as well as the sacrifices, surprises, gratifications, and objectives of the ethnographers in their one-year's sojourn among the Mundurucú. The Murphys found that putting those experiences into words on paper, long after the fieldwork had been done and the scholarly theses, treatises, and articles had been printed, involved, as they put it, "stepping through the looking glass."

Women of the Forest is a sophisticated study of Mundurucú women within Mundurucú society at a given point in their history. It is also a cogent assessment of the enduring duality of the sexes, regardless of geography, language, and culture. Thus, the book is comparative in a pointed sense. The authors ask their readers—many of whom are reading their first ethnography—not only to peer outward onto an indigenous Other but to focus inwardly on themselves and their own culture, to grasp its multiple instantiations of male/female conflict, accommodations, and potential.

The Murphys see culture dialectically. As Bob put it in *The Dialectics of Social Life*, "the structure of reality is a structure of oppositions, of elements that contradict each other and limit each other's possibilities" (R. Murphy 1971:95). The given duality of the sexes underlies a certain tension that by design remains unresolved. Among the Mundurucú, the dialectic is clear in the inherent tensions between matrilocal residence, patrilineal descent, the men's house, men's concepts and fears, and women's less than venerating views about men. These cultural particularities within a more universal framework of gender oppositions make Mundurucú culture a singular fragment in a kaleidoscope of cultures.

The Murphys' dialectical approach involves an explanatory model that incorporates the unpredictability of history, on the one hand, and the legacy of form, or structure, on the other. The concept of structure presupposes an ongoing order. The Murphys found that for the Mundurucú, what "we call culture had a fixity that moderns would find difficult to comprehend" (this volume,

21). Yet they juxtapose this ordered system of surety with concerns about culture change and culture loss, as in threats to residence pattern, family organization, ritual paraphernalia, and concepts of male domination of a society. The Murphys experienced this contrast between the original, formal order of Mundurucú society and what was emerging in a spatial sense. They spent time in both a traditional village of the interior forest and a village that was experiencing rapid cultural change along the Rio Tapajós, the Mundurucú outlet to the world and the source of Western influences on them.

The Murphys conclude that traditional Mundurucú men used symbols of the past to create a Freudian other-order of male domination of domestic life to counter their living in a village where women were close relatives among themselves—as mothers, sisters, and daughters to one another—but men were not. These were extended matrilocal families. But in the newer order then dawning, the nuclear family and neolocal residence seemed to be becoming the norm. While the symbols of male domination were being extinguished with the changing culture, an artifact of contact and economics, the domination of males within the household as represented by the earlier symbols was possibly turning into reality.

The formal order in the interior village embodied basically dichotomous relations between women and men. The Mundurucú, in their sharp division by gender of labor and other phenomena (such as housing, ritual, song, property, and dance) are, the Murphys tell us, "unusual" (this volume, 233) in the world's societies. In most societies, then as now, the sexes are not so sharply contrasted in terms of the roles they fulfill in relation to one another, and the sexes do not form such segregated collectivities. Yet in traditional Mundurucú society, matrimonial harmony perseveres in the permanence of structure. It is eroded by the dynamics of history, and encroaching Western civilization is the principal mechanism. In reading *Women of the Forest*, in stepping through the looking glass with the Murphys, it is important to recognize that the looking glass provides a reflection of us as well. Gender is the most basic of all sociocultural divisions, but it is always understood locally. When the Murphys reveal a very different system of gender relations and show how it changes as it comes in contact with our world, readers are challenged to reflect on the pattern and meaning of gender in their own lives.

The Murphys interest in history is consistent with their anthropological training at Columbia University, which also included an emphasis on the environment. The complex interplay of structure and history presupposes a physical setting and a technology involved in extracting natural resources. Bob's graduate advisor and dissertation sponsor, Julian Steward (1902–1972), was an original thinker who invented cultural ecology, a general theory of relationships among culture, environment, and technology. Bob honored Steward's theoretical and anthropological legacy (R. Murphy 1977).

A subtle concept of ecology is present in *Women of the Forest*. Relations between the sexes in Mundurucú society do not unfold in a vacuum of abstract thought but are grounded in linear (historic) and environmental realities. The Murphys conjoin the unilocal residence pattern of the interior Mundurucú and the nucleated residence pattern of the riparian Mundurucú not only with the historic and economic impact of the rubber trade but also with the distribution of the rubber tree itself. The rubber tree has a dispersed distribution in flooded forests, and that dispersal, together with the tapping technology for extracting the latex, is linked to the nucleation of riverine households and settlements. Or, one should say, it once was so linked (Murphy and Steward 1956). Mundurucú society did not vanish because of inroads by settlers and the rubber trade. Bob's graduate student, the late Brian Burkhalter, went back and studied the Mundurucú in the late 1970s and early 1980s (this volume, lxiv) and found that many Mundurucú men living near the Rio Tapajós had abandoned work in rubber extraction and taken up gold mining instead. They continued to experience an intimate if tense relationship with surrounding non-Indian society and displayed a yen for cash and the myriad consumer goods it could buy. Yet interior villages remained, and these still maintained matrilocal residence and other aspects of more traditional ways (Burkhalter and Murphy 1989). In a sense, Bob studied Mundurucú society first as an eyewitness while a student of Steward, and second, years later, as an indirect observer, through his student's eyes.

Fifty years have now gone by since a young, recently married pair of graduate students lived among the Mundurucú people. In his later years, Bob was fond of saying to his graduate students that some anthropologists are interested in why things stay the same while others are intrigued by why things change. Some are interested in structure, others in history. But in true dialectical fashion, the Murphys themselves contradict this generalization. In this book, they have written an ethnography of women that absorbs persistence and change, structure and history, in a dialectically meaningful, relevant way. *Women of the Forest*, a collaboration of wife and husband, well deserves its resilient reputation against the merciless test of time. It momentarily resuscitates a lost but fathomable world of relations between the sexes in an Amazonian society. And it contains a general theory of gender relations applicable to human societies worldwide. That is why it's a classic.

Co-authoring Culture

Janet M. Chernela

It was 1952 when Yolanda and Robert (Bob) Murphy set out for a Mundurucú village on the upper Tapajós River, a southern feeder stream of the Amazon in Brazil. In the same year, Mamie Eisenhower modeled a *peau de soie* inaugural gown with pink rhinestones as Republican "Party Girls" worked to bring out the women's vote. Mamie may never have cooked, as some journalists noted, but her campaign underscored the role of wife as homebody. She once said she was "perfectly satisfied to be known as a housewife." *Good Housekeeping* magazine published her brownie recipe. Buttons with the slogan "I like Mamie" appeared with her picture. Dwight, the five star general who was to become president of the United States, wore one. In the same year, Rosalind Franklin was carrying out X-ray analyses of DNA that would reveal its double-helical structure. Her findings would be later overshadowed by an article interpreting her results by James Watson and Francis Crick. The renowned Brazilian anthropologist Berta Ribeiro was typing her husband's diaries as he mailed them to her from the field; it would be twenty-six years before she would publish her own (1979). It would be another year before Gertrude Dole would begin her ethnographic fieldwork in an equally remote region of the Amazon basin, an effort that earned her the reputation of "first American woman to carry out anthropological fieldwork along a headwater stream of the Xingú River in the Amazon of Brazil" (Barnes 2003). Betty Friedan, still unpublished, was a full-time wife and mother. In this context of constrained normalcy and cherished domesticity, the Murphys left for central Brazil. They were in their mid-twenties. They had married two years before on April Fools' Day.

Access to the region was difficult. The couple traveled by plane, riverboat, then raft and pole into the remote Mundurucú territory. This was anthropology as envisioned by Franz Boas, and it was his students who were the mentors of the Murphys.

The Murphys' purpose in living among the Mundurucú was to gather data for advanced degrees in anthropology at Columbia University. Columbia was then the most prestigious anthropology department in the country, having been established by Franz Boas, the reputed founder of American anthropology. But although many of Boas's students were women, the department, by 1952, had never granted tenure to a woman. Two accomplished female anthropologists, Margaret Mead and Gene Weltfish, were part-time instructors. Weltfish became Yolanda's principal mentor. In her 1972 thesis, "The Mundurucú Women of the Village of Cabruá," Yolanda writes: "The importance of working with the women was

impressed upon me by Gene Weltfish, who . . . reminded me that
most ethnographies have been collected by men and that it would
be extremely important to have data on women as seen through the
eyes of a woman" (1972:3). When Yolanda completed the manuscript as a master's thesis, Weltfish urged her to expand it into a
Ph.D. dissertation. Yolanda preferred to write a book.

Although co-authored, it can be argued that *Women of the Forest*
is an extension of Yolanda's original work. Were he alive, Robert
himself would say so. His own contributions and prestigious career
not withstanding, on more than one occasion he insisted that many
of the insights that bore his name were not possible without her.
For example, one article has the following note: "I wish to express
my deep appreciation to my wife, Yolanda, not only because of her
continuing encouragement and support, but because she collected
all the data upon which this article is based" (R. Murphy 1974:208;
italics in original). Although not universally accurate, the statement
is nowhere closer to truth than in *Women of the Forest*. It is not coincidental that Yolanda's name, which would have followed Robert's
had the criterion been alphabetical, is listed first in the book's joint
authorship.

A principal theme for the Murphys was the dialectic that characterized the relationship between the individual and the collectivity. This concern is related to the larger issues of structure and
practice at the center of anthropological debate during the 1950s
and 1960s. Over three decades, the work of Robert Murphy addressed the necessary contradictions between that which is collective and normative and that which is practical, quotidian, and
individual. A dialogically produced work on gender where each
author contributes fully may be regarded as a logical extension of
this project as well as an allegorical commentary on itself.

Residence, Relationship, and Power

In writing about the Mundurucú, the Murphys had entered an existing debate about women and power. In 1949, three years prior

to the Murphys' expedition, Robert Lowie referred to "the antifeminist flavor" in the ritual and belief systems of the Mundurucú and other Amazonian societies. Based on reports sent to him by the German-born Brazilian ethnographer Curt Nimuendajú, Lowie writes, "Mundurucú . . . myths depict an early matriarchate, [with] women controlling the mysteries (the Munducuru clubhouse and wind instruments . . .) and thus lording it over their husbands. The men, however, discovered the secrets and turned the tables on their wives" (Lowie 1949:337).

In her thesis Yolanda attempted to deconstruct these conjectures. One of the insights of Yolanda's 1972 monograph is that the spatial separation of the sexes among the Mundurucú, thought to be the root of their subordination, was, instead, an important source of women's cohesion and autonomy:

> The relative autonomy of the women derives principally from the separation of the sexes in both work and residence. . . . The women slept in separate dwellings from the men and associated principally with each other. In most of their daily activities, they worked together as a group without any direction from the men and their work was fundamental to village subsistence. . . . This group cohesiveness, strong separation of the sexes and strong kinship ties within the village forged the women into a bloc . . . [that] was self-regulating. (1972:4)

She concludes, "Separation of the sexes would seem, on the surface, to be a symptom of male dominance, but it is actually the source of female strength" (1972:67).

Mystification

A Mundurucú charter myth provided the basis for Lowie's allusion to an early matriarchy overturned by men. In this myth, women first occupied the clubhouse at the center of the village and controlled the instruments that imbued their possessors with power. When women brought out the sacred trumpets, they shunted men to the periphery to hide in the dwelling houses (as men order women today). The men rebelled. They occupied the meeting house and secured the instruments for themselves. Once the instruments of power were transferred to the men, roles were reversed and men became ascendant. Since then, noninitiates were forbidden to see the sacred instruments.

Early travelers made much of the dangers involved in witnessing the ritual objects. They impressed upon their readers that women and boys might be put to death if they accidentally caught a glimpse of the powerful instruments (Koch-Grunberg 1917:219). But Yolanda was not convinced. In her 1972 manuscript she had this to say regarding the ritual and its demonstrations of power and subordination: "The men blow their sacred trumpets and the women are appropriately cowed. This is a ritual statement of one aspect of Mundurucú culture, but a complete picture must include the fact that the women are not really awed or mystified in the least bit" (1972:67).

Two years later, in *Women of the Forest*, the Murphys together reworded the argument to state that although the formal canons of Mundurucú culture would place women in an inferior position to men, this is "a matter of official creed—male creed to be sure. . . . The women . . . do not agree with the men and, in spite of the sanctity given by tradition to their role, they neither like it, nor do they accept it. The relation between the sexes is not, then, one of simple domination and submissiveness, but one of ideological dissonance and real opposition" (113).

In pointing to the disparities in men's and women's views of Mundurucú ritual, values, and social universe, the Murphys challenged the fundamental assumption that sharing common values was requisite to the overall coordination and integration of a society as a coherent whole. Small-scale societies, such as those of Amazonia, were thought to be homogeneous and consensual, lacking internal diversity. *Women of the Forest* set siege to these assumptions. The Murphys were among the first to point out that by neglecting unauthorized participants of society and presenting only the normative perspective, anthropologists represented the notions of groupness presented to them by a subset of stakeholders. "Because they are excluded from so much of what is reported by anthropologists as 'the culture,' we assume that they [women] do not have one of their own. . . . We seem to have forgotten that the very essence of the relationship between the sexes is struggle, opposition, and socially useful, however, unconscious, misunderstanding. . . . Our description of 'Mundurucú culture' should be understood as a point to the counterpoint of the female realm, a foil for the play of social life" (78).

The Murphys departed boldly from anthropological dogma when they wrote that much of "traditional Mundurucú culture as it is recognized, conceptualized, and stated . . . is male ideology and lies within the sphere of masculine activity. . . . The social perspectives of the women are different, and they do not wholly identify with, nor feel bound by, that from which they are systematically excluded" (77). According to the Murphys, radically different cultural realities may coexist, as they do for Mundurucú men and women, without threatening the coherence of a society. Instead, they maintain social interaction as an ongoing dialectic characterized by misinterpretation, tension, and intrigue.

Sex, the Mundurucú, and the Collective/Individual Divide

But, if by "culture" one means a creed that is "masculine" in origin and design, then women would be its alienated subjects. The Murphys found the source of intracultural dissonance in socialization. They followed Freud in maintaining that socialization was a sloppy process and the internalization of social values is incomplete. Successful socialization—producing individuals who share group values and systems of belief and meaning—requires submission of the ego to a collectivity. Only a motivational structure that could generate behaviors that favored group life over self-gratification could achieve this end. It seemed to the Murphys that socialization was particularly sloppy when it came to women. If, as the Murphys maintained, women did *not* subscribe wholly to or believe completely in the dictates of society, the inescapable explanation was their partial and incomplete socialization. If the processes of socialization, incumbent as they are on motivations that do not reward women, failed when it came to them, then where are women situated vis à vis culture? The Murphys would say that the flaw lies in facile definitions of culture.

The early 1970s was a significant moment for new emerging fields in gender studies. The differences attributed to women and men by the Murphys in *Women of the Forest* were noted in the same year by feminist researchers Sherry Ortner and Nancy Chodorow. In spite of similarities in the descriptive findings, however, the conclusions arrived at by these pairs of authors were profoundly different. All four authors appear to agree with the perspective that women are "less mediated" than men. All describe women as everywhere more practical, pragmatic, particularistic, and this-wordly than men.

Ortner writes,

Chodorow demonstrates to my satisfaction at least that the feminine personality [is] characterized by personalism and particularism. . . . The feminine personality . . . may have contributed further to the view of women as being somehow less cultural than men. That is, women would tend to enter into relationships with the world that culture might see as being more 'like nature'—immanent and embedded in things as given—than 'like culture'—transcending and transforming things through the superimposition of abstract categories and transpersonal values.

(Ortner 1974:82)

On the subject of agency, however, the two pairs part company. According to Ortner and Chodorow, women, as the principal agents in socialization, must subscribe to the same low evaluations of their own positions in society as men. This early feminist viewpoint, then, held that the subordination of women emerged from the construction of personhood, with women bearing the greater responsibility for it.

Although in agreement with Chodorow and Ortner about the cultural construction of gender difference, the Murphys diverge in their analysis, with important implications for cultural theory and process. If women were subject to, but not full participants in the "superimposition of abstract categories and transpersonal values," to use Ortner's phrasing, it was because they did not subscribe to what Robert Murphy had earlier referred to as the "collective delusions" of ideology (1971:229). According to Murphy, women did not subscribe to or believe in the dictates of a society that rewards men and is created largely by them. In the writings of the Murphys women are skeptical and less self-delusional than are men; they are more closely situated to an unsocialized or unmediated (though the latter is not their word) "truth." Rather than being "inferior" and "dominated" the Murphys found in women a freedom from the normative grasp. It is precisely *because* women are less motivated and less mediated that they may be said to have a degree of freedom from cultural constraint not had by men, who are both creators of and actors in their own creations. One can read the Murphys to find in women an existential freedom. Since they do not fully succumb to the "illusions" of ideology, women provide a metacommentary on culture. This in itself should provide them with a power.

While the signifier in any act of signification is empowered by the act, the signified may be victimized by it. The Murphys' solution to the dilemma of unequal distribution of power in the creation of meaning is to postulate that women do *not* participate in the system of significations recognized as "culture" when these do not concern them or fly in the face of their own beliefs. In the process of creating meaning, women do not necessarily subscribe to the significations of men—particularly to those sets of meanings in which they themselves are the signified. Although obviously aware that norms are a very real part of the real world (with death or rape consequences for women who would disregard them), women did not regard rules with the peremptory obedience often attributed to them.

Gender and Power in Amazonia: Influences

Women of the Forest inspired a new school of anthropology. One of
the closest followers of the approach established by the Murphys
is Thomas Gregor. In *Anxious Pleasures* he writes, "The legend of
matriarchy . . . reveals a dangerous truth: the men's house as a
symbol of male identity is a citadel of papier-mâché. The secrecy,
the intimidation, and the use of force are the shims and gimcracks
that shore it up . . . The cost of maintaining the façade runs high.
The price the men pay is in anxiety: fear of their own sexual im-
pulses and fear of women" (1985:115).

In her work among the Xinguan Bakairí, Debra Picchi furthers
these themes. Like a Mundurucú village, a Bakairí village is organized with a men's house at the center and a periphery of residential houses. Although women avoid the ritual-political spaces
at the center of the village and may not witness the sacred flutes,
Picchi argues that these factors alone do not indicate a domination
by men over women (2003:28). Picchi points to the many female
rites of passage that mark puberty, pregnancy, and birth, stressing
that each sex passes through life cycle rituals which render them
temporarily vulnerable.

Since Robert Murphy was my advisor at Columbia University, it
is not surprising that the influence of the Murphys is apparent in my
own work on the northwestern Amazon. There, among the Tuka-
noan Wanano, where women are also prohibited from viewing the
potent initiation flutes that were once their own, I found reciprocal
narratives involving monopoly and appropriation of instruments of
power (Chernela 1997). My comparison of two myth performances,
one by a woman and the other by a man, suggested the Murphyesque finding that the differing perspectives of women and
men in Wanano culture produced different narrative constructions
and configurations of power. The male version called attention to
the hidden dangers of women who may intercede between a man
and his claim to paternity. The female version revealed the treach-
ery of men as a man disguised as a woman steals from women the or-

naments imbued with the power of "knowledge." The simplest reading of these myths reduces each to an essential theft-and-loss narrative. Each sex's relation to a source of potency is portrayed as indirect and precarious. For males, the loss is reproductive rights; for females, the loss is the right to speak and to know. The differences between them suggest what the Murphys told us thirty years ago: The most fundamental dilemmas of existence are not the same for men and women. Nevertheless, the two may be mutually determined.

Conclusions

By neglecting the unauthorized participants of society and presenting only the normative perspective, anthropologists had obscured the complex relationships and social realities that are the objects of anthropological analysis. By considering the roles of women, Yolanda and Robert Murphy restored women to their rightful status as social actors. Yet in so doing, they raised fundamental questions regarding ideology and common ground. The viewpoints of women are important here, not just because they have been generally neglected, but because they provide insights not available through the authorized views of either male informants or outside analysts. They draw critical attention to persisting assumptions that underlie anthropological convention. When the perspectives of women are considered a previously unseen picture of society emerges.

Women of the Forest:
The View from Morningside Heights

Judith Shapiro

> The battle of the sexes is not carried on by individual gladiators,
> as in our society, but by armies.
> —*Women of the Forest*, 136.

The first time I read *Women of the Forest*, back in what we now refer to as the last century, I was riding high on the second wave of feminism, along with many close colleagues and friends. Inspired as a graduate student by the Murphys and by Charles Wagley, I had traveled down to the Brazilian tropical forests myself for fieldwork in the late 1960s, first with the Tapirapé of Mato Grosso and then with the Yanomami of Roraima.

When I embarked on my dissertation research among the Yanomami in 1967, I had no thought of focusing on the social roles of women and men; this was not, at that time, one of the going topics of anthropological discourse. "Sex roles," to use the language of the era, seemed to be relegated more to the domain of "nature" than "culture" or, to put it another way, seemed so obvious as to be beneath notice. In any event, gender differences were—with a few notable exceptions—part of the background, not the foreground, of ethnographic analysis. What could not be clearer, however, when I actually began looking at Yanomami life, was that it was the central pivot of the social order, what we might call the elephant in the living room. And thus I set about trying to describe it in the most basic terms I could. Robert and Yolanda Murphy became my guides, my inspiration, and my fellow travelers as we struggled, in the succeeding years, for a language with which to describe gender hierarchy and as we sought to address both the similarities and differences among societies with regard to this core domain of life.

They themselves were always acutely aware of the challenges to this enterprise. As they wrote in *Women of the Forest,*

The problem of hierarchy, which is comparatively transparent in the case of the master–slave or ruling class–plebian relationship, becomes muddied and opaque in the complex and emotion-laden tie—or breach—between the sexes. To cap it all, the anthropologist is just as enmeshed in the false veneer of sexual ideology as are his informants, and he or she is additionally encumbered with that enormous and largely unconscious baggage of fears, frustrations, hatreds, and longings that characterize sex roles. There is no easy solution to the problem, and we can only suggest caution and skepticism in its discussion. As in all things, the first step toward wisdom is the awareness that we really do not know what we are talking about. (234–35)

This passage reflects the Murphys' distinctive psychoanalytically informed wariness of our conscious efforts to make sense of the world and also clearly reveals their immunity from any form of irony-deficiency anemia. But it is overly modest, since they themselves have contributed significantly to our having a far deeper and more nuanced sense of what we are talking about when we talk about sex and gender. As Clifford Geertz has liked to remind us, even when we cannot arrive at definitive answers, we can certainly refine the terms of our debate.

The Murphys' contribution to debate refinement in the area of sex and gender falls under the rubric of what Robert Murphy liked to call "Irish social anthropology," defined very much in opposition to British social anthropology. Whereas British social anthropologists viewed societies in terms of patterns, rules, norms, and the functioning of structures, Irish social anthropologists viewed social life in terms of conflict, contradiction, lies, and illusions. As the Murphys put it in *Women of the Forest*, "the very essence of the relationship between the sexes is struggle, opposition, and socially useful, however unconscious, misunderstanding" (78).

The first time I read *Women of the Forest*, I was also one year away from what has now become close to three decades of life in women's colleges: first at Bryn Mawr, where I arrived in the fall of 1975 to join the anthropology faculty and where I was to serve, for the last eight of my nineteen years there, as provost of the college; then, at Barnard, where I have been president and professor of anthropology since the summer of 1994. The Murphys, and the Mundurucú, have been very much with me all along the way. The questions they raised and the perspectives they offered found an echo in the way I have come to see the central, ongoing mission of women's colleges.

My entry into the world of women's colleges occurred in the spring of 1975, when I made the decision to move to Bryn Mawr College instead of returning for my second term as an assistant professor at the University of Chicago. Having been the first and only woman in Chicago's Department of Anthropology (and the first to teach a course on "sex roles," as it was then called), I found the environment to be rather daunting at that stage in my career.

The anthropologist I was succeeding at Bryn Mawr, who had just retired, was Frederica de Laguna, one of Franz Boas's last students, who is, as of this writing, still going strong well into her nineties and continuing to publish up a storm on the Tlingit. The senior colleague I was joining, Jane Goodale, had published a significant contribution to the growing anthropological literature on women, *Tiwi Wives* (1971), in which she was able to make new sense of a highly complex Australian system of kinship and marriage by looking at it from the women's point of view. Interestingly, the major earlier work on this Melville Islands group, which had focused entirely on men, was entitled simply *The Tiwi of North Australia* (Hart and Pilling 1979). Clearly, the time had come for women to move out of the shadows and for men to cease being an unmarked category representing a society in its entirety.

The move to Barnard in 1994 was a homecoming—to my native city and to the neighborhood in which I had done my doctoral work in anthropology. I was also drawn to Barnard as an institution that had had the courage of its convictions and identity, having maintained its independence from a very powerful big brother, Columbia University, in the face of great odds and uncertainty.

To the east, across Broadway from Barnard, I could see the familiar sacred symbol of Columbia: the majestic seated statue of Alma Mater, her head crowned with laurel and her arms upraised, in front of the University's iconic, domed Low Library. To me, she was very much like the Mundurucú "mothers of the game," an object of ritual veneration by the men who had hunted for her (in forests or in libraries) and who, at the same time, had carefully shielded her from any degrading contact with actual living women deemed unfit for her company (in Columbia's case, until the various programs of the university were successively and very successfully opened to women, mostly, but not always, at the urging of Barnard—a story for another day). Were I as psychoanalytically inclined as the authors of *Women of the Forest*, I might even have thought to characterize the stately rotunda of Low Library itself as a highly visible, reassuring, never-to-be-withdrawn breast.

The argument that I have made over the years for the enduring mission of women's colleges has had much in common with the Murphys' approach to the role of women in Mundurucú society. It has centered on the lived social experience of women, the need to look at a society's gender arrangements in terms of whose interests are being served, and an emphasis on the power of female solidarity. In taking such an approach, I have sought to avoid what I see as the Scylla and Charybdis of much feminist discourse: on the one hand, an androgynizing approach to equity that underplays the powerful role of gender in sociocultural systems and, on the other hand, idealized essentialist visions of womanhood that partake of what I call the "feminist mystique."

In *Women of the Forest*, the Murphys drew a basic existential contrast between the condition of women and men, most notably asserting that women, as givers of life, partake in the only human activity that has intrinsic meaning. At the same time, however, their analysis of gender focused primarily on the social organization of work and everyday activities. Mundurucú relations of production involved women in the group activity of processing manioc flour together. The uxorilocal extended family made communal houses the province of women. Mother-daughter relations, said the Murphys, were the most solid and enduring bonds in traditional Mundurucú society.

This focus on patterns of work and solidarity was also central to the way I had been approaching the respective positions of men and women in Yanomami society. In my view, a central difference between the condition of Mundurucú and Yanomami women was that the latter lacked the communal power base—built on patterns of residence and work—that Mundurucú women enjoyed. To put it another way, if women were not going to be equal, there was something to be said for their being separate.

So, similarly, I have seen the purpose of a women's college as the proverbial "room of one's own" for women in a society in which they still do not enjoy the same benefits as men. I do not see them as places where women can think differently or learn differently, an approach taken by some proponents of women's colleges, but rather as places that serve women's interests and serve them well. Like the Murphys, I ask the question: Where do women get the strength to operate within, and even confront, a system of male dominance and privilege? Like the Murphys, I answer: They get it from one another.

But, in the case of women's colleges, they do not get this strength only from one another. They also get it from the men who have chosen to ally themselves with these institutions—on the faculty, in the administration and staff; from the fathers who are gratified to see their daughters thrive; and from the many other male friends who have been a source of support.

Indeed, when one looks beyond the student body, one sees that women's colleges have been the very model of true coeducation. In this, they can be distinguished from many colleges and universities labeled "coeducational" because they admit women as students even though they have remained places where gender inequity persists, first of all, in the numerical representation of men and women in other segments of the institution's population (faculty, senior administrators, trustees), and, secondly, in terms of the respective experiences of women and men in those institutions.

In saying this, I do not minimize the great progress that has been made in opening a wide range of opportunities for women in what were formerly bastions of male privilege. I say only that coeducation, like gender equity more generally, is a work in progress and requires eternal vigilance. Women's colleges have an ongoing role to play in this work. Why? Because it is women who have the greater interest in achieving gender equity and it is women's colleges that can be counted on to pursue that interest. Though they are only a tiny minority of all institutions of higher education, they are, to use a religious metaphor, the leavening in the dough.

Women, as the Murphys told us in the case of the Mundurucú, can develop a sense of distance from those aspects of their own culture in which they have little vested interest; "they do not wholly identify with, nor feel bound by, that from which they are systematically excluded" (77). This subversiveness can make women effective agents of social transformation. *Women of the Forest* thus addressed familiar stereotypes of women as social conservatives, inherently resistant to change. Women were the ones initiating a move to the Cururú River and a greater involvement in rubber tapping. The explanation given by the Murphys was that women seemed to have less to lose. Since traditional patterns of life in the Mundurucú village supported a system of male privilege in which women had far less reason to feel invested, the rewards of acculturation seemed more obvious to them. And, indeed, in the short run men seemed to be the bigger losers. The men's house was gone and men appeared to experience the greater degree of downward mobility.

But the Murphys did not stop with the short run. They moved on to consider the issue of unintended consequences and the paradoxes they entail. They argued that the longer term effect of the involvement in rubber tapping would be to benefit men by strengthening their economic position in relation to the women. The Murphys argued that Mundurucú women and men had yet to become aware of this transformative power of the new relations of production in which they had become enmeshed (238). The most obvious and consequential change would be women's loss of the social and economic basis of their solidarity: the uxorilocal extended family and communal patterns of manioc production (241).

We can see comparable unintended consequences of social changes championed by feminists in our own society, one of the most dramatic being so-called no-fault divorce laws, which show what happens when women and men are treated as social equals when, in fact, they are not: men get richer while women and children get poorer. The move of women into higher strata of the labor force has involved unsolved problems of its own; as Lily Tomlin put it in *The Search for Intelligent Life in the Universe*, portraying a successful career woman trying to manage both work and family: "If I had known what it would be like to have it all, I would have settled for less." As the noted writer and Barnard alumna Anna Quindlen likes to point out, women have earned the right to do as much as men, but not the right to do as little.

We can also see some unintended consequences of the move from single-sex education to coeducation in some of our colleges and universities. A striking case was revealed in a recent study of the situation of women at Duke University, undertaken at the direction of the president of that institution, formerly the president of a distinguished women's college. The segment of the study dealing with undergraduates documented the persistence of gender stereotypes and a pervasive sense of insecurity among young women. Women who had graduated before 1972, when Duke had a separate women's college, expressed higher levels of self-confidence than women who had graduated in the era of coeducation (Rimer 2003).

The assumption that coeducation is in and of itself a positive development and a sign of progress—or, to put it another way, the inability to distinguish between true and illusory coeducation—may also pose dangers to the education of women in developing countries. These countries may be tempted to view their own traditions of single-sex education as somehow backward, rather than as building blocks of the future. The challenge will be to find ways of bringing women and men together while making use of strategic forms of separation.

The understanding at the heart of *Women of the Forest* is that things are rarely what they seem as far as sex and gender are concerned. Nor will one go far in penetrating the mysteries of this domain of the human experience unless one is armed with wit and a high tolerance for ambiguity, as has always been the case with the

Murphys. In characterizing male dominance as an "uneasy overlordship" (121); in perceiving that those viewed as inferiors are also especially threatening and thus arguing that male dominance is "pervaded by doubt and contradiction" (137); in noting how male solidarity itself calls forth effective forms of female antagonism; in recognizing the effectiveness of those weapons available to the relatively powerless, notably ridicule (something humorless feminists have ignored at their rhetorical peril); in providing an analysis at once cold-eyed and warm-hearted, the Murphys have given us a study of a particular moment in the history of a lowland South American people that is valuable company for other times and other places.

Male Supremacy and Female Collective Strength

Orna Johnson

> If the men really were all that powerful,
> they wouldn't need such rigmarole.
>
> —Margaret Mead

The above quotation, cited in *Women of the Forest*, represents an early recognition of the contradictory nature of gender roles. It questions the validity of masculine ideological superiority and suggests that if men were really dominant by nature, they would not need so many cultural props to support their superior gender status. Indeed, according to Mundurucú myth, men have power because they are hunters and can make ritual offerings of meat to the spirits that reside in the sacred trumpets which were once owned by the women. Their position is tenuous and fraught with apprehension because there is always a danger that if they could no longer hunt, the women would regain control of the trumpets and the men would revert to a passive, weakened state.

I first read *Women of the Forest* in manuscript form when I was a graduate student just back from my research among the Matsigenka Indians of Peru. The Matsigenka, who are a family-level society, living in dispersed hamlets, are very different from the Mundurucú; they live in nuclear family households with a high degree of cooperation and mutuality between husbands and wives. Yet, there were lessons to be learned from the Murphys' work that apply not only to gender roles among the Matsigenka but to contradictory nature of gender relations inherent in all human societies.

Robert Murphy, who was my advisor, taught me that that social life was more complex than it appears on both the ideational or the behavioral level, or between norm and action. Social life is derived from the "interplay of activity and consciousness" (R. Murphy 1971:219). The task of the ethnographer is to understand the mundane quality of people's lives, which entails the pragmatism of their everyday activities and the imagery of their symbolic world and the rituals that shape societal institutions.

My reading of *Women of the Forest* helped me understand my own research in terms of three important concepts. First and foremost, it provides the concept of a new "language" (to echo Judith Shapiro) for discussing gender hierarchy. In the early years of gender research, there was an effort simply to find ethnographic descriptions of women because before the 1970s, most anthropologists did not provide a balanced view of gender roles. Gender relations were evaluated in terms of gender hierarchy: male dominance and female subordination or male authority and female submission. The Murphys, however, tell us that women are powerful in unexpected ways. Although the Mundurucú have an explicit ideology of male superiority expressed in myth and ritual, male superiority is not evident in daily life. "A husband seldom gives orders to his wife, for his sphere of interest and hers do not intersect deeply" (184). Furthermore, although men have one idea about which gender is more valuable, women have quite a different idea. In fact, it could be said that women have their own gender ideology. The women are apathetic to the myths and rituals of the men. They are bound by much stronger emotional ties and affective relations and are not impressed by the myths and rituals that affirm male dominance. "It is as if they had investigated the secret sources of men's power—and had found absolutely nothing" (167). It is the power of women's solidarity that provides them with their greatest strength. When men try to assert their ideological superiority as expressed in the myth of the sacred trumpets, they only increase women's cohesion and hostility toward them.

The second concept illuminated in the book is the question of why men need myths and rituals to validate their position and why male activities and occupations are deemed more important than those of women. In *Male and Female*, Margaret Mead wrote, "In every human society, the males' need for achievement can be recognized. . . . Men's sureness of their sex role is tied up with their right, or ability, to practice some activity that women are not allowed to practice. Their maleness, in fact, has to be underwritten by preventing women from entering some field or performing some feat" (1968:168). The reason why men monopolize prestige and perpetuate a veneer of superiority is because manhood is almost universally seen as problematic. Manhood is a critical threshold that boys must pass through, and the achievement is tenuous. It is a career fraught with apprehension because there is always a danger that a man could lose his ability to live up to culturally imposed standards of masculinity (Gilmore 1990). As Mead (1968:165) notes, a boy must "master a great variety of skills and strengths, before he can compete with grown males." Attaining full rights as a man is conditional on learning to act in specified ways, some of which may seem difficult. Real manhood is more than anatomical maleness; it requires proof of action through skill and endurance, the ability to overcome danger, and in some cases, violent testing. Furthermore, full masculinity has to be proven again and again, for it requires continual affirmation, not just proof of past success. Being a man does not come easily and failure to live up to the stringent standards of manhood leaves a man without a valid role or sense of belonging, which is equivalent to emptiness.

Womanhood, by comparison, develops more naturally, without need for cultural intervention. A women has no similar challenge; in most societies her role is validated through her ability to bear children, a task that comes naturally to her by virtue of her being female. This in no way reflects on the value of women's roles. As the Murphys note, a difference in kind does not necessarily mean a difference in quality. The sexes are different, but there is no innate inferiority or superiority of one over the other. The reason mothering is self perpetuating for women is because women themselves were mothered by women. This is what Nancy Chodorow (1978) calls "the reproduction of mothering." Women develop capacities for mothering based on their prolonged relationship with their own mothers. This, as we will see, is both a source of strength and of conflict for women.

Because woman are exclusively responsible for childcare, children of both sexes depend on and identify with the mother during the earliest stage of life. This means that both boys and girls form a primary identification with a female caretaker. During this period of "infantile dependence," the infant is incapable of distinguishing him or herself from the mother. At around age three, both boys and girls go through a process of separation and individuation and become receptive to gender-appropriate demands. For girls, this process is continuous; a daughter proceeds along the established path, which is identification with the mother. To develop masculine identity, however, boys must sever their early identification with the mother and replace it with a secondary masculine identification. Yet, as the Murphys point out, "the Oedipal transition is never a complete success" (this volume, 252). The male figure, who is generally the father, is often less physically present in a boy's everyday life, making it more difficult to grasp and construct a masculine identity. The fact the father's role is not so clearly defined may explain why masculinity is often defined in negative terms—as not female—in order to repress the original identification with mother (Chodorow 1974).

The implications of this psychodynamic process are twofold: (1) boys define masculinity in negative terms; they use females as a negative example of what they are not supposed to be or do, thereby devaluing women; and (2) girls continue to identify with their mothers, which provides a more secure gender identity. Yet because a girl does not break away, her relationship with her mother perpetuates dependence and less clearly defined ego boundaries. A boy, on the other hand, must overcome his identification with his mother by repressing or negating whatever is seen as feminine or childlike (Chodorow 1974). As the Murphys point out, "the mother figure is sensed ambivalently as a negater and destroyer, as well as a giver of life. . . . There is, then, in every male a struggle between his maturation and his status as a man, on the one hand, and his return to passivity and then to nothingness on the other" (this volume, 252–53).

The third concept addressed in the book is how to account for cross-cultural variation in gender roles. The Murphys show how the organization of work accounts for women's solidarity. Mundurucú women form a cohesive group in work and residence. "The solidarity of the mother–daughter and sister–sister dyads extends itself in diminished degree to a union of all the women of a household and, ultimately, of the village. One of the chief sources of this cohesiveness is, very simply, the work process" (149). Bitter manioc—the Mundurucú food staple—must be processed into manioc flour in order to be edible. The most efficient way to prepare large amounts is through communal use of facilities and collective labor. Women also have effective control over the economy of food distribution, including the distribution of meat provided by the men. Men do not intrude upon domestic activities because they are the province of the women. In sum, women's work entails affective bonds of cooperation and mutual loyalty that are much stronger than the more diffuse ties of the men.

Hunting is the most essential activity of the men. Skillful hunters are honored and meat is the favored food. In fact, it was the ability to hunt that made it possible for the men to seize the sacred trumpets from the women, who were unable to properly feed the spirits that resided in the trumpets. Hunting, however, is a precarious activity; unlike with gardening, which is consistently dependable, not all men are effective hunters and there are times when men are unlucky and meat is lacking. In the past, hunting was closely associated with warfare. The Mundurucú were fierce warriors known for raiding distant villages, taking trophy heads, and capturing children who were brought back and raised as Mundurucú. The trophy head was valued because it "pleased" the game spirits and promoted the fertility of animals. Historically the Mundurucú cooperated with the Portuguese through trade and raiding against hostile Indians to make the region safer for commerce and missionaries. The Mundurucú in turn received valued commercial goods, which greatly enhanced the status of individual warriors. Warfare against enemy outsiders thus provided a means for constructing hierarchies among successful warriors and hunters who benefited through the capture of trophy heads and the acquisition of western trade goods.

The practice of warfare is cross-culturally associated with male-supremacist behavior patterns. The male-supremacy complex entails, among other things, male monopoly over weapons, training of males for bravery, rewards for masculine performance, patrilineal descent, and the denigration of women. It is evident in the military service and is activated in such male-centered social groups as fraternities and athletic teams. These behavior patterns are not human universals but are found in situations of intense competition, where men engage in activities from which women are excluded. Male supremacy, in its fullest form, is brought about through warfare, where peoples lives are in danger and defeat is costly. Warriors have to be "real" men, stand up to challenges, show physical strength, not be afraid of danger, and take courageous action. Such heroic behavior does not come naturally. It is instilled through socialization and requires a good deal of shoring up and repression of inner insecurity. As Gilmore (1990:106) notes, "Real men do not simply emerge naturally over time . . . they must be assiduously coaxed from their juvenescent shells, shaped and nurtured, counseled and prodded into manhood." Outside of combat, male groups that engage in ritual activities, sports, or other collective endeavors work to shore up masculine identity.

In the Mundurucú case, certain conditions may exacerbate the male-supremacy complex. As discussed earlier, masculinity is the universal conflict associated with the Oedipal complex that makes male gender identity problematic. Additionally, there is gender segregation that results in an intense isolated relationship between young boys and their mothers before they are ready to transition into the men's house. Once adolescent boys join the men's house, they are confronted with male bantering and idealized tales of past bravery. The Murphys tell us, "Warfare was the predominant male occupation—one might say obsession . . . although the last hostilities occurred almost four decades before our visit, the men still talked about it as if it were yesterday. . . . [They] recounted in vivid detail the techniques . . . that went into warring; one had the feeling the entire complex could have been reactivated at any time" (this volume, 105). Comparing men's cults in Amazonia and Melanesia, Gregor and Tuzin (2001:332) note that both regions have settlement and subsistence conditions in which boys are typically unable to perform heavy or dangerous men's work, namely, hunting, the clearing of forest, or defense of the community, leaving them separated from the women yet not part of the men's world. It is during this time in their development that boys need to find reassurance in achievement yet remain uncertain of whether they will be able achieve full status as men. The only clear indicator of masculine selfhood is that they are superior to females and that external objects and rituals symbolizing masculine power will help them overcome the fears and anxieties associated with fulfilling their masculine role.

Men's Cults and the Mundurucú

Thomas A. Gregor

First published in 1974, *Women of the Forest* was ahead of its time in attempting to examine women's roles in an ethnography of an indigenous people. Although the Murphys succeeded in documenting Mundurucú women's lives, they also provide us with a vivid portrait of a defining institution for gender relationships within the community, the Mundurucú men's cult. When they arrived among the Mundurucú for the first time in 1952, they discovered a cult, which, thanks to their efforts, is one of the best known in the ethnography of Amazonia.

Indigenous men's cults are one of the more remarkable social institutions known to anthropology. The Mundurucú version represents a social form that is widely distributed among tribal peoples, especially in Melanesia and lowland South America. The features of the cult include a club house and temple in the center of the community. Inside are sound-producing sacred objects, including trumpets, bull-roarers, flutes, and other paraphernalia that are absolutely taboo to the women of the community. Some of these devices—notably the bull-roarer, which is slat of wood that makes a droning noise when whirled about on a cord—are nearly identical in Melanesia and Amazonia. All of the cult objects are used in a ritual that is regarded as essential to the well-being and productivity of the village. The women and children are often told that these sounds are the voices of spirits. The cults and their attendant mystification and secrets have broad implications for gender relationships in these societies. A woman who so much as glances at these objects would be gang raped by every member of the community or, in some instances (as in New Guinea), raped and then put to death.

As Robert Murphy noted in a classic article (1959), men's cults exist in a setting that is deeply misogynistic. Gang rape is the extreme end of a range of conduct that Murphy identified as "gender antagonism," which includes individual rape, the taunting of women, and their general deprecation. Among many societies, the hostility of these acts is also reflected in anxieties and taboos that the men have with respect to the women, including fear of menstrual blood and a belief that sex is dangerous to male vitality. While the Mundurucú share some of these beliefs, they are much diminished in comparison with similar societies (see this volume, 135–36).

Perhaps the most remarkable feature of men's cults is their claimed origin. In both Melanesian and Amazonian societies, the villagers claim that in mythic times the cult was invented by women. They were the ones who founded the men's house, learned the secret of the cult objects, and, in some cases, actually acted men's roles. Ultimately, the men rose up against them and tricked or forced them to give up the cult objects and established a male-dominated society. The Mundurucú version of this myth, skillfully narrated by the Murphys, is one of the richer and better-documented tales of the origins of the men's house.

What can account for the similarity of men's institutions that are half a world apart in terms of geography? The earliest ethnographers of the two regions, who were the first to notice the remarkable parallels, believed that they must have diffused from a common source. Robert Lowie (1920:313) remarked that they are "an ethnographical feature originating in a single center, and thence transmitted to other regions."

From the perspective of cultural history, Lowie's theory seems improbable. The distance alone would seem to preclude diffusion. Moreover, even if the cults were an ancient invention that spread to the New World, why did they retain their essentially similar form in different environments? It has been more than 40,000 years since the peoples of Melanesia and Amazonia were one, and we know there is no credible evidence of significant contact between them since that time.

The Murphys answer to the puzzle of the similarity of the myths associated with men's cults is that they reflect neither actual history nor common origins. Rather, they are representations of universal gender psychology, in which men, who are raised in intimacy by their mothers, must learn to identify themselves with their more distant fathers. The men must separate themselves from their mothers, who represent dependence and immaturity. The disparagement of women in general is "protest masculinity," which reflects insecurity over gender identity rather than strength. The myth of an ancient matriarchy thereby reflects the reality of the earliest years, in which males are largely raised by women. Life in the nursery, from this point of view, is the only historical truth that lies behind the myth. The walls of the men's house, which appear at first blush to be of solid granite, turn out to be a façade. From a psychoanalytic perspective, which is used by Murphy (1959) (see also Gregor's study of the Mehinaku [1985] and Gregor and Tuzin's approach to men's cults [2001]), the men's culture and cult has a dreamlike, fantastic quality. Ultimately, it is defensive in nature, and it embodies and elaborates classic defense mechanisms of projection and reaction formation.

If the Murphys find the roots of the men's house to be in the universals of child rearing, why is it that the pattern is not found more broadly, or in Robert Murphy's words, "why are we not all swinging bull roarers?" His answer is that men's cults mainly appear in societies of an intermediate size. In the smallest of human communities, those comprising only a few families, gender takes second place to bonds of close kinship as a basis of organizing social life. In large, politically complex societies, however, the unity of men vs. women is blurred by competing ways of organizing individuals, such as class, religion, ethnicity, race, and politics. It is in midrange societies such as the Mundurucú that we find men's cults. Admittedly, no society is free of a measure of tension and conflict between men and women. Among the Mundurucú, however, gender opposition is a matter of organized aggression. In other societies, as the Murphys put it, the battle of the sexes is fought between "individual gladiators" (this volume, 136).

Upon looking at the Mundurucú men's cult, one is shocked at the extent and intensity of gender violence and separation. The men sleep in the men's house, away from the women and their children. The community is matrilocal (the men marry in from other villages), so that men stand apart from the women who are united by kinship. Gang rape is the ultimate sanction not only for intruding on the men's space but also for a woman who in any way threatens the men's status. Hence a girl who might attend a mission school and thereby begin to question the values of the men's culture is a likely target. Moreover, women who are alone are fair game for rape by any man who happens to encounter her. The Murphys describe how one young man lay in wait in a tree looking for a vulnerable woman (136).

Notwithstanding the apparent oppressiveness of this relationship, the Murphys discovered that the women had a certain unity in sisterhood. They were openly contemptuous of the men's pretensions and the ritual of the men's house. "There they go again" was one woman's comment regarding the start of a new ritual sequence.

Looked at in the broad cross-cultural perspective, the Mundurucú are toward the far end of the range of gender opposition and antagonism. In the union of men vs. women, in their residential separation from their wives and families, in the brutality of the sanctions that they imposed upon them, and in the apparent emotional distance and contempt that men and women shared (one of the Mundurucú men claimed men tamed women as wives with "the banana" [120]), the Mundurucú are a remarkable case study of the institutionalization of aspects of gender relationships that we deny or abhor in our own and other cultures. Comparatively, the best examples of societies similar to the Mundurucú are from Tierra del Fuego (Chapman 1982) and especially from New Guinea, such as the Sambia who are described by Gilbert Herdt (1981). Among the Sambia, the union the men is further supported by mandatory homosexual relations between boys and bachelors, as well as continual aggression against other tribal communities.

The intensity of aggression and sexual opposition diminish as the social basis of the cult changes. Residential separation seems to be at the foundation of the most extreme forms of the cult. When men and women live together, their common humanity is more apparent, and it is hard to sustain the rigid divisions that the culture of gender generates. The peoples of the Upper Xingu river in central Brazil, some five hundred miles distant from the Mundurucú, are a good example of this more muted form of the men's cult, in that spouses live together. There is nonetheless opposition and tension in the relationship of men and women. The center of the men's social and political life is in the men's house in the center of the village. Any woman who sees the sacred flutes is raped. Even though this has not occurred for more than fifty years, it has happened in the other tribes of the region. As a threat, it is perpetually present. The Mehinaku part ways with the Mundurucú and Sambia in that their men's cults and their sanctions are more or less compartmentalized. The Mehinaku are enthusiastically heterosexual, and virtually all of the villagers are engaged in affairs that generally do not threaten the stability of marriages. Family relationships, affection, and even love between the genders is as much of a reality as the men's institution. Nothing is more common in the area than a family traveling together. Upon a death, the love that husbands and wives share is institutionalized in the year-long period of seclusion of in which the bereaved spouse is known as "the owner of sadness."

Moving still further from the relatively pure examples of cultures with men's houses like the Mundurucú, we come to societies whose exclusive male cults are now pale shadows of what they may have been in the past. Such is the case of the northwestern Amazon, as described by Stephen Hugh-Jones (2001). He finds that the rituals of the Barasana are reflections on the interdependence of men and women. They retain some of the ideology of male-female opposition and antagonism, but the myths may no longer be directly read as reflecting the psychology of gender differences. Similarly, the exquisite tortures once used for the initiation of boys into the cults in these regions—including the lash and stinging ants—are no longer used.

What is also striking about men's cults in cross-cultural perspective is that they are unsteady edifices, partly because they depart from reality. The world of the myth and the cult are factually wrong. Sex is not dangerous, menstrual blood does not in fact make one sick, women do not have to be gang raped, nor does female sexuality actually threaten the security of the men. In the words of two Melanesianists, men's cults are based on "error"

(Keesing 1982), and they are objectively "preposterous" (Hays 1988). As such, the cults are fragile if dark flowers, easily disrupted by positive and intimate relationships between men and women. Donald Tuzin (1997), in the *Cassowary's Revenge*, relates how Ilahita Arapesh men gave away the secrets of the men's cult and displayed the sacred bull-roarers and fetishes to the women to deliberately destroy the cult. For their part, the Sambia initiated their last cohort of boys in the 1980s, and the cult is in eclipse.

In *Women of the Forest*, the Murphys describe the same process among the Mundurucú, where many of the villagers have chosen to abandon their communities and live in family groups. Part of the lure was access to trade goods, but it is also clear that the opportunity for husbands and wives to live together was also significant. As the Murphys and Tuzin demonstrate, both the Mundurucú and the Ilahita Arapesh got more than they bargained for, in that the conflict between men and women, which had formerly been played out at a group level, was now inserted directly into marital relationships. Although liberated from some of the culture of gender misunderstanding, there remained a nostalgia for the richness of symbolic life and the "sanctuary" offered by the men's house.

It is doubtless true that in the near future societies that are based on men's cults will disappear. With them will also go a purity of social form in which gender is the organizing template for both social structure and a complex and "gender-inflected" culture. From the perspective of comparative anthropology, this is surely a loss. But from a frankly value-oriented perspective, one might well also see traditional Mundurucú social organization, with its obsessive concern for sexual separation, as mutually punishing for both men and women. Lest we become too prideful, however, the Murphys remarkable account not only allows us to see the Mundurucú but also ourselves, since we struggle with many of the same issues of gender conflict, albeit in different ways and with different resolutions.

The reader now begins a narrative that is both a contribution to social science and a beautifully crafted work of ethnographic liter-

ature. Written with great sensitivity and attention to detail, it suc-
ceeds in conveying the life ways of a people whose lives, even
when disturbingly different from our own, had richness and depth.
As such, the Murphys' *Women of the Forest* is a work of appreciation
for their subjects.

References Cited

Barnes, Monica. 2003. "Gertrude Evelyn Dole, 1915–2001." *American Anthro-pologist* 105 (2):484–86.

Burkhalter, S. Brian. 1988. "Sexual Antagonism and Play in Mundurucú Soci-ety: The Fun Is in the Chase." *In Dialectics and Gender: Anthropological Ap-proaches*, ed. Richard R. Randolph, David M. Schneider, and May N. Diaz, 57–65. Boulder, Colo.: Westview.

Burkhalter, S. Brian, and Robert F. Murphy. 1989. "Tappers and Sappers: Rubber, Gold, and Money Among the Mundurucú." *American Ethnologist* 16 (1):100–116.

Chapman, Anne. 1982. *Drama and Power in a Hunting Society: the Selk'nam of Tierra del Fuego*. Cambridge: Cambridge University Press.

Chernela, Janet. 1997. "Ideal Speech Moments: A Woman's Narrative Perfor-mance in the Northwest Amazon," *Feminist Studies* 23 (1):73–96.

Chodorow, Nancy. 1974. "Family Structure and Feminine Personality." In *Women, Culture, and Society*, ed. Michelle Zimbalist Rosaldo and Louise Lamphere, 43–66. Stanford, Calif.: Stanford University Press.

——. 1978. *The Reproduction of Mothering*. Berkeley: University of California Press.

Eagly, Alice H., and Wendy Wood. 2003. "The Origins of Sex Differences in Human Behavior: Evolved Dispositions Versus Social Roles." In *Evolu-tion, Gender, and Rape*, ed. Cheryl Brown Travis, 265–304. Cambridge, Mass.: MIT Press.

Ferguson, R. Brian. 1988. "War and the Sexes in Amazonia." In *Dialectics and Gender: Anthropological Approaches*, ed. Richard R. Randolph, David M. Schneider, and May N. Diaz, 136–54. Boulder, Colo.: Westview.

Gilmore, David. 1990. *Manhood in the Making: Cultural Concepts of Masculinity*. New Haven, Conn.: Yale University Press.

Goodale, Jane. 1971. *Tiwi Wives: A Study of the Women of Melville Island, North Australia*. Seattle: University of Washington Press.

Gregor, Thomas A. 1985. *Anxious Pleasures: The Sexual Lives of an Amazonian People*. Chicago: University of Chicago Press.

Gregor, Thomas A., and Donald Tuzin. 2001. "The Anguish of Gender: Myths of Matriarchy and Men's Cults in Amazonia and Melanesia." In *Gender in Amazonia and Melanesia: An Exploration of the Comparative Method*, ed. Thomas A.Gregor and Donald Tuzin, 309–36. Berkeley and Los Angeles: University of California Press.

Hart, C. W. M, and Arnold R. Pilling. 1979. *The Tiwi of North Australia*. New York: Holt, Rinehart, and Winston.

Hays, Terrance E. 1988. "'Myths of Matriarchy' and the Sacred Flute Complex of the Papua New Guinea Highlands." In *Myths of Matriarchy Reconsidered*, ed. Deborah Gewertz, 201–38. Oceania Monograph 33. Berkeley: University of California Press.

Herdt, Gilbert H. 1981. *Guardians of the Flutes: Idioms of Masculinity*. New York: McGraw Hill.

Hugh-Jones, Stephen. 2001. "The Gender of Some Amazonian Gifts: An Experiment with an Experiment." In *Gender in Amazonia and Melanesia: An Exploration of the Comparative Method*, ed. Thomas A.Gregor and Donald Tuzin, 245–78. Berkeley and Los Angeles: University of California Press

Keesing, Roger M. 1982. Introduction to *Rituals of Manhood: Male Initiation in Papua New Guinea*, ed. Gilbert H. Herdt, 1–43. Berkeley: University of California Press.

Koch-Grunberg, Theodor. 1917. *Von Roraima zum Orinoco. Reise durch Nordbrasilien zum Orinoco in den Jahren, 1911–1913*. Vol. 3. Berlin: Verlag Dietrich Reimer.

Lowie, Robert. 1920. *Primitive Society*. New York: Boni and Liveright.

———. 1949. "Social and Political Organizations of the Tropical Forest and Marginal tribes." In *Handbook of South American Indians V: The Comparative Ethnology of South American Indians*, ed. Julian H. Steward, 313–69. Smithsonian Institution Bureau of American Ethnology Bulletin 143. Washington, D.C.: Smithsonian Institution.

Mead, Margaret. 1968 [1949]. *Male and Female: A Study of Sexes in a Changing World*. New York: Dell.

Lyons, Patricia J. 1985 (1974). *Native Americans: Ethnology of the Least Known Continent.* Prospect Heights, Ill.: Waveland Press.

Murphy, Robert F. 1957. "Intergroup Hostility and Social Cohesion." *American Anthropologist* 59:1018–35.

———. 1959. "Social Structure and Sex Antagonism." *Southwestern Journal of Anthropology* 15 (1):89–98.

———. 1960. *Headhunters' Heritage: Social and Economic Change Among the Mundurucú Indians.* Berkeley and Los Angeles: University of California Press.

———. 1971. *The Dialectics of Social Life: Alarms and Excursions in Anthropological Theory.* New York: Basic Books.

———. 1974. "Deviance and Social Control II: Borai." In *Native South Americans: Ethnology of the Least Known Continent,* ed. Patricia J. Lyon, 202–8. Boston: Little, Brown.

———. 1975. "The Quest for Cultural Reality: Adventures in Irish Social Anthropology." Paper presented at the Department of Anthropology, University of Michigan, Ann Arbor. 27 October.

———. 1977. "Introduction: The Anthropological Theories of Julian H. Steward." In *Evolution and Ecology: Essays on Social Transformation by Julian H. Steward,* ed. Jane C. Steward and Robert F. Murphy, 1–39. Urbana: University of Illinois Press.

———. 1987. *The Body Silent.* New York: Henry Holt.

Murphy, Robert F., and Julian H. Steward. 1956. "Tappers and Trappers: Parallel Processes in Acculturation." *Economic Development and Culture Change* 4:335–55.

Murphy, Yolanda. 1972. "The Mundurucú Women of the Village of Cabruá." Master's thesis. Columbia University.

Rimer, Sara. 2003. "Social Expectations Pressuring Women at Duke." *New York Times,* 24 September.

Ortner, Sherry. 1974 "Is Female to Male as Nature Is to Culture?" In *Woman, Culture, and Society,* ed. Michelle Zimbalist Rosaldo and Louise Lamphere, 67–88. Stanford, Calif.: Stanford University Press.

Picchi, Debra. 2003. "Brazilian Indigenous Gender Constructs in a Modern Context." *History and Anthropology* 14 (1):23–39.

Ribeiro, Berta. 1979 *Diário do Xingú.* Rio de Janeiro: Paz e Terra.

Randolph, Richard R., David M. Schneider, and May N. Diaz, eds. 1988. *Dialectics and Gender: Anthropological Approaches.* Boulder, Colo.: Westview.

Rosaldo, Michelle Zimbalist, and Louise Lamphere, eds. 1974. *Women, Culture, and Society*. Stanford, Calif.: Stanford University Press.

Tuzin, Donald. 1997. *The Cassowary's Revenge: The Life and Death of Masculinity in New Guinea Society*. Chicago: University of Chicago Press.

Preface to Second Edition

The second edition of *Women of the Forest* contains a new chapter in which we present a chronicle of our fieldwork and a description of our methods. The book is otherwise unchanged, except for minor editorial revisions. When we initially wrote *Women of the Forest*, we had not fully anticipated that it would be so widely used in introductory cultural anthropology courses. The language of the work was intentionally nontechnical, making it accessible to the beginning student, but we had not considered the possibility that a substantial segment of our audience would have only a vague idea of how data are collected. The new chapter meets this need.

Chapter 3, "Beyond the Looking Glass," gives the reader an idea of the nature of ethnographic fieldwork as both personal experience and scientific practice. In recent years, anthropologists have turned increasingly toward the study of life in modern industrial societies, and the recounting of our own adventures is a remembrance of the classic fieldwork situation of novices living with a primitive tribe in a total wilderness. We hope that the reader will catch some of the flavor of our odyssey. The beginning student will also learn something about anthropological methods of data gathering, as well as some of the pitfalls in interpretation. In this sense, our intention has been to increase the educational value of the book.

In the thirty-two years since our field trip, many profound changes have taken place in Mundurucú society. These have been masterfully described and analyzed by Dr. Brian Burkhalter, now of the University of South Florida, who worked among the Mundurucú in 1979–81 (Burkhalter 1983). We have not, however, incorporated his findings in this edition, which remains a description of the Mundurucú in 1952–53. Dr. Burkhalter is now preparing a book based on his later research, and we look forward to its publication.

A few further notes are in order. All personal names of Mundurucú individuals in this book are pseudonyms, starting with Borai, the fictitious heroine of our composite "Woman's Day." We hope, too, that the addition of a chapter on our research will give proper recognition of our indebtedness to Sr. Francisco Manhuari, our field assistant. We also note with appreciation the services of Ms. Elizabeth Astwood, who prepared the manuscript of the new chapter. And we acknowledge with gratitude the fact that it was our colleague Dr. Elliott Skinner who first suggested the book's title. Finally, to all who have read the book over the years and told us of your reactions, our deepest thanks.

July 1985

Preface to First Edition

Over two decades have passed since we studied the Mundurucú Indians, a time during which our data, both the truths and the errors, have of necessity remained the same, but during which we have changed. We were still in our twenties and recently married when we first walked into a Mundurucú village—we were students, and we lived in a world that, for all its problems, seemed somehow or other more predictable and orderly than today's. And we had studied an anthropology which, however relativistic, was expansive and optimistic in outlook, as befitted the times.

This book is written by different people than the young ethnographers who went to Brazil in 1952. The authors are middle-aged, they have raised a family in the interim, they have experienced the failure of confidence that has occurred in America in the last ten years, and they teach an anthropology that lacks the certitude and consensus of the one they learned. It is a science that, like this book, now takes a somewhat skeptical view of our common-sense perceptions, sees illusions where we once saw hard facts, and views society not as a clockwork but as a series of binds and contradictions. But it is a science that is in search of new directions, and we hope that where it has lost in exuberance it has gained in depth of reflection.

It is for all these reasons that this book will present a somewhat different view of Mundurucú society than in Robert Murphy's previous publications (1956, 1957, 1958, 1959, 1960). Of even greater importance, however, is that the subject matter has shifted, for we turn now to the role of the woman, a topic that Yolanda Murphy has discussed elsewhere (1972).

The project had its incipience when we were graduate students, long before the current rise of interest in "women's studies." Dr. Gene Weltfish, who was a professor at Columbia University at that time and an early and steadfast proponent of the rights of women, invited Yolanda into her office and told her in no uncertain terms that she should do a thorough study of the life of the Mundurucú women. Ethnographies have such a strong male orientation, Dr. Weltfish argued, that one could well wonder who or what gave birth to the men.

She was, of course, absolutely right, for most anthropological field research has been done by men, and there has been a distressing tendency for even the work of women to have the same bias toward male values and activities. This was not in the least true of Weltfish and the other great female anthropologists who trained at Columbia under Franz Boas but, until very recently, the later generations of women anthropologists attuned their interests to the theoretical and substantive issues posed by the men.

In their defense, one can note that they had career goals and livings to make, and these were the directions for advancement in a male world; one goes where the action is. But it is good to remember that the anthropological study of women is not one of the social phenomena of the 1960s, for decades earlier the research had been pioneered by such persons as Ruth Bunzel, Ruth Landis, Margaret Mead, and Gene Weltfish, and had been urged by them upon their students.

Following Gene Weltfish's advice was not difficult for Yolanda. As we will show, social life among the Mundurucú was sharply dichotomized by sex, and we drifted quite naturally into the same pattern in our interaction with the Indians. Our experience was hardly unique among ethnographers. Most have found that male anthropologists have poor success in establishing rapport with females. No matter how antiseptic their advances, these are often misinterpreted by the women, and sometimes by their husbands. Often, too, women feel a sense of embattlement against their men, and a male who also asks persistent questions becomes doubly threatening.

Female anthropologists actually have better results with men than their male colleagues do with women. First, from the point of view of the women, she is one of them. Second, from the point of view of the men she is a Martian, somebody they really do not have to fit into the arrangements and values that guarantee their superiority; in this sense she is like an African in the American South. In the same spirit, the Mundurucú men thought that Yolanda was Robert's worry, not theirs, and she could do as she wished. Besides, the essential colonialism of the relationship between anthropologists and informants sees the male-female status difference canceled out by the fact that the female anthropologist comes from the more powerful society. An unpleasant observation, but true.

Most of our days were spent by Yolanda among the women and by Robert among the men. She sat with the women in their houses, worked with them in making manioc flour, went with them to the gardens, bathed with them, and helped them take care of the children. When she was not off with them, one or more women were usually in our house. Mundurucú women are eminently gregarious, and she soon became included in most of their activities. She did not have to search for informants or seek ways to intrude herself in their midst. Quite to the contrary, she sometimes wished for more privacy. Even today, she recalls nostalgically the hot afternoons when she would settle in her hammock for a nap only to be aroused out of slumber by the women, who would shake her hammock insistently, calling out, "Iolantá, are you awake?"

The fieldwork, lasting from June 1952 to June 1953, was carried out in two villages, one a traditional community of the savannahs far inland from the Tapajós River, and the other a more acculturated village along one of the Tapajós tributaries. The contrasts between the two were an essential part of Robert's book *Headhunter's Heritage* (1960), a study of social change, for they showed in a slice of time the history of the inroads of Brazilian society upon Mundurucú culture.

The two communities were equally valuable for limning Mundurucú sex roles, for one of them had a men's house and the other did not. We had thus found two very different modes of sexual interaction in the same group of people and at the same time. It might be added that though we lived in Mundurucú villages in Mundurucú houses, following a pattern of existence not too different from that of the Indians, Robert never lived in the men's house. We ate like the Mundurucú, but we still had a typically American marriage.

Our account of the life of the Mundurucú woman will, hopefully, reveal a great deal about their men as well, but from a different angle. One of the great faults of cultural descriptions that center upon males, whether they do so intentionally or not, is that they are one-dimensional, not just in their neglect of the female but in their treatment of the men. Elementary logic tells us that to know light, you must have a concept of darkness, for they are relative to each other and intelligible only in terms of each other. In the same sense, one cannot understand one sex role except in its interaction with the other, for they define one another, they beget one another, and they become actualized only vis-à-vis one another.

The relationship is a dialectical one in the exact sense of the term, and our book will then, in a broader framework, be an analysis of sex relations among the Mundurucú from the standpoint of the female. It has been written in what we believe is conformity to the proper standards of anthropological scholarship, but its language has been left deliberately simple and untechnical in order that it will be easily read by the student or layman. The book pretends to be a study only of the Mundurucú, and we make minimal reference to the voluminous literature on women in our own and other societies. Nonetheless, the general significance of the study will become evident, and the final chapter will explore its ramifications.

The substantive conclusions of this book belong properly at its end, but it should be said at the outset that one of its primary lessons is that the subject matter, for all the ink that has been spilled over it, remains obscure and refractory—perhaps because everybody is too close to the problems of sex roles and sex identities to think effectively about them. This bodes ill for all of us, for the depth and magnitude of the modern transformation of sex roles in our own society is greater than most of us are able to perceive.

In looking at the position of women in another, totally different, society, we hopefully can stand off from ourselves as well, and see the cant and illusion that invade our own thinking on sexuality. And in doing so, we must keep in mind that there are awesome gaps between our images of life and life as it is lived, between the rules of society and the course of daily events. This is one of anthropology's most elementary teachings; its relevance to the problems of females and males was lucidly expressed by Robert H. Lowie (1920, p. 188) over half a century ago: ". . . it is important to ascertain what customary or written law and philosophic theory have to say on feminine rights and obligations. But it is more important to know whether social practice conforms to theory or leaves it halting in the rear, as it so frequently does."

We have had the opportunity in other prefaces to other publications on the Mundurucú to express our sense of debt to colleagues, teachers, and institutions, and to friends and associates in Brazil who contributed to our research. It is, however, a pleasure to once again acknowledge the fellowship support of Columbia University and the Social Science Research Council which made the research possible. A draft of the present work was read by Orna Johnson, who helped greatly with her comments, and we have prevailed upon many others to listen to our ideas. John Moore of the Columbia University Press lent his encouragement to the project and his trenchant observations to the manuscript. We also wish to express our thanks to Mrs. Jessie Malinowska for her editorial assistance and typing.

The myths on pages 114–15 and 124–25 are reprinted, with permission, from "Mundurucú Religion," *University of California Publicatijons in Archaeology and Ethnology*, Vol. 49, No. 1, Berkeley and Los Angeles: University of California Press, 1958.

One of the great joys of writing the book has been the revival of dormant memories of the Mundurucú, for it has allowed us to relive the most fascinating year of our life. Yolanda, especially, remembers the kindness, good humor, warmth, and generosity of those lovely people, the Mundurucú women. They accepted her as a friend and as a sister, and she will never forget them. This book is her witness to their lives.

Y. M.
R. F. M.
Leonia, New Jersey
May 1974

Women of the Forest

1.

Woman's
∧∧∧∧∧∧∧ Day

Dawn came first as a shift of light and shadow in the eastern sky, etching out of the blackness of the night the outline of the hills on the watershed of the rivers. With it, the forest fell silent, the raucous noises of the night creatures faded, and the great quietude separating the life of the night from that of the day reached its brief ascendancy. As the eastern sky turned a dark, then a lighter, gray, the houses of the Mundurucú village of Cabruá began to emerge from shadows into pale images, and the first stirring of the people was heard.

Borai tossed in her hammock, wrapped it tightly around and snuggled her baby closely against the chill dawn. The child began to whimper, and she took a breast from under her worn dress and placed it by his mouth. While he suckled, Borai lay half-asleep, gazing out through the space between the walls and roof of the house, watching the light strengthen in the east. The eight-month-old baby finished feeding, fell back to sleep, and Borai gently disengaged herself from it and eased out of her warm cocoon into the cold of the wakening house. She yawned and stretched, scratched herself luxuriantly, and then kicked at the dogs nestled around the smoldering household fire.

The earth around the hearth was still warm, and she stood close to it, warming the bottoms of her feet. Borai then took some kindling and placing it next to the fire, took a still glowing end of a piece of wood from last night's fire and blew it into flame. She placed the kindling carefully around the small flame, like spokes about a hub, and when the fire crackled into life, brought over larger pieces of firewood to prepare for the day's cooking. She swung rather halfheartedly with a piece of firewood at the lingering dogs, chasing them out of the house, and then went to stand at the back door, pensively watching the breaking day.

The sky in the east had by then turned to delicate and striated bands of mauve and pink, and the land in the valley below was beginning to appear from the gloom. The hills beyond the headwaters of the river could now be seen in sharp relief, and the islands of forest in the rolling savannah appeared as dark blotches, their trees gaining distinction as the light grew stronger. The valleys were still covered with the mist of the dawn, and small pockets of fog moved slowly across the faces of the hills. It was a calm and serene period, and the other women of the house only spoke to each other in whispers, lest the stillness of the natural world be torn by human beings.

The life of the village gained momentum as the natural order of the day asserted itself. Before the sun had edged over the horizon, a rooster crowed from somewhere in the underbrush bordering the village, another in the brush near the *farinha*-making shed answered, and the morning litany of cock-crowing was joined by the first snarling fight of dogs competing for a shred of tapir intestine outside the village. In the men's house many of the men were stirring, though a few were still lying in their hammocks, their feet dangling over the small fires they had built beneath. Most of them planned to hunt that day, and they were already testing bow strings and sighting down arrow shafts for straightness. Others squatted by a fire to discuss where to hunt, passing from one to another the single cigarette one of them had rolled.

Borai's husband, Kaba, broke away from the group of men and came to the house. He sat on a log that served as a seat, and Borai brought him a half gourd of farinha, flour made from bitter manioc, mixed with water. He tilted the container back, pushing the farinha toward his mouth with a hunting knife, and passed it back to her when he had finished. Borai had warmed up, over the fire, two monkey legs left from the previous night's dinner, and she passed one of the legs over to him with a small gourd of salt. He dipped the scrawny and heat-shriveled meat in the salt between each bite, washed it down with water, and went back to join the gathering hunting party. Few words had been exchanged. The baby had a slight cold; Kaba asked how he had spent the night, and he played with the child for a short time before leaving.

Borai's older son by a previous marriage, a boy of twelve, arrived from the men's house for food and water, but left quickly to join the other boys, who were planning a day of stalking fish with bow and arrow in a nearby stream. The boys would roast the small fish near the stream and eat palm fruits, so she did not expect to see him again until the men began to return from the hunt, bringing the boys out of the forest to examine the day's kill. The baby having begun to cry, she picked him out of the hammock and gave him the breast again, then passed the child to her sister's ten-year-old daughter, who put the now squalling baby in a carrying sling passed around her shoulder, forming a seat for the baby on her narrow hip. Freed of her burden, Borai gnawed on monkey bones, took some farinha and water, and then went off some 200 feet from the village to relieve herself. Three thin and mangy dogs, not suited for hunting and thus reduced to scavenging garbage and human waste, followed her, sat patiently on their haunches, and waited.

The sun had cleared the hills and the house was in full motion when Borai returned. Children were laughing, crying, and shouting, emerging from their houses to wander through the village and explore the other four dwellings. Wherever the little ones went, they were offered a bit of food and fondled, for in this village of ninety people, every child was well known to each adult, and most of them were related in ways that people could not quite specify, however much they categorized their kinship ties. The men by this time had left the village, winding single file down the path that led from the grass-covered hill into the still mist-shrouded forests bordering the stream below. The column of hunters passed out of sight, but the women and children could still hear the barks of the hunting dogs and the deep sounds of the horns of the hunters signaling to each other, ever more faintly until only the low murmur of village life broke the calm that had settled on the community.

As the sun rose, it evaporated the mists, driving away the cool of the dawn and touching the village with a promise of the oppressive heat of midday. It was May, and though the worst of the rains had passed from the uplifted drainage south of the Amazon River, the air remained humid, and afternoon thunderstorms were still frequent. But the streams had receded to the confines of their banks, their waters had cleared, and the small rivulets of the high savannahs flowed cool through the tunnels of forest they watered. The women of Borai's house—her mother, two sisters, the wife of one of her brothers, and a maternal cousin of her mother—gathered up their gourd water containers and, bidding the children to follow, went down to the stream below. As the procession wound through the village and past the back doors of other houses, more women joined them, calling out to each other, while the little children ran down the grassy hill, playing as they went; the boys were empty-handed, but their small sisters carried their own little gourds. As they neared the stream, the older boys finished their morning swim and began to work their way downstream to one of the better fishing holes.

The smallest children, who were naked, ran into the water with shrieks of glee, while their older sisters shucked off their thin dresses and followed them. The older women eased into the stream, taking off their clothes as the water rose higher on their bodies. The water was stinging cold at first, but they soon became accustomed to it, ducking under the surface and splashing each other happily. The women rubbed their bodies with the water and scrubbed the backsides of the smallest children to clean them. They splashed about for another half hour and then slipped on their cotton Mother Hubbard dresses and sat in the sun to warm and dry.

Their ablutions done, the women filled the water gourds, and most started back up the hill to the village. A few stayed behind to wash clothes, dipping them in the water, rubbing their folds against each other, and smacking the wet clothing against flat rocks. Last week, the village had run out of the soap they had gotten from the trader, but most of the dirt was washed out without it. Borai had only two dresses, the one she was wearing and the one being washed; Kaba had promised her another after he had sold some rubber to the trader during the coming months of the dry season.

The washing done, the remainder of the women returned to the village together. Both propriety and fear of lone and wandering males kept any from remaining behind, forcing them to stay in small groups on almost any venture beyond the immediate vicinity of the village. Back at the house, Borai hung her tattered wash on a small cotton bush near the back door and began to clean up garbage, which she simply threw in the underbrush, from the cleared area around the house. She started to sweep out the house with a broom improvised from a few branches, but the baby began to cry in earnest, and she took him from her niece. This time, however, instead of offering the breast to the child, she mashed up a piece of banana with a chunk of boiled sweet manioc and spooned it into his mouth. She then put the baby in its carrying sling and swept the floor in a rather desultory way with one hand, while stroking the baby with the other. One of her sisters joined in the house-cleaning, and they swept the remains out the door, where a tame parrot and two hens immediately began to pick through the trash for pieces of grain and fruit. The women watched in amusement as the hens tried unsuccessfully to drive off the parrot, who reared back in outrage and squawked at the menacing fowl. The sisters then sat in their hammocks and talked to their mother about the day's work ahead; housekeeping in the large, uncompartmented, and dirt-floored dwellings was the least of their chores.

The sun had risen full into the morning sky, but the peak of the day's heat was still four hours away, making most of the women anxious to get their garden work done. The supply of manioc flour in the house had already been eaten, and for the last two days the women of Borai's house had been drawing on the larders of their neighbors. Borai's mother went to the open-walled shed in the middle of the village where manioc flour was made, and began to build a fire in the large earth-walled oven on which the farinha was toasted. She directed her three daughters to fetch tubers from the stream, where they had been soaking in water for the past three days, and sent her daughter-in-law for more firewood. The daughter-in-law put an axe in her carrying basket, which she carried on her back with a bark-cloth tumpline hung across her forehead, and went through the village to ask her cousin to come help her. Borai and her sister stopped at another house to tell the women where they were going and enlisted the support of two of the occupants. The four then set out for the stream on a path which took them well below the area where they bathed and drew water, and they began to load their baskets with the softened, almost crumbling, manioc tubers. The children had been left with their grandmother, allowing the women to take another, more leisurely, bath and to discuss some of the shortcomings of their sister-in-law.

The carrying baskets were heavy with the water-laden manioc, and they squatted in a genuflecting position with their backs to the baskets, passed the tumplines across their foreheads, and slowly stood up, using the full strength of their torsos and necks to lift the burdens. The sun was beating down on the path as they made their way laboriously back up the hill to the village, walking in silence to conserve their strength. Arriving at the farinha shed, they gratefully dropped their loads into a long hollowed-out log used as a tub and sat down in the shade to rest. Borai's baby began crying as soon as he saw her, quickly escaping from his older cousin to crawl through the dirt to his mother. She nursed him, more for comfort than food, and then let him crawl back and forth across her lap. The sister-in-law and her helper returned from the garden, where they had gathered felled, but unburned, wood and chopped it into stove lengths, and dumped the contents of their baskets next to the farinha oven. They too sat in the shade against one of the shed uprights and joined the conversation. Three other women drifted across the weed-choked village plaza to help, and to tell of their own plans to make farinha in two days' time.

The work party having increased to eight, the women decided

that the dull and laborious chore could be put off no longer. Borai and her mother stepped into the trough filled with soft manioc and began to walk back and forth, working their feet up and down, to break up the tubers and separate the pulp from the skins. As they worked, the water oozed out of the broken tubers, mixed with the pulp into a thick mass, and squished rather pleasurably between their toes. Another woman began picking out the skins and throwing them to one side. The sister-in-law and her cousin went off to the old garden for more firewood, and three of the other women went down to the stream to get more manioc. One woman remained seated in the shade, helping Borai's niece in keeping the children from underfoot.

Despite the tedium of the work, the conversation in the farinha shed never slowed. Borai's mother brought up the possibility that the trader might pay a visit to the village in the near future, a story she had heard from the wife of a young man who had been visiting on the Tapajós River. One woman added that it seemed to make little difference whether he arrived or not, as he rarely brought very much desirable merchandise. Another commented that on his last visit the trader had brought nothing but *cachaça*, the regional cane rum, and that the men had exhausted all their credit in becoming thoroughly drunk. Borai's mother reminded the critic that she, too, had drunk her fair share of the trader's rum on that occasion, and the onlookers dissolved in laughter. Given the fact that many of the women had drunk as much as the men would let them have, the subject was quickly turned to the men. One of the chief topics of conversation at the time was the visit in the village of a young man, who was in a late stage of courtship of one of the village's girls. The progress of the romance was carefully examined by the group in the farinha shed, and the young man's merits mercilessly evaluated. One of the women noted that the suitor had a small penis, bringing forth the sour remark that he was not much different from the other men. At least, said another, his penis showed more life than those of most of the other men. The women laughed and all looked over with amusement toward the men's house, where two or three occupants still lingered. The men, aware of the derision, became furiously intent on whatever they were doing, their eyes turned carefully away from the farinha shed.

In the meantime, the work was progressing at a slow and steady pace. Large wads of wet pulp were taken from the trough and placed in the open end of a *tipiti*. The tipiti was a long tube made of loosely woven palm leaves, with an open mouth at the top and closed at the bottom. The top end was suspended from a rafter, and a long pole was placed through a loop at the bottom. Two of the women sat on the end of the pole, the other end of which was secured near the ground, and the resultant lever pulled powerfully downward on the tipiti. This caused it to elongate and constrict, squeezing out the water from the pulp and leaving the contents still moist, ready to be sieved. When only a dribble of water came from the tipiti, the women emptied the pulp into a large sieve placed over a shallow basin and gently worked it through the mesh with their fingers. It dropped into the receptacle as a coarse, damp cereal, and the pieces that did not go through were taken by another of the women and pounded with a wooden mortar and pestle.

The day's production of farinha would not last the household much more than a week, and the women agreed that they should put more tubers in the water to soak. Borai and three of the other women took their carrying baskets and machetes and headed out of the village to the gardens. They followed a path from the village plaza that passed in back of one of the houses. The path narrowed through the dense underbrush surrounding

the village and emerged suddenly into the open savannah. The
land ahead rolled gently. The sandy soil was covered with
clumps of short grass and small flowering shrubs, and here and
there were small islands of trees, some of which marked the sites
of old and abandoned villages. These were easily identified by
the scattered fruit palms in their midsts, the end products of
palm pits thrown away decades ago. As the women walked
single file along the narrow path worn through the grasses, they
commented on almost everything they saw—a pair of doves
cooing in a distant grove, a parrot flying from one tree clump to
another, the activity around a termite hill, a curious cloud formation.

The trail entered suddenly into the forest and dropped to a
small stream that bubbled among rocks. A log served as a bridge
across the water, but the women stopped to bathe before going
on to the garden. The path wound for a while among very tall
trees, whose leafy branches almost 100 feet above kept out the
sunlight and left the forest floor clear of underbrush. As the trail
rose, it became lighter and the underbrush became thicker, for
they were entering a tract that had been farmed many years ago
and was still under the cover of lower, secondary forest.
Shadow gave way to brightness, dark greens to light hues, and
coolness to heat as the women broke out of the forest and into
the garden.

The garden was no more than two acres in extent, and along
with two other producing gardens provided the main source of
vegetable food for the household. This garden had been cleared
two years earlier and was yielding only manioc on its second
planting. One of the women, however, spotted a pineapple
growing among the weeds and picked it for her children to eat.
The garden was rank with weeds and, since no further planting
would be done in it, nobody bothered any longer to keep it

cleared. To the women, it looked like any other garden, though an outsider would see nothing more than stumps, felled and charred tree trunks lying at various angles, and a clutter of undergrowth. Most of the higher vegetation, however, was bitter manioc, the tall stalks of which had grown to six feet and over.

The women set to their harvest work, taking the machetes from their baskets and cutting the manioc stalks near their bases. They put the stalks aside, and then proceeded to dig out the tubers clustered at the base of each stalk, like fingers from a hand, with the machetes. Each plant yielded two to five tubers, ranging in size from six inches to over a foot in length; if the manioc had been left in the ground to grow for a few months longer, some would reach a length of two feet or so. After knocking the dirt from the manioc, the tubers were put in the baskets. Before going back, the women made a brief reconnoiter of the garden in search of more pineapples or an unharvested squash. Unsuccessful, they took up their burdens and, with another stopover for a drink of water, went directly to the stream near the village where they put the manioc in a quiet pool to soak.

By the time this chore was done, the sun was almost directly overhead, and the morning breezes had died completely. The village lay beaten down by the sun, quiet and somnolent under the noonday heat. The roosters and chickens were not to be seen, and the few dogs remaining in the village were lying in the shade. One of the men in the men's house was still working on a basket, but the other two had retired to their hammocks in its shady recesses. Borai and her companions went to the farinha shed, where she found her baby crying lustily from hunger. She sat in the shade to nurse him, while watching her mother and another woman slowly turning and stirring the manioc flour, which was being toasted on a copper griddle above the furnace.

The women each had a canoe paddle which they used as a spatula to prevent the manioc from burning on the pan and to turn under the flour on top to expose it again to the heat. It would take well over an hour for each panful to become dry and toasted brown, and other women took up the task at intervals of about fifteen minutes to relieve the heat-parched workers.

As the work dragged on, most of its preliminary phases, such as bringing in the manioc, mashing it, running the pulp through the tipití, and sieving the resulting mash, were already largely completed, and many of the helpers from the other houses had drifted away to escape the heat of the oven. Borai was hungry after her morning's work and she went to the dwelling, where she put the baby in her hammock. One of her sisters had cooked some plantains in the coals of the fire and offered her some, and Borai rounded out the meal with manioc mixed with a drink made of palm fruit. She then lay down in the hammock to rest with her child and almost immediately fell into a light sleep.

Borai drowsed in the heavy heat of the afternoon and finally awakened after the baby's fitfulness had turned into crying. She fed him and then went out to the farinha shed, where she gave the baby to one of the young girls and took a turn at toasting the manioc flour. The rest of the farinha-making process was now completed, but two five-gallon cans filled with damp sieved pulp remained to be put on the griddle, and it would be almost dark before they were finally done. Though only one or two women at a time were required for the work, others drifted out from the houses to join in the conversation. The sun was already halfway between its zenith and the horizon, and dark cumulus clouds were beginning to build up in the west. The breezes freshened as the storm approached, dispelling the heat and lifting everybody from their afternoon torpor. One of the women suggested that it was time to get water for the evening meal, and the group scattered to their houses to gather up gourds and children. Some twenty of them trooped down to the stream to bathe off the day's sweat and to immerse themselves in the cold stream, lolling in it until their teeth chattered and they had to seek the warmth of a sun-bathed rock.

From the distance, still deep back in the forest, the faint sound of a horn was heard, followed a short time later by another, somewhat closer. The women quickly filled the water containers and shooed the children ahead of them as they hurried to get back to the village before the hunting party. The storm, too, was approaching, and the silence of the forest and savannahs was broken by still remote rumbles of thunder. Borai went to her house and placed more wood on the fire, put the baby in the hammock, and waited for the return of her husband.

The hunters split up just outside the village and took the separate paths that led to the back entrances of their houses. Borai was waiting there when Kaba walked through the door carrying a wild pig, weighing about 100 pounds, across his shoulders. He dropped the pig to the floor, put his bow and arrow on a platform under the rafters, and sat to wait for Borai to bring him a half gourd of water and manioc. She commented on the fatness of the wild pig, asking her husband where he had taken it. "We cornered the herd at a crossing of the River of the Wild Turkey, not far from the Cabruá River and at a place where there are still ripe *burití* palm fruit," he replied. "The arrow of my brother Warú hit this one in the flank, and I brought him down with another over the heart." He went on to tell Borai that four pigs had been killed before the herd broke and ran, and individual hunters had also taken two monkeys, an agouti, and a paca. One of the dogs had been gashed by a boar, but the wound would probably heal. It had been a good hunt.

Kaba saw two men leave the men's house for the stream and

hurried after them to take a bath before the storm hit. The other women of Borai's house joined with her in butchering the wild pig. They took long knives, finely honed on smooth rocks, and drew incisions down the stomach and along the legs. Two of them then carefully pulled back the hide, cutting the gristle at points where it stuck to the flesh. The skin was stretched out with sticks and hung up outside to dry and cure for later sale to the trader. The pig was then sliced through the ventral section to the viscera, the intestines removed and thrown outside to the ravenously hungry dogs. They fell on it ferociously, snarling and fighting while they gulped down whole chunks of the offal. The rest of the pig was quartered, the head and neck put aside as a fifth portion. Pieces of meat were then taken by the women to all the houses in the village, and by the time the usual reciprocity had been observed, almost a whole wild pig was ready for cooking in each dwelling.

The fire was now burning strongly, and Borai half filled a bell-bottomed ceramic pot with water and placed it in the center of the hearth, the flames licking up its sides. As the water heated, she cut a hind quarter of pig into chunks, which she placed in the pot for the evening meal. When the water came toward a boil, she threw in several pinches of salt. Her mother and one of the young girls, in the meanwhile, were cracking Brazil nuts and grating their meats, throwing the fragrant and milky pulp into the pot. The women then sat by the fire, stirring the pot, savoring the smells, and talking happily about the excellence of the meat. The men had by this time returned from their baths and were resting in their hammocks in the men's house, recalling events in the day's hunt, and laughing at some of their misadventures.

The sky had now turned completely dark, though there was still an hour and a half before the sun would set, and a cool breeze blew in advance of the storm. Suddenly the storm struck, with brilliant flashes of lightning and sharp claps of thunder which reverberated off the hills across the valley. The rain fell in sheets, the wind driving it into the open sides of the men's house, forcing some of the occupants to move further into the back and others to run for the walled dwelling houses. The roofs all leaked in places, but the residents had already arranged their hammocks and belongings in dry locations, and nobody paid much attention to the puddles forming on the floor. Borai's mother, nonetheless, took the occasion to ask her sons-in-law when they were going to build a new village. "The roofs are old and leak, the house poles creak in the wind, and one of the children was almost bitten by a scorpion in the underbrush," she said. "Do we have to wait until our gardens are a half-day's walk away before you men decide to move?" Kaba stared intently at his toes and muttered that they were talking about building another village during the next rainy season. There was no time now, for soon after the next full moon most of the people would be leaving to collect rubber on the larger rivers. Enjoying his discomfiture, the old woman reminded him that this is what the men had said last year and then went back to stirring the pot.

The front of the storm had passed, the wind died down, and the rain became lighter. Several of the men wandered back from the dwellings of the women to the men's house and climbed into their hammocks under the shelter of the overhanging roof. Many of the little boys trailed after them to play among the hammocks, and one three-year-old girl toddled along, too; her father took her into his hammock and played with her while talking to the other men. Everybody was in good spirits. There was enough food in the village for at least two days, the rain had made the day's end cool, and the smells of cooking wild pig occasionally wafted over from the houses. The men chatted with each other from their hammocks, and, in one, three teenage boys were rolling about in obvious sex play, unnoted by the adults.

In the houses, the boiled meat was now cooked, and Borai took a large half gourd, filled it with meat and broth, while one of her sisters filled another with freshly made farinha. They brought them across the plaza to the cleared area in front of the men's house, where Kaba took them and called to the other men. Other women were bringing food to their husbands, too, and the men, with most of the boys squatting around them, sat on their haunches in a ring about the bowls. The men took spoons and scooped up meat and broth from the common bowls, occasionally dipping their hands into the farinha bowls and throwing the manioc flour into their mouths with quick tosses. The hunters were hungry after a long day with little more than farinha and water and ate steadily, but quietly and soberly; boisterous and noisy behavior while eating would offend the spirit protectors of the game animals. Other spirits had to be appeased, too, and one of the men took a gourd of meat into the closed chamber adjoining the men's house, where he offered the meat to the ancestral spirits, saying, "Eat grandfathers, and make me lucky in the hunt." The offering made, he brought the bowl of meat back out and placed it with the others.

After the meal had been cooked, the women of Borai's house placed a babricot over the fire. This consisted of a tripod with a horizontal rack of green wood strips running across it a foot from the base. The remaining meat was placed on the babricot, where it would slowly roast and smoke until bedtime. The meat would then be removed, but it would be placed over a low fire again in the morning to complete the cooking process and prevent rotting. One of the women stayed by the fire to turn the meat occasionally and to hit any dogs that approached it. The other women, and the girls and little boys, sat around the pot of boiled meat, filling little half gourds with the stew and eating. The meat was tender, and the sauce of broth and Brazil nut milk delicious. There had been little meat in the village for the past few days, and they all gorged themselves. They also knew that by the third day, the remaining meat would be tough and barely chewable.

Dusk is very brief in the tropics, and the sunset glowed brilliantly against the broken clouds in the clearing western sky. The colors shifted, modulated, changed, and were suddenly gone. Night rapidly enfolded the village, and the people who were watching the setting sun remained a moment in silence and reentered their dwellings. In each house, the women lit small kerosene lamps which cast a flickering glow over the interiors, supplementing the flames of the fires. Borai sat in her hammock, talking with her mother about plans for the next day's work, while her baby sat in the sling on her hip and nursed, more for solace than for food. A few of the children of the house were playing with a puppy, pulling its tail, twisting its legs, and preventing it from running away from them.

Borai and her mother went back to the farinha shed in the middle of the village to finish toasting the manioc flour. They stoked the fire back to life and after letting the oven warm up, poured in the remaining pulp. The glow from the open front of the oven cast a dim and flickering light over their work as they slowly turned and stirred the flour. Other women wandered from their houses to join the group, though the women of the chief's house, who were miffed because they felt they were being gossiped against, stayed home. Finally, unable to bear the thought that the farinha-shed group really was talking about them, two of the chief's daughters joined them. Everybody took a turn at stirring the farinha, but interest centered on a plan to gather *assaí* palm fruits the next morning at a grove a few miles away. The fruit drink, and the abundance of roast meat, would make the day a festive one, and they would hold a dance in the evening.

Across the village plaza, a small fire was burning in front of the men's house. A poorly played guitar was trying to pick out the strain of a Brazilian song heard at a trader's post, and another man was softly playing one of their own songs on a traditional flute. The conversation of the men drifted across as a low murmur, broken occasionally by a raucous cry from one of the boys. After a while, the music stopped, but the silence was soon broken by a deep vibrant note from one of the *karökö*, the long tubular musical instruments which contained the ancestral spirits and which the women were forbidden even to see. The first notes were joined by the second and then the third karökö, playing in counterpoint to each other, slowly, repetitively, and in measured cadence. The men fell silent for a moment, then the conversation picked up again, the guitarist tried futilely to catch the elusive melody, and one of the boys dumped another from his hammock. But the mournful notes of the karökö dominated the village, shut out the night noises, accentuated the calm.

"There they go again," said Borai, as the first sounds of the karökö reached the farinha shed. The women listened for a moment, trying to identify the players by style and skill, laughing at an off-note played by one of the younger men. They then turned back to their conversation and the work of farinha toasting. Many of the little ones were becoming cranky from tiredness, and their mothers caressed them, or nursed the infants. One five-year-old climbed onto his mother's lap to nurse, but giggles from the older girls made him give up after a few minutes. The farinha was finally finished, scooped out of the pan with the paddles into loosely woven baskets lined with palm leaves, and placed on a storage rack in the house. A large bowl of the freshly made flour was kept in the shed, and the women occasionally dipped their fingers into it, enjoying the tanginess of the still hot grains. Some of the women brought their children back to their hammocks and remained in the houses; the rest of the group lingered a while and then went home, two by two, leaving the farinha shed to a few dogs huddled near the warmth of the oven.

The men's house had grown quiet as people drifted off to sleep, and finally the last sounds of the karökö faded. The players emerged from the enclosed sacred chamber, climbed into their hammocks, talked a while, and then fell asleep. One of the men drowsily told the boys to be quiet, and they, too, rolled up inside their hammocks, still whispering to each other. The dying fire cast in flickering outline the arching, open-ended roof of the men's house and the two rows of hammocks.

Borai took the meat off the babricot, placing it in a covered basket, which she put on a storage rack. She threw a bit of dirt on the fire to bank it for the night, removed the babricot, and then slid gently into her hammock so as not to waken the already sleeping baby. Two of the other women went outside to urinate, but they stayed near the house, as the underbrush in the night was a hiding place of the *Yurupari* and other evil spirits. They reentered, blew out the kerosene lamp, and the house fell into silence.

The hills in the east began to emerge from the total blackness as a three-quarter moon rose, bathing the countryside and the village in pale light. The circle of houses around the village plaza could now be clearly seen; yet nothing moved, and the only sounds were an occasional cough or a baby's whimper. Traces of smoke from the smoldering fires were picked up by the moonlight, and the inside of the farinha shed was tinged with orange by the glowing embers of the dying fire. The village was silent, but the forests were not. From far off in the distance, a band of howler monkeys made an ululating uproar, and the noise of tree frogs near the stream was a steady backdrop of tone, broken by the cries of night birds and the chirping of crickets in the brush around the village. Borai listened for a very short while before tiredness overtook her; her last thought before drifting into full sleep was a hope that her husband would not decide to pay a night visit. A woman's day had ended.

2.

The Land
/\\.\\.\\.\\.\\.\\.\\.\\.\\.\\.\\and the
People

The deep and seemingly endless forests of the Amazon River basin have been for centuries a sanctuary of societies having simple technologies and relatively uncomplex social fabrics. It was a way of life that derived its sustenance from horticulture, hunting, fishing, and collecting of wild foods, and populations were small and scattered. The Indians lived off nature without destroying it, and they adapted themselves to the environment without irredeemably altering it. While great civilizations grew in Europe, Asia, Africa, Middle America, and on the crest of the Andes, to the west, the peoples of the Amazonian forest region maintained a simpler existence, changing, to be sure, but at a pace almost imperceptible within the lifetime of an individual. And since they had no system of writing, and therefore no records of their histories, their societies appeared to be frozen, crystalline, and immortal. Wars occurred, people were born and died, but life was seen to move in seasonal cycles, and the social guidelines and institutions that we call culture had a fixity that moderns would find difficult to comprehend. Thus, as parts of the outside world underwent deep and dramatic transformations, starting with the growth of urban centers and states 5,000 years ago and continuing to the Industrial Revolution, the Amazon remained one of those pockets of humanity that had been blessedly bypassed. Changes in the outer world had affected the people of the forests, but they filtered in slowly and in attenuated form. What was left behind were populations that, in economy and overall form of society, were continuations of the condition of much of mankind millennia in the past.

The Indians of the Amazon enjoyed relative isolation—not to be confused with pristine innocence—until recent centuries, when colonial exploration and settlement shattered their autonomy and doomed them to eventual extinction. They were shielded from the Old World to the east by a still untraversed sea and from the native empires to the west by the sheer wall of the Andes. The natural obstacles of the region proved sufficient to keep the Inca armies confined to the high peaks at the Amazon's headwaters, despite several attempts to penetrate the lowland areas. But the Incas lacked both the weaponry and the peculiar singlemindedness and intensity of purpose of the Spanish and Portuguese explorers and conquerors of the sixteenth century, who saw the Amazon as a source of great wealth in gold and slaves, and also undertook to save the souls of the Indians in the process of relieving them of their lives.

The early European settlement of Brazil was restricted almost wholly to the Atlantic coastline, but its repercussions were felt throughout the vast forests to the west. The intrusion of the conquerors sent Indian groups fleeing into the interior, adding greatly to an earlier, precolonial migration from the coast into the Amazon. There followed massive displacements of people, which undoubtedly aggravated the already endemic warfare between the native tribes. At the same time, groups of adventurers, *bandeirantes* in Portuguese, set out from São Paulo and other new colonial settlements in search of gold and human captives for enslavement. The bandeirantes ranged through the interior of eastern Brazil, penetrating well into the Amazonian forests. They pillaged, burned, and killed as they went, scattering those Indians whom they did not enslave. And with them came the entire gamut of European diseases, some of which, like smallpox, were new to the continent and had deadly effects upon a population without natural immunity. The number of Indians in Amazonian Brazil dropped from an estimated 1,500,000 in the sixteenth century to only about 75,000 today. Slavery, assimilation, and warfare accounted for some of this population loss, but disease was without doubt the principal source of the decimation.

As the Portuguese colonization of Brazil continued, the Indians were pushed westward, reduced in numbers, and in many cases whole societies disappeared. Fortunately for the surviving Indians, however, the Amazon remained poorly known and sparsely settled by the whites. The dense forests made overland access almost impossible, restricting travel to the major waterways. Brazilian settlements spread up the main stream of the 'Amazon itself and penetrated the tributaries as far as the heads of navigation.

In the areas adjoining the lower Amazon, between Santarém and Belém, there are extensive uplands reaching northward to the Guiana massifs and southward to the Planalto of Mato Grosso, a vast uplifted area of forests and savannahs. The rivers issuing from these uplands tumble down toward the Amazon through a series of cataracts and rapids which make travel difficult and have inhibited settlement beyond the lower reaches of the streams. The regions above the rapids remained practically uninhabited by whites, except for occasional miners, until the rubber boom of the late nineteenth and early twentieth centuries. Even during this time of great economic activity, however, the Brazilian population of the upper reaches of the Amazon tributaries was thin and scattered and restricted to the banks of the major waterways. The interior regions between these rivers and along their upper shores were either uninhabited or the territory of Indian tribes.

In the early 1950s, when we traveled to study in Brazil, South America was one of the last fastnesses and refuges of primitive peoples. They were found in isolated pockets along the frontier between the Guianas and Brazil, in the rugged uplands of the Venezuelan borders, along the streams issuing from the Andes in Perú, Colombia, and Ecuador, and on the upper waters of the Amazon's great southern tributaries. Only thirty years have passed since that time, but there are far fewer autonomous Indian societies today than there were even then. Governments and missionaries have reached out to establish control over some of the most isolated groups, and only a very few uncontacted and unpacified tribes remain. With the Western world have come clothing, Christianity, new influxes of disease, and absorption of Indians into the labor force of the region.

The technology of the industrial world will ultimately destroy the remaining Indian societies. The rubber extraction trade almost did this at the turn of the twentieth century, but the cultivation of plantation rubber in Malaysia soon caused the collapse of the Amazonian industry, which exploited only wild trees. But this provided no more than a half-century reprieve, and our modern technology, having drained the resources of so much of the rest of the planet, has now turned to the oil, metal, and timber reserves of the Amazon. Burgeoning populations have also pushed deeper into the Amazon drainage in search of agricultural and ranching land.

The penetration of the forests has been facilitated by new technology. Areas that could be reached only after journeys of weeks by boat and on foot are now only hours away from the great cities by airplane; almost every mission station, company outpost, or government installation now boasts its own small landing strip, and pontoon planes can reach any that does not. Even more ominous for the surviving Indian groups, a system of roads which will one day link the cities of the Atlantic and Pacific coasts is now being pushed through the region. The Peruvian government has already constructed roads that extend from the Andes down into the heart of the Amazonian lowlands, and the Brazilians, using giant earthmoving machinery, are slashing a highway through the forests south of the Amazon and parallel to it, and are constructing feeder roads from it which will pierce the practically unknown areas between the rivers. Behind the roadbuilders will come farmers and ranchers, who will clear the forest and displace the Indians from what little territory remains to them. The entire ecological balance of the Amazon is uncertain and threatened, but there is no doubt about the fate of the Indian's way of life: it is doomed.

The new Trans-Amazonian highway crosses the lower Xingú River near the town of Marabá, then swings westward through untrodden wildernesses and ferries the Tapajós River at the town of Itaituba. South of the road, and before it reaches the Tapajós, is a countryside that we remember as remote, peaceful, and untouched, a tract of magnificent wilderness, of deep forests, broad savannahs, and countless rivers, the homeland of the Mundurucú Indians.

In 1952 and 1953, when we studied the Mundurucú, they numbered about 1,250, a population level that was more or less stable, though far below the 5,000 or more estimated for the nineteenth century. Their present homeland is the region east of the upper Tapajós River, one of the principal southern tributaries of the Amazon, in an area circumscribed by the das Tropas and Cururú Rivers, both tributaries of the Tapajós (see Map 1). Of the 1,250 Mundurucú, 200 lived scattered among the Brazilians on the Tapajós River, another 450 were located in a dozen small villages on the Cururú River, about 200 lived at a Catholic mission on the Cururú River, and 50 more were found at the Mundurucú Post of the Brazilian Indian Protection Service. The balance of the population, some 350 people, lived in seven traditional-style villages in the high ground between the headwaters of the Cururú and das Tropas Rivers (see Map 2). Our research took us to both the Cururú River and the savannahs, allowing us to compare and contrast the radically altered life style of the Cururú River villages, invaded as they were by missionary, governmental, and commercial influence, with the relatively unchanged ways of the savannah communities. We were thus able to see social change represented in their contemporary life, to find the Mundurucú past and present side by side.

The Mundurucú are linguistically related to the far-flung Tupí-speaking peoples of South America. The Tupians at one time occupied almost the entire Brazilian coastline, as well as large areas of the lower Amazon River and the shores of its southern tributaries. However, the surviving Tupians, now vastly reduced in numbers, are found only in isolated pockets in the forests of the Araguaya, Xingú, Tapajós, and Ucayali rivers, as well as in Paraguay and French Guiana. Most of the Tupí-speaking peoples were either wiped out by warfare and disease or assimilated into the *caboclo*, or backwoodsman, population of the Amazon valley. Traces of their former suzerainty over this great wilderness are evident in the pronounced Indian features of

MAP 1

REGION OF THE TAPAJÓS AND LOWER MADEIRA RIVERS

Óbidos

AMAZON RIVER

Alemquer

Parentins

Santarém

Mirim

R. Maué-Assú

Paraná

Maués

Boím

Belterra

R. Madeira

R. Curauhy

Borba

R. Cunani

R. Abacaxis

R. Amaná

R. Parauary

Aveiros

R. Cupari

R. Secundurí

TAPAJÓS

Itaituba

Fordlandia

Cachoeira De Maranhão ⚓ São Luiz

Cachoeira Do Apuhý

Cachoeira Da Montanha ⚓

RIO

R. Jamaxin

Bacabal Mission
(abandoned)

AREA SHOWN
IN MAP 2

Cachoeira Do Chacorão

R. Das Tropas

R. Cadiriri

R. Cabituá

R. Crepory

Cachoeira Das Capoeiras ⚓

Barra

Government Indian Post

R. Juruena

R. São Manoel

R. Cururú

Cururú Mission

Miles
0   50

Amazon R.

AREA OF
MAP 1
SHOWN IN
SOUTH
AMERICA

MAP 2
PRESENT TERRITORY OF THE MUNDURUCÚ INDIANS

KEY:
o Mundurucú villages of the Cururú River
● Trading Post
□ Mundurucú villages of the Savannas

São Martinho

Caroçal

TAPAJÓS

Sai Cinza

RIO

Porto Alegre

Vila Nova

Cachoeira Do Chacorão

Ig. Dacheuri

R. Das Tropas

Cabruá

R. Cadiriri

R. Cabitutú

Arö

R. Cabruá

Aipká

Dekodyém

Ig. Parauarokti

Cabitutú

Parauaroktiká

Cabruá

Patuazal

Careca

R. Cururú

Government Indian Post

Cauí

R. São Manoel

Morro

Missão Velha

Maloquinha

Cururú Mission

Parataktí

Uadyemtí

Moiussú

Terra Preta

Cababí

Cachoeira De Crepotiá

João Rebeca

Lucio

0   Miles   10

many local Brazilians and the large number of Tupian words that have been absorbed into the local Portuguese. Some groups located deep enough in the fastnesses of the hinterland of the Amazon maintained their languages, most of their customs, and a considerable degree of autonomy, and they have survived as distinct social and cultural entities until the present day; the Mundurucú are one of these groups.

The Mundurucú first came to the attention of the Portuguese colonists in 1770, when they initiated a series of attacks on settlements along the Amazon River. We know nothing of their earlier history, but their strongest cultural affinities are to groups further south. This, and the sudden explosive expansion of the Mundurucú into the valleys of the lower Tapajós and Madeira Rivers in the late eighteenth century suggest that they may well have been moving northward from an earlier home in the Planalto of Mato Grosso. Whatever their origin, they quickly developed a reputation for tremendous prowess in warfare, and the colonial government sent a successful expedition to the upper Tapajós River in 1795 to pacify them. It hardly seems likely that one defeat by the Portuguese would have quelled permanently the still powerful Mundurucú, but they did indeed stop warring against the whites, finding, perhaps, greater advantage in siding with them.

During the next century, ties between the Mundurucú and the whites grew closer, and the dependence of the Indians upon commerce with the Brazilians grew more complete. Those who had moved into the waters of the lower Madeira and Tapajós Rivers at the end of the eighteenth century fell under the influence of missionaries and traders and were soon busily selling manioc flour and guarana and sarsaparilla bark, used to flavor soft drinks. They maintained friendly relations with the whites and even undertook raids against hostile Indians to make the area safer for commerce and Christian missions. They were, of course, paid for their mercenary services by the local business interests, who found this a cheap and, for them, completely safe way of opening up new areas for exploitation. By 1820, the Mundurucú had scattered the once feared Mura and Arara from the lower Madeira and sent the refugees fleeing into the Brazilian settlements, where they became part of the labor force.

These episodes will hardly win the Mundurucú an honored place in future histories of the Brazilian Indians, but it must have seemed a perfectly logical thing for them to have done at the time. From the Mundurucú point of view, almost all of the surrounding Indian societies were their enemies, and the destruction of enemy villages, the capture of their children, and the taking of trophy heads were traditional and hallowed ways of dealing with a foe. That they should receive axes, knives, guns, cloth, and other avidly desired items for doing what they had always done was probably an unusual boon. And, from the perspective of time, friendly relations with the whites probably saved the Mundurucú from violent destruction of their society.

The Mundurucú of the lower Tapajós River had been almost wholly assimilated into the Brazilian population by the end of the nineteenth century. Those on the Madeira waters still maintained a separate identity, but they had lost their capacity for warfare by the middle of the century and lived in Brazilian-style villages which served as home bases for the gathering of wild products. Louis Agassiz and his wife found only a few bilingual Mundurucú in the area in 1865 (Agassiz, 1869, p. 312), but today, the native language has practically disappeared, the people are almost completely Brazilianized. The last bastion of Mundurucú culture, then, is in the upper Tapajós valley, and the survivors have only vague traditions recalling their former domination of a region extending north to the Amazon.

The Mundurucú of the upper Tapajós, though more isolated than their fellows to the north, were not immune to the changes occurring outside. They, too, were occasionally enlisted by the whites in raids against other tribes, but they also pursued warfare on their own without encouragement or pay. We do not know for certain when the first itinerant traders penetrated the Tapajós River above the rapids, but by the 1850s, the *regatões*, as they are called in Portuguese, were trading Western articles with the Mundurucú in exchange for manioc flour and wild products. Large-scale penetration and permanent settlement of the upper Tapajós began during the 1860s. The Brazil–Paraguay War of the late 1860s made it necessary to supply the city of Cuyabá, far to the south in Mato Grosso, by way of the Tapajós River, and large convoys of canoes pushed up the stream through country that has not been traversed since, all the way to the headwaters of the Tapajós and down the Paraguay. At roughly the same time, a development of even more fundamental importance was taking place: the growing demand for wild rubber had attracted collectors and traders into the upper Tapajós valley proper.

The Mundurucú found a market for their surplus manioc flour in the rubber collectors and traders who drifted in increasing numbers into the upper Tapajós after 1860, and a few Indians began collecting the latex of the *hevea brasiliensis* during the dry season months of June to September. The Brazilian collectors at first came during the dry season and left when the floods made their collecting activities impossible, but some began to stay throughout the year. In 1872, a Silesian mission was established at Bacabal on the upper Tapajós; the Mundurucú were by then so deeply involved in trade that the missionary spoke out against their exploitation. This apparently cost him his post, and the mission was abandoned in 1876. As the rubber trade grew into the boom of the late nineteenth century, the Mundurucú were absorbed more completely into collecting activities, and significant numbers of Indians were attracted by the lure of Western goods, resulting in their eventual assimilation into the caboclo population.

Mundurucú society then and today was not suddenly or dramatically destroyed by the rubber trade, as happened in some parts of the Amazon, where virtual slavery was practiced. Rather, the population was slowly leached away and absorbed, and diseases further diminished the ranks of those who remained. The Indians who chose to stay in their original savannah habitats were also able to take a marginal part in the rubber economy without abandoning village life. Rubber can be collected only during the dry season, for the trees grow near the rivers and the annual floods make access to them difficult and the yields low. This seasonality made it possible for the people to clear their gardens from March to May, go to the river banks to collect rubber for two or three months, and then return in September for planting at the beginning of the rainy season. The new pattern fitted in well with tradition, for the Mundurucú commonly scattered afield during the dry season for warfare and fishing, returning to village life for planting. The initial effects of the rubber trade were not, then, totally or immediately disruptive, and life in the savannah villages persisted, albeit with metal pots and pans, steel axes, some firearms, and the assorted trinkets and gadgets brought by the traders. The whites lived near the rubber trees adjacent to the main stream of the Tapajós River, but the interior grasslands and forests where the Mundurucú villages were located remained completely in their possession.

Catholicism had been introduced to the Mundurucú at the time of the Bacabal mission and through their Brazilian neighbors, but its influence was weak until the establishment in 1911 of a mission on the Cururú River by German priests of the Franciscan order. The mission had an impact beyond mere catechization. First, the priests discouraged the practice of head-hunting, and by 1914 warfare had ended. The success of the missionaries was due in large part to the fact that the years of the rubber boom had decimated and scattered the neighboring tribes. Moreover, the rubber boom ended in 1914, and nobody was particularly interested in encouraging the Mundurucú to war on the remaining hostile Indians. The fall in the price of rubber undoubtedly slowed the progressive involvement of the Mundurucú in commercial relations, but by the 1920s the villages nearest the Cururú River were trading again—this time with the mission. Selling rubber and hides to the priests proved to be more attractive than dealing with the commercial interests for the priests were honest and fair, whereas the traders unscrupulously juggled accounts in order to keep the nonliterate Indians in permanent debt. The commerce benefited the mission as well; they derived revenue from it, and they used the ties of mutual dependence to draw the Mundurucú closer to their preaching. Through no accident, Saturday and Sunday became the time when trading was conducted at the mission, and it was a simple matter to get the clients into the church.

The shores and flood plain of the Cururú River are rich in rubber trees, and most of the Indians who traded with the mission collected rubber near its banks. In the beginning they worked out of temporary dry season houses, returning to the inland savannah villages with the rains, but as their desire for trade goods increased, so also did the time they spent in rubber collecting. When their stays extended into the planting season, some resorted to making gardens near the Cururú River instead of returning to their villages. Ultimately, their dry season residences became year-round dwellings, and small villages grew up along the shores of the Cururú. The migrants, however, did not move their traditional social arrangements along with their belongings, for the family forms and the very division of labor itself in the Cururú villages differed from traditional Mundurucú institutions, being more appropriate to rubber gatherers than to hunters and warriors.

At the time of our writing, the Trans-Amazonian Highway is still being built along the northern and western fringes of Mundurucú country. But Brazilian society had established itself firmly in the upper Tapajós valley at the time of our fieldwork in the early 1950s. The mission station on the Cururú River had three priests and a lay brother in residence, and there were four nuns living in a separate convent. In addition to the church, there was a small school taught by the sisters and attended by about thirty Mundurucú youngsters, some of whom boarded at the mission, while others were the children of resident families. About 200 Mundurucú lived adjacent to the mission, making this the single largest settlement in the region. Many of the Indians served as employees of the mission, but others farmed and fished in the vicinity and tapped rubber at various points along the Cururú. The closest contacts of the missionaries were with those Indians residing along the Cururú River, though one priest, who spoke Mundurucú fluently, made an annual visit to the interior villages to perform baptisms and, when he could, marriage rituals.

The other major outpost of Western civilization among the Mundurucú was a post of the Indian Protection Service, the Brazilian equivalent of the American Bureau of Indian Affairs (see Map 2). The post was established in 1941, and its ostensible purpose was to offer protection to the Indians from outside forces, primarily commercial interests, and to provide health and educational facilities. Schooling was rather sporadic at the post as only about fifty Indians lived there, and no children were being boarded. As for medical attention, this was the responsibility of the radio operator, who had little else to do, the radio being chronically broken. For that matter, his medical practice was also limited by the fact that the post always seemed to be short of medicine. Since the nearest certified physician was at the old Fordlandia plantation some two weeks' travel downstream, and no doctor at that time ever traveled to the upper Tapajós, the main sources of Western medicine were the missionaries and ourselves. Wanting as it may have been in its educational and medical functions, the Indian post did serve to keep outside traders off the Cururú River, thus preserving the commercial monopoly of the mission—and the Indian post. The two were in lively competition with each other, but it must be said that the priests had cornered most of the Indian market.

The Indian post and the mission were the only two settlements of whites within the borders of Mundurucú country. All the other whites of the region lived along the Tapajós River or the lower reaches of some of its larger tributaries. The largest settlement in the area was the town of Barra, a large trading post at the confluence of the São Manoel and Juruena Rivers. Barra was the principal entrepôt for an area larger than some American states. That it consisted of a small warehouse and some twenty houses is a commentary on the development of the region. Some fifty miles or so south of Barra, white settlement ended on both the Juruena and São Manoel Rivers; beyond this point, the country was occupied by only a few hostile tribes as far south as the headwaters of the rivers. Brazilian penetration of the region had actually shrunk since the nineteenth century rubber boom, as had the size of the population, and a substantial length of the upper waters of the Tapajós system has not been reached by outsiders for several decades. North, or down-stream, from Barra, the Tapajós River, now a mighty stream one-half mile to a mile in breadth and flowing deep and swift, courses through a valley that in a length of over 200 miles had a population of no more than 1,500; this is admittedly an es-timate, as census takers were as rare as any other kind of govern-ment official.

The Brazilian population of the Tapajós valley is a potpourri of physical strains, running the gamut of racial stereotypes from the typical Iberian Caucasoid through the Indian to the African; actually, most of the people are mixtures of two or three of these lines of ancestry. Culturally, they are Brazilian caboclos, mean-ing they speak Portuguese, practice a form of Catholicism that is unencumbered by clerical hierarchy or formal dogma, and share a life style common to most of the impoverished inhabitants of the Amazon basin. Their homesteads are scattered along the river banks at distant intervals, consistent with the fact that they must locate near the wild rubber trees, which are thinly dis-persed throughout the flood plains bordering the river. A rub-ber-tapper settlement usually consists of just one house, never more than two, set in a tiny clearing on the river bank. Most have small gardens nearby, but the pressures of collecting rub-ber rob time from agriculture, and many have to buy part of their food from traders.

The only approximation to villages in this vast region are the traders' houses, located at intervals of twenty miles or so from each other. These small settlements rarely have over five or six houses, comprising the trader's dwelling, his store, and the houses of a few of his rubber-tapping clients. The classical tie be-tween the patron and his clients is indebtedness leavened by a traditional sense of mutual responsibility. It is understood that the client will sell his rubber only to the trader, who exercises a loose control over the lands in his district, and that he will occasionally perform services for the patron as well. The trader, in return, is obligated to provide for the client's bare necessities whether or not the client has sufficient credit to cover the expenses. The trader must extend credit to allow a new client to become established, he must care for the needs of the client and his family in case of illness or accident, and he commonly serves as godfather to the client's children. It is a diffuse kind of relationship, but the seeming paternalistic benevolence must be viewed in light of the fact that the client is almost always in debt to the trader. It is a form of debt servitude from which the rubber tapper cannot escape, for if he leaves his patron for another, his debt goes with him. And he cannot leave the region without the funds to cover at least transportation for himself and his family. In all fairness to the traders, however, they themselves were not getting rich, for the system kept them in debt to the commercial houses in Belém and Santarém.

Most of the traders were tied to a single company that controlled navigation on the Tapajós through its possession of the lands adjoining the Cachoeira de Maranhão, a tremendous set of rapids that block access to the upper Tapajós from the placid and unobstructed lower reaches of the river. These rapids must be portaged, and to do so, company facilities and lands have to be used. The company town of São Luis, located at the lower end of the rapids and accessible by steamboat from the Amazon, thus served as the main distribution point and commercial center for the entire Tapajós River above the rapids. For a "metropolis," São Luis was a depressing place. A collection of frame and adobe warehouses, office space, and dwellings, it baked torpidly in the sun by day and was somnolent by night. The bareness of its storehouses, the quiet of the town, and the emptiness of its port bespoke the economic backwardness of an entire region.

The mood of the caboclo population ranged from stoicism to

despair. They were in debt, impoverished, living at the very edge of subsistence, and they knew it. There was little hope among them, and life stretched out as an endless round of their rubber trees, grinding work, continual insecurity, and no reward or surcease. Only death would liberate them. When a child died, they drew comfort from the fact that he would not have to live in the misery of his parents, and this was a genuine sentiment, not a convenient sop. Solitude and loneliness were their most commonly expressed grievances. The rubber tapper's family might go for weeks without seeing another human being, and when an occasional boat stopped briefly at one of their houses they unfailingly produced coffee for their guests out of a small supply that may have been saved for months for just such an occasion. Most of the families on the upper Tapajós waters had not even been as far as Barra in years, and the rest of Brazil was either a distant memory or a still unseen Camelot.

If the rubber tapper never reached the world outside, neither did that world extend itself to him. Except for the mission and Indian post schools for Mundurucú children, there were no educational facilities of any kind above São Luis. Children learned to read, write, and do arithmetic from their parents, and if they were illiterate, so also would be the children. Needless to say, the general inability to understand the trader's bookkeeping was one of the reasons why the caboclo was always in debt. Moreover, there were no medical facilities on the upper Tapajós; the ill simply died or got better. Many, of course, were chronically ill most of the time with malaria, dysentery, and pulmonary diseases; one meets few old people in the Amazon.

The upper Tapajós country was part of the Municipio of Itaituba, but government rarely reached above the rapids. Law and order were maintained by the traders and those they could enlist in support. This posed no great problem as crime was usually a result of drunken violence; fortunately, poverty and a poor supply system made liquor relatively scarce. With rum in short supply, the only comfort left was religion, but, except for the missionaries to the Mundurucú, there were no churches or clergy above Itaituba. Worship was restricted to prayer sessions, usually held at the small shrines found in most trader's houses. The people placed their faith in a god from whom they had no great expectations in this world, and their prayers sought relief from temporal suffering and a better life in the hereafter. But in all the squalor and hopelessness of their lives, the backwoodsmen were a warm and kindly people who accepted their lot because they had no choice.

The new road system will end the isolation of the caboclos, but most students of the Amazon will agree that only the form of suffering, and not the intensity, will change. The penetration of the modern age actually began during our stay, when a landing strip was cut in the jungle near the trading post of Jacaré Acanga, on the Tapajós River. The field, which was able to accommodate only DC-3s and light planes at the time we left, was designed to serve ultimately as an emergency landing strip for intercontinental jets enroute from the United States to Rio de Janeiro and São Paulo. The construction of the field drew many rubber tappers into wage labor, and a few even managed to hitchhike out on the Brazilian Air Force transports which supplied the base. The old ties with the traders were already being broken by the appearance of an alternative and a form of escape, but work as unskilled laborers hardly promised deliverance any more than will agricultural homesteading when the road opens up the interior regions. The Amazon is indeed a new and rapidly expanding frontier, but it is well to remember that our own American frontier was, contrary to the popular image, a threadbare and desperate place where poverty and economic failure were the norm. The Amazon has a long way to go.

This is the milieu into which the Mundurucú will eventually

assimilate, and they will lose by the exchange. But the very nature of Brazilian society on the Tapajós makes understandable the quite considerable retention of their culture through a century of contact. Unlike their North American cousins, the Mundurucú have not yet experienced the inroads of hordes of land-seekers, railroads and roads, automobiles, motels, hamburger stands, and so forth, which have left our own native cultures shattered. The Mundurucú of the Cururú River come into contact with few whites besides missionaries and government employees, and those of the interior savannahs encounter only the Tapajós River traders and occasional rubber tappers. There is a kind of tacit peaceful coexistence between Indians and whites. They get along well enough, but they do so largely by staying separate. As for the cultural differences, the blighted society of the whites offers few attractions. Those things that the Indians want, such as knives, axes, guns, and so forth, they can acquire through trade. For the rest, they eat better than the whites and they know it, they live in larger and more cohesive communities, and the results of a half-century of catechization indicate that they have been less than eager for the Christian message.

The very nature of their commerce with the whites has allowed the Mundurucú to keep their distance. They are not wage workers, but independent rubber collectors on lands generally recognized as tribal. They work apart from the whites without outside supervision, and the traders come to them just as often as they visit the posts. An Indian may, thus, spend only three months of the year collecting rubber, while the remaining three-quarters of the year are spent in traditional activities. Two or three visits from the trader, or to his store, are enough to conclude a year's negotiations. Those Mundurucú who live at the mission and the Indian post have experienced the greatest cultural change, of course, as have a few who have spent rather long periods working for traders.

Most of the Indian–white contact occurs between men. A small number of Mundurucú speak a fairly fluent, if broken, backwoods Portuguese, but practically no women have a knowledge of more than a few trade words. This includes many who have gone to the mission school, after which an almost deliberate effort is made to erase from their memories everything they have learned. Some young adults had spent up to five years at the mission as youngsters and, though they understood more Portuguese than they would acknowledge, found themselves almost mute when called upon to speak the language. Their amnesia for reading and arithmetic was even more striking. Given the Mundurucú way of life, almost everything they learned in school was irrelevant; it is conceivable that Portuguese and arithmetic could be useful for the boys in their later trade transactions, but for the girls, such subjects had no earthly purpose whatsoever. The school, however, left its imprint, for though its products were hardly Brazilians, neither were they fully Mundurucú. There was always about them a sense of alienation and removal, a lack of certainty and assuredness, which was most manifest in the virtual withdrawal from all interaction of youngsters newly returned to their villages. "They are ashamed," the older Mundurucú would say; the shame lasts for years.

Culture change has affected different Mundurucú villages, and individuals, to varying degrees, but no sector of the population has escaped it. The extent of these changes will become manifest in the rest of this volume, but it should be stressed that its chief vehicle has been the dislocations caused by rubber tapping and the impact of the new technology that has come to them through trade. A steel axe or a gun is more than just another material item or a means toward greater productivity. Both the axe and the gun can change the very social relationships that go into production; both have had the effect of loosening ties of cooperation between families by making individual effort more efficient. And rubber collection can be accommodated to the traditional yearly round only as long as it is limited to three months. Beyond that, it interferes with the agricultural cycle and tends to draw people away from their villages to a new life along the larger streams. The social and cultural demise of the Mundurucú was foreseeable twenty years ago, and the new road will only speed the process.

The social setting of the Mundurucú is a shifting and transient one, but the natural environment of the upper Tapajós River has been virtually undisturbed for millennia. It is a land of great and complete wilderness, scratched here and there at its edges by man, but largely unknown and ineffable. The extent of its forests staggers the outsider. One can travel along its rivers for weeks, even months, and encounter only occasional breaks in the wall of forest along the shores. The traveler in an airplane sees below him a blotchy green sea that unfolds under the wings for uninterrupted hours, except where it is broken by a river or, at rare intervals, by a clearing. This may be a village site or a spot where an Indian or a lone Brazilian has borrowed a piece of garden land from the jungle—"borrow," for the omnipresent forest creeps in and reclaims the tract after only a few years. The river, too, is awesome. Though the Tapajós is not by any means the largest of the Amazon tributaries, its size, in terms of length, breadth, and water flow, is surpassed in the United States only by the Mississippi and its two principal affluents, the Missouri and Ohio. Indeed, some of the tributaries of the Tapajós are larger than such American rivers as the Sacramento, the Hudson, and the Platte. In its lower reaches, below the Cachoeira de Maranhão, the Tapajós broadens out into a bay ten miles wide, its shores lined in the dry season by white sand beaches. Above the rapids, it ranges up to a mile in width, though occasionally it is squeezed by the abutting hills into a channel only a quarter-mile wide, through which the water races at frightening speeds. Like the forests, the river conveys a sense of grandeur, of untamed power, of unknowable depth.

The majesty and mystery of this raw nature are conveyed in stories told among both Brazilians and Indians of dark, bottomless areas in the river where dwells the *cobra grande*, an anaconda as large as a steamboat with eyes that have a fiery glow. And the forests are populated by strange and dangerous creatures that must either be avoided or placated if man is to maintain his delicate balance with nature. The Indians have a keen sense of the tenuous quality of the relationship between human culture and the natural environment. One Mundurucú myth tells of a young man named Perisuat, who left his home and traveled through the forest for years, having remarkable encounters with the animal kingdom along the way. At the end, he returns to his village covered with insect bites and bee stings, really more animal than human, and dies shortly thereafter. There is an allegory here of man's regression from his delicately contrived cultures, of the irreversibility of his progress from the natural to the human state, of the death that lies within nature. But it is an attractive regression that appeals to the atavistic tendencies in all of us. The jungle exercises a pull to enter more deeply, to penetrate beyond man into unknown wildernesses, to become enfolded in the great forests. Seemingly an impulse to set out, it is really a call to return—back into nature, back into ourselves and our origins. It provides the realization of what, to most of urban mankind, is fantasy, and it is not adventitious that twenty years later it appears to us in retrospect as a dream.

Unlike the muddy Madeira and Negro Rivers, the Tapajós is a blue-water river, ranging in clarity from a slightly roiled state in the floods to a beautiful pellucidity during the dry season. The river rises ten to twenty feet during the rains and extends far into low-lying forest areas along its shores; its recession in May and June leaves behind long stretches of sandy beaches and bars, used by the turtles to lay their eggs. Navigation is difficult because of a number of powerful rapids that in the dry season require either portaging or perilous threading between the rocks in swift waters. In the rainy season, most of the rapids are covered by the flood, but the currents are far stronger, making ascent of the river time-consuming and dangerous. In places the river is like a cauldron, yet in long stretches it is broad and calm and so unruffled that the forest and the clouds are reflected in it as in a mirror.

The rapids of the Tapajós mark stages in its descent from the Planalto of Mato Grosso to the Amazon, a fall of about 2,000 feet in its course of over a thousand miles. The Planalto proper lies far to the south in the watershed between the Paraguay and Amazon systems, but it extends long fingers of highlands northward between the rivers, ending in bluffs of some 300 feet overlooking the Amazon behind the city of Santarém. Along most of its length, the upper Tapajós River is flanked by low hills, though there are many stretches that correspond to most notions of the Amazon region as unbroken, flat and dank jungle. The presence of large tracts of land that are well above the seasonal floods makes the area favorable for agriculture, and for habitation in general, but the rocks of the rapids are notorious as favored places for the *borrachuda*, certainly one of the most ferocious of all gnats.

As it flows toward the Amazon, the Tapajós is swelled by a number of quite large streams; most of these flow in from the east, as the headwaters of the Madeira River are only a short distance west of the Tapajós itself. The largest of the eastern affluents of the Tapajós below the community of Barra is the Jamaxím River, which at the time of our research was largely uninhabited because of forays by the Gê-speaking Northern Kayapó. Fear of the Kayapó had actually driven several rubber tappers away from the east bank of the Tapajós between the mouth of the Jamaxím and the beginnings of Mundurucú country, at the point where the Rio das Tropas enters.

The Mundurucú live on the watersheds of four eastern tributaries of the Tapajós: the Rio das Tropas, the Rio Cabitutú, the Rio Cadiriří and the Rio Cururú. The latter is the largest and southernmost of the four and is the locale of the mission and Indian post; some 700 Mundurucú live along its shores. Only a few scattered Indian families reside throughout the year on the banks of the other three streams, though they are used for dry season rubber collection, and the 350 Indians located in their drainage live in villages far inland on open savannahs.

The forests of the upper Tapajós country wall the river with trees over 100 feet tall. The jungle is especially high in the *igapó*, or annually inundated lowlands, but the fact that the land is covered with water for over four months of the year combines with the absence of sunlight to inhibit the growth of underbrush. Every tree fights against the other to extend its foliage to the sun's rays, and the branches and leaves form a solid cover at the top of the forest, which prevents branching and leafage below. The light filters dimly through the forest roof, and the jungle floor remains in a half-light, cool and damp. The trees thrust their great trunks upward from fantastic root systems, standing like pillars in a cathedral whose vaulting roof soars far above the congregation. But as one leaves the flood plain, the trees become lower, though still enormous by most forest standards, and the penetration of sunlight allows the growth of thick rank underbrush. This is the more typical Amazonian rain forest, less majestic than that along the shores, but more resistant to man.

The traveler into the interior of Mundurucú country ascends one of the four tributaries, all of which are navigable by small launch, and debarks at a settlement or a house on its upper reaches. From there he sets out through the igapó forest along a well-used, though narrow, trail which ascends gradually above the flood line and through thick underbrush and jungle. After a march of anywhere from a half-hour to several hours, he suddenly breaks out of the forest into an open grassy plain, dotted here and there with small clumps of brush or a little grove of trees. From the Madeira River west to the foothills of the Andes, the jungle is continuous, but in the interior uplands east of the Madeira, between the Tapajós, Xingú, and Araguaya Rivers, extensive stretches of savannah are found, and in some locales the forests grow only along the rivers. After long periods in the jungle, the savannahs are a welcome relief. Unsheltered from the sun though the savannahs may be, on them the air feels less heavy and humid and the breezes that blow across their open reaches alleviate the oppressive heat. This is rolling country, where one can look from the top of a grassy knoll and see the land stretch away for miles. By comparison, the jungle closes in, encroaches, smothers. One feels that he has broken out and escaped when he leaves the jungle for the savannah, though in actuality he has really folded himself more deeply into the wilderness.

The Mundurucú are located only 7° south of the equator, and the weather is hot all year long. The temperature never reaches extremes, however, and the daytime highs generally range between the upper 80s and the low 90s. Nights are commonly in the mid-70s, though lows of 63 degrees have been noted in June, when a cool wind occasionally blows from the far away winter-shrouded Andes.

Seasons are marked by a wet and dry cycle, rather than by

great temperature differences. The rains begin in mid-September, reach a peak between January and March, and taper off through May. Very little rain falls during the three to four months between mid-May and early September. The climate is not particularly enervating, and most evenings are cool and pleasant. The most uncomfortable period comes just before the arrival of the rainy season, when the breezes still, the humidity climbs, and the sun beats down unmercifully. Most white residents of the tropics know the pre-rainy season weeks to be the time when the very sky seems to lower, tempers become shorter, and everybody is reduced to torpor. The Indians feel this way, too. The coolness of the first rains brings instant relief, but as they grow in frequency and intensity, as the forests become more sodden, the rivers more flooded, the houses more mildewed, the heat of early September is forgotten, proving that people everywhere get tired of the weather.

The most disagreeable, annoying, and painful aspect of the Amazon country, and the upper Tapajós valley, is not the climate, but rather the insect life. The borrachudas that swarm in rocky areas near rapids bite so fiercely that scratching risks major infection. Their smaller cousins, a gnat called the *pium* in Tupian and Portuguese, have a less painful sting, but they compensate for this by their numbers. When the gnat hordes leave at the end of each day, they are replaced by mosquitos, malarial, of course, and when the traveler retreats to the relative safety of his mosquito net, he finds that on moonlit nights there emerges a little gnat, called the *marouim da lua*, which is so small that it can get through the mesh of the netting. There are also various ticks, fleas, ants, and so forth, which contribute to the misery, but the flying creatures, appropriately referred to by the generic term *praga*, or "plague," in the local Portuguese, are the bane of the region. Their continual stings eventually build up some immunity in their victims, but even the Indians spend a great deal of time swatting themselves. No photograph can convey the real Amazon to the person who has not experienced it, for the most memorable features of the region are too small to be caught on film.

The insects were less bothersome on the open, breezy savannahs, making the villages there at once more endurable and less malaria-ridden. The Mundurucú appreciated these advantages, but it was probably not health and comfort that made the open terrain their traditional homeland. Rather, the savannahs and the neighboring forests provided enough ecological diversity to make the area rich in game while allowing farming, and the situation of their villages on open grasslands reduced the danger of surprise attack from the cover of forest.

The reader may have guessed that the savannah villages were also our favorites, a bias which should be freely confessed. They harbored the remains of traditional Mundurucú culture, an irresistible attraction for the anthropologist, but the region also had a profound, deeply quiet beauty. Our house in the village of Cabruá looked out across a wooded valley to a grassy hill and beyond that to higher hills and uplands, said by the Mundurucú to have been created long ago by a god. The shadows of the clouds marched across the landscape, shifting the colors of the hills through shades of green to a dark purple; the distant vistas wavered in the middle of the day through humidity and heat, but as the sun lowered, each aspect of the horizon shone with a clarity that conveyed the absolute purity of the air. In the mornings we sat behind our house drinking coffee and watching the mists rising from the hillside in thin tendrils that were said by the Indians (who knew that it was really mist) to be the campfire of a mythical *inambú* bird. And the evenings often closed in brilliant, iridescent sunsets, kaleidoscopes of shifting colors. It was an enchanted land existing in a distant place and peopled by descendants of a remote age. To enter it was to step through the looking glass.

3.

Beyond
/\/\/\/\/\/\the
Looking Glass

Ethnographic research, or fieldwork, is at the heart of the anthropological enterprise. It is our primary means of data collection, the source of our now encyclopedic knowledge of the cultures of the world, but it has a significance that goes beyond this obvious purpose. Fieldwork gives the discipline its very unity, and much of its flavor. The anthropological method of total immersion in the culture being studied entails full-time, long-term residence of the investigator among the research subjects. He or she does not "go native," but does exist much like the people, living in their dwellings and eating their foods. And the fieldworker often does this in strange and remote places, among people whose ways are wondrous to us. Anthropology is indeed a science but, paradoxically, it is conducted under romantic circumstances which weld its practitioners into a true fellowship.

This bond of common experience extends beyond cultural anthropology to the other three branches of the discipline: archaeology, physical anthropology, and anthropological linguistics. Specialists in all three areas carry on fieldwork, often in places just as distant and isolated as the ethnographer's. Of course, most

anthropologists today do their fieldwork in more accessible locales, some even in their own cities, but the prototype of field
research is work in a primitive culture, remote and exotic. And
such was the nature of our year with the Mundurucú.

Research among primitives—a term meaning only that a society has a simple technology, is nonliterate, and is socially uncomplex—has provided anthropology with an enormous catalogue of human customary behavior. It documents a range of
practices so diverse as to call into question tidy definitions of human nature, while expanding the outer limits of what we consider humanly possible. Our data are also the raw material of
anthropology's comparative method, through which we study
cross-culturally recurrent, and divergent, customs to discover the
underlying order of cultures and keys to an understanding of their
development. The small size of most primitive societies also allows us to study them in their entirety, as wholes, and thus to
be able to see their component parts in relation to an overall social and cultural system.

The last reason for anthropology's absorption with primitive
cultures is the most urgent, though not the most important. This
is that each year sees the destruction of such cultures through
the extinction of their bearers or their incorporation into a dominant society. And even when they survive as identifiable populations, they are no longer "primitives," for they have usually
adopted much of the life style of their conquerors. The Indian
tribespeople of the United States are still Indians, and they still
have somewhat distinctive cultures, but they go to schools, drive
cars, and watch television—they are not at all primitive. Indeed,
in a generation or two, there will no longer be primitive cultures
anywhere in the world, and we will have lost touch with some
of our roots. The world will also be deprived of variety and en-
chantment; our species will have been impoverished. It is a pri-

mary mission of anthropology, then, to capture a record of these simple cultures before they are forever gone.

In 1952, we were both graduate students in anthropology at Columbia University; Yolanda was specializing at the time in physical anthropology and Robert in cultural, with a particular interest in native South America. We had married only three months after meeting in the physical anthropology laboratory in 1950; it was a thoroughly anthropological union. We were both New Yorkers whose experience in the wilds was limited to hikes in Bear Mountain Park, and we were not only new to roughing it, but to each other. In the coming year, we were to learn a great deal about both subjects.

By 1951, Robert's studies had advanced to the stage when one does fieldwork to gather material for the doctoral dissertation. Yolanda still needed more courses, so she decided to suspend her work in physical anthropology and try her hand at ethnography. We next had to make two big decisions: where to do fieldwork and why. The two choices were closely linked. Robert was interested in studying economic and ecological change, and the Mundurucú were an ideal case study. We also wished to go to an unstudied group, and the only reports on the Mundurucú came from missionaries and early travelers. The data were fragmentary, but we learned that the Mundurucú had clans, moieties, patrilineality, totemism, and men's houses—all of which will be explained in their proper place—making them wonderful subjects for students of primitive social organization. Our minds were made up; all we needed was money.

Armed with a proposal that included a detailed theoretical rationale for our research, we went to the foundations for support. To our surprise, we succeeded, getting funds early in 1952 from the Social Science Research Council, the Institute of International Education, and a Columbia traveling fellowship. Most of that spring was spent feverishly learning Portuguese, obtaining visas, and shopping. As our departure date drew closer, we became panicked, not so much from a sense of what remained undone as from a growing realization of the enormity of our undertaking. Despite all this, we somehow managed to leave for Brazil early in May 1952.

Most anthropologists today find endless delays and horrendous bureaucratic tangles in their struggles to get official clearance for their research, and a few have had to give up in despair. Our own experience was totally different. We were met at Rio de Janeiro's Galeão Airport by our friends Eduardo and Clara Galvão; Galvão had been a fellow graduate student at Columbia and was then chief of operations in the Serviço de Proteção aos Indios (SPI, Indian Protection Service), the forerunner of today's Fundação Nacional dos Indios (FUNAI, National Indian Foundation). Galvão then introduced us to anthropologist Darcy Ribeiro, then head of the SPI's study section, and to the director of the agency. That was it; permission was granted in twenty-four hours.

After a couple of weeks, we tore ourselves away from the charms of Rio and went by plane to Belém, the gateway to the Amazon and its principal city. We had brought only cameras and clothing from the United States, and our principal shopping was done in Belém. It was an awesome task, complicated by the fact that, aside from some general advice from our mentor, we had only a vague idea about what we needed, and in what quantity. Fortunately, Darcy Ribeiro was in Belém on business and personally took us from store to store, bargaining the prices downward and making sure that we were fully outfitted. Belém was a wonderfully decadent backwater in 1952, and the only remnant of its World War II role as an American air and naval base was that every time we walked into the hotel dining room, the band would play a wheezy rendition of "Anchors Aweigh." Yolanda thought this was wildly funny, but Robert, who had ambivalent memories of his Navy years, was less amused. But Belém and its denizens were intrinsically interesting, and we met SPI pacification agents, gold and diamond prospectors, bush pilots, animal dealers, Indians, and other anthropologists, all while drinking beer in sidewalk cafes.

Shopping mostly completed, we set out for Santarém, some 500 miles up the Amazon, by a slow, wood-burning steamer. We were awed by the great river, which flowed deep and swift between shores three to ten miles apart; it was well named the Rio Mar (Ocean River) by the early explorers, for one can look upstream and see a watery horizon. The trip took a full seven days, but it seemed longer, for Yolanda came down with a bad case of dysentery. She left the boat in a weakened state, longing for a clean hotel with a bed. She was not to find it.

The best hotel in Santarém at the time was an infamous fleabag located above a store whose loudspeaker blared music and commericals all day and part of the night. The beds were an entomologist's delight, and we took to our new hammocks, which were to be our beds for a year. The rooms had no ceilings, allowing us to listen to our neighbors, and the communal bathroom was adjacent to the kitchen, though not even this could explain the atrocious food. We finished our purchases in Santarém and then looked for passage up the Tapajós River, grateful to be liberated from our septic lodgings.

In the course of our shopping, we had acquired sixteen small crates of supplies, aside from our personal baggage. We had done a year's shopping, for there were only small rubber-trading posts upstream, and we were actually traveling light. In the boxes there were: knives, axes, machetes, fish hooks, line, scissors, cloth, needles, thread, perfume, glass beads, pots, pans, cutlery, fire-arms for hunting, tobacco, canned food, rice, beans, sugar, salt, and other items beyond counting. In addition to the presents for the people and our own supplies, we also brought a complete medicine kit, including penicillin and hypodermic syringes.

There was no regular passenger service on the Tapajós River in 1952, but we found space on a trader's launch, a small steamboat very similar to Humphrey Bogart's *African Queen*; we actually slung our hammocks on a *batalão*, or barge, that was tied to the steamer's side. It took a week for the boat to reach São Luis, the head of navigation on the Tapajós, for the trader stopped at hamlets and houses along the shores to do business; besides, the *Maralita* could only do about five miles an hour and the current flowed at three. The Tapajós is a delight during the dry season, and we didn't mind our slow pace. For the first time, we learned to suppress our New Yorker's impatience and fell into the slower tempo of the Amazon region.

São Luis was less a town than a warehouse and transfer point of the Companhia Alto Tapajós (Upper Tapajós Company), the company that controlled trade on the river. It was, as we said, a forlorn, sun-beaten, fly-ridden place, and we were delighted to find that a boat was loading for the upper Tapajós. Our sixteen crates of suplies were trucked around the rapids, and we walked behind; we were under way by noon.

The upper Tapajós River is broken by strong rapids at several points, and our small diesel launch, which was loaded to the gunwales with cargo and people, had to battle its way upstream through flumes between the rocks. At times the boat was stopped dead by the current, and the crew would help out with long poles. These were tense moments, for if the boat were swept backwards, it could strike a rock and sink. The pilot ended all estimates of arrival times with the well-chosen words, "Si Deus quiser" (If God is willing).

As we ascended the river, trading posts became more infrequent, the houses of rubber tappers more scattered. And soon after leaving São Luis, we found that there were no Brazilians along the entire east shore of the river; they had abandoned good rubber areas out of fear of the Mekranoti Kayapó, who had been sighted in the nearby forests. We thought that at last we were seeing the heart of darkness, not knowing that this was only a pallid taste. Our trip took us through hilly, pleasant country, and we even had a two-day *friagem*, the cool spell that comes every June from the south. The heat returned, however, and we arrived at our next portage after a week of travel. Another five days took us to the trading post at Barra, where the Tapajós is created by the confluence of the Juruena and São Manoel Rivers, and from where we hoped to find transportation to the Cururú River and the SPI's Mundurucú Post. In a stroke of luck, the SPI launch arrived the day after we did, and we landed at the post three days later. At last we were among the Mundurucú— a month after leaving Santarém.

We had spent weeks in the cramped spaces of the traders' launches and were delighted to be back on land. Our days were passed on the boats, but each night was spent ashore, and we slept in the houses of traders and rubber gatherers, people whose poverty was softened by calm dignity. We became the center of attention at every stop, for few foreigners went so far into the interior in those years. Besides, we had a battery-operated shortwave radio in the pretransistor age, and we also dispensed free medicine. There was little to do except talk to our new Brazilian friends about the region and their lives, and we did this day and night.

Our month of travel was really the beginning of our ethnography, for during this time we learned of the outside society to which the Mundurucú were exposed, and we learned, too, how much better off materially the Mundurucú were, as compared to their exploited caboclo neighbors. We also met our first Mundurucú at a trader's house on the Tapajós: three young girls who came into the room, looked at us with hands hiding their mouths, and ran away shrieking with laughter. It was an inauspicious beginning. Finally, it was the most remarkable trip we would ever take—and there were to be many more—for each day we gazed raptly at a wilderness beyond our comprehension, at a landscape barely scratched by humans, at a profusion of nature that enveloped us.

The Mundurucú Post (the Government Indian Post on Map 1) was located in a sandy clearing on the Cururú River, where it sat baking silently under the equatorial sun. It was a godforsaken place, the kind of setting that inspired the title *Tristes Tropiques* for Claude Lévi-Strauss's account of his Brazilian field trips. The agent, as we said, was locked in competition with the Catholic mission some fifty miles upstream and he appeared to be losing, for most of the Indians of the Cururú traded with the mission, and the post had only sporadic contact with the savannah villages. This gave the post a backwater, run-down atmosphere, and it became clear to us that the agent's good offices would be of little help in introducing us to the Mundurucú. We spent a week at the post compiling our first word lists and were glad to accept the agent's offer of a ride to the mission. He, in turn, was happy to get rid of us.

In addition to the priests and nuns at the Missão São Francisco, over 200 Mundurucú were in residence, though many had scattered out to their rubber-avenue dwellings during the dry season. The Catholic Church indeed sought to capture the minds and hearts of the Indians, but the priests knew, as we have noted, that the best way to do this was to make them economically dependent through a monopoly of their rubber trade. Each Sunday, families came to the mission with balls of smoked latex, which they traded for objects of outside manufacture. And they also attended Sunday Mass, as did we. Although we had both been raised as Catholics, neither of us was still a communicant, but a good ethnographer takes part in the culture he is studying. It had its rewards, for we learned, among other things, that one of the mission's staunchest converts, a man who knew when to stand, kneel, and sit so well that he was always five seconds ahead of the nuns, was also the shaman who identified sorcerers for execution.

Most Mundurucú had little difficulty in believing what the priests taught them, while maintaining much of the native belief system. They managed this, in part, by modifying Christian creed to make it fit into preexistent Mundurucú culture patterns, a process called syncretism. Thus, Christ was identified with the culture hero Karusakaibö, and the serpent in the Garden of Eden was a benefactor to humanity, for he taught Adam and Eve how to perform the sex act. They knew that the missionaries told the story differently, but they preferred their own version. So did we.

The two priests in residence, both of whom were German, were hospitable and cooperative. The older one had spent almost forty years with the Mundurucú and was fluent in the language. His annual tour of the savannah villages made him a valuable source of information on these communities, as well as on those of the Cururú. The old priest also introduced us to the chief of the village of Missão Velha (Old Mission), so named because it was the site of the first Franciscan mission. We explained, as best we could, our purpose in studying the Mundurucú, and asked permission to live in his community. A quiet and dignified man, he readily agreed, and we arrived a few days later.

Missão Velha is only about five winding miles upstream from

the mission, and we suspected that the priests arranged our stay there so that they could keep an eye on us. They did not interfere with our work, however, and the village, which had eleven houses and a population of ninety, suited our purposes well. Many of the inhabitants had left the community for rubber collecting, but there were enough left to enable us to study the full round of daily life.

We arrived in the village in a mixed state of eager anticipation and anxiety. It was a dramatic moment for us, but the spell was shattered by about ten dogs, which went for our legs with fangs bared. Fortunately, some little children had come out to see us, and they drove the dogs off, leaving us feeling shaken and vaguely foolish. But from that moment, we had to carry cudgels to beat off the dogs whenever we left our house; they were vicious, but, happily, they were also cowards. In the village, the chief came forward to greet us, extending his hand in the standard Euro-American manner, but then shaking with a limp wrist. Robert gave the usual American firm-clasp, eye-to-eye handshake, which only made the chief wince. And so, we learned, cultural differences intrude even when you think you are on common ground. This was only the first of our errors, for ethnography is conducted in good part through overcoming misunderstandings.

The chief brought us to his house, like the others a rectangular, thatch-roofed, mud-walled dwelling; it was compartmented into three rooms, one of which was assigned to us. We hung our hammocks from the walls and went outside to the unwalled cooking shed behind the house. Few adults came out to greet us at first, which caused us some concern, for we only learned later that it is considered impolite to go directly up to a newly arrived person. They soon came in ones and twos, however, and after a couple of hours the whole village was gathered in our new abode, talking animatedly about us in a language we did not understand. We had no idea what was going on and even less about what to do next. It was at just about that moment that we first asked ourselves, "What in hell are we doing here?"

All ethnographers ask themselves this question, but the reasons given at the beginning of this chapter were far too abstract for people in our circumstance. Our worries were more immediate, urgent, and earthy. Where does one go to carry out the mundane and nondeferrable body functions? How do we start a fire? Doesn't anybody here speak Portuguese? How and what do we eat tonight? Where does one get water? Will the people let us stay? And even if they do, will they talk to us? Each of these questions found good answers in the months ahead, but when they occur to one all at once, in the first hour, the instinctive reaction is to run away and hide. And there was no way that we could do so. This was the beginning of what anthropologists call "culture shock."

Culture shock occurs when someone is thrown into a new and alien cultural milieu, a setting in which the familiar meanings and symbols within which one has lived, and to which she or he was socialized, are totally absent. This leaves the person floundering in a social situation that is opaque, amorphous, and incomprehensible. Sojourners in exotic places become more than mere strangers; they are outsiders and "aliens" in the sense the term is used in science fiction stories. This was our dilemma. We could not speak Mundurucú, and the few people who knew some Portuguese did not like using it. To make matters worse, we could not interpret gestures or facial expressions, and most of the actions of the people around us were without meaning. Indeed, we had entered a meaningless (to us) world, and we would never again underestimate the tyranny that culture holds over our behavior, our sense of self, and our consciousness.

The usual response to culture shock is depression and withdrawal, and we had symptoms of both. Some fieldworkers stay in their houses for days or find some pretext for going to town, but we were far, far away from town, and the people pursued us to our room when they couldn't find us outside. Unlike many ethnographers, however, we were not alone, and we spent hours in conversation with each other as a substitute for flight. We weathered the psychological aspects of culture shock well enough, but we were fish out of water in the practical matters of survival. The people watched, at first in disbelief and then in well-concealed mirth, as Robert tried to make a fire on our first day. After a while, a young woman came forward, disassembled the huge pile of barely smoking wood that he had put together, placed ten pieces of firewood in wagon-spoke fashion, and lit a fire at the hub. From then on, the Mundurucú knew that they had to help us adjust, which they did—to our eternal gratitude.

During those early days in Missão Velha, we continued our language learning, which was complicated by the fact that we were still learning conversational Portuguese. As anybody who has learned a language by the total immersion method knows, it is an exhausting process, and our problems were compounded by having to work in two foreign tongues. After about a week in the village, we realized that we were spending most of our time in just staying alive, and we looked for an assistant. Luck was with us again, for we found Francisco ("Chico") Manhuari, a young Brazilian who had spent most of his life among the Mundurucú and was fluent in the language. He joined us in Missão Velha, and our expanded household moved into a vacant, but still habitable, dwelling.

Chico served as our manager, factotum, and interpreter throughout our stay with the Mundurucú, becoming almost too indispensable. He took care of all the practical problems of daily existence, engaging village women to do some of the chores that would have violated the division of labor, were he to do them.

He also served as our interpreter, making our early fieldwork far more productive than it would have been, but making our language learning slower than it should have been. Our funds were only enough for one year, and it takes at least six months to acquire even a middling command of a non-Indo-European language. Rather than having only a few months of high-quality fieldwork, we made a trade-off and used an interpreter at the beginning of our interviewing. Today, we encourage graduate students planning research in societies whose languages cannot be studied beforehand to spend at least eighteen months in the field.

Our new house was the only one in the village with rounded ends, the once standard form of the Mundurucú dwelling. Unlike traditional houses, however, ours was built of wattle and daub, that is, clay applied to a wood frame. Our living arrangements were simple; we slept in one room of our two-room house, and Chico hung his hammock in the other. We had brought only a limited supply of food in the expectation that we would be able to barter with the Indians for manioc flour and fresh meat and fish. This was not as simple a process as we had anticipated, for buying and selling food was alien to them and they had no scale of equivalences. This was complicated by the fact that we were exchanging trade objects rather than money. Money was totally foreign to the Mundurucú in 1952. Their trade with whites had always been on a credit basis, and, though the traders kept their books in monetary terms, the people thought of it as barter. We tried to explain why a twenty cruzeiro note could buy two knives and a ten only one. "Is it because the man on this paper has a beard and the other doesn't?" they asked. "How could a scrap of paper have such power?" To further complicate matters, only those few Mundurucú who had attended the mission school could handle the arithmetic, and the traditional counting system only went up to ten. We put our money away and bartered.

During our year with the Mundurucú, we barely touched our

stock of two dozen cans of meat. There was good fishing in the Cururú River, and we ate fish every day. The Mundurucú kept chickens, but the dogs ate the eggs. As for the birds themselves, one woman explained that they were only killed when somebody had a cold, for which chicken soup had great curative properties. This left us dumbfounded until further questioning revealed that they had learned this from the German nuns. Except for an occasional chicken, we ate a completely Mundurucú diet, cooked in their way. We slept in hammocks, as did they, we lived in one of their houses, and we followed their routines. We even performed our bodily functions Mundurucú style, in the underbrush outside the village; this created no public health dangers, for the dogs ate the feces. Our pattern of daily activity was adjusted to that of the people, and we became part of the community.

Our worries about whether the people would accept us proved groundless, for they visited us in twos and threes during the days and en masse in the evenings—and we reciprocated. Life can be quite humdrum in an Amazonian Indian village, and we were the most exciting thing that had ever happened to them. The people found us just as interesting as we found them, and they asked continual questions about *Ameriko-be*. Our radio was a great drawing card, and they queried us at length about programs. The first Eisenhower–Stevenson campaign was going on at the time and we tried to explain the electoral process to them; we probably succeeded only in raising questions about our sanity. But we had become a focal point of community life and won acceptance beyond our hopes.

The hallmark of the anthropological method is participant observation, a ponderous term that means only that we live among the people we are studying, take part in their activities, watch what they are doing, and ask questions when we don't understand. It is an eighteen-hours-a-day, seven-days-a-week, month-after-month job. Our first weeks in Missão Velha were spent primarily in people-watching, in an attempt to discover regularly recurrent patterns in their daily lives. This was not an easy task, for everybody seemed to make his or her own schedule in a life uncomplicated by overseers or clocks. Rather than discovering rote compliance with traditional norms, we found that everybody did their own thing—or so it seemed at the start of our research.

We also trailed after couples on their way to their gardens, not realizing at first that these excursions were often pretexts for private love-making. Despite the fact that our presence was sometimes unwelcome, we gathered a great deal of information on horticulture. Other work that required little linguistic facility included a household census, a survey of material culture, and observations of technology, fishing, and rubber-tapping. Assisted by Chico, we began to conduct interviews, at first to fill in some of the holes in our observations of economic activities, and then to explore the realms of values and standards of conduct. In this way we were able to study the relationship between attitudes and expectations, on the one hand, and actual performance on the other. That is the great strength of participant observation, for survey research questionnaires cannot do this. And as the reader will see, there are great disparities between the Mundurucú ideology of sex roles and what actually goes on between men and women.

The complexity of relations between the sexes was brought to our attention vividly through participant observation. During gatherings in our house the men always sat in front near us and the radio, and the women sat behind them on the ground. One day, however, a woman who appeared to be in her sixties visited Missão Velha. She walked straight up to us, shook hands and, looking Robert directly in the eyes, told him that she wanted coffee and a cigarette. He hurriedly complied with the request— really a command—and one of the men got off a seat up front and gave it to her. She then proceeded to dominate the conversation, paying not the least deference to the opinions of the men. We had discovered that the nominal inferiority of females only applied to women of child-bearing years; older women become "sociological males," and the symbolic abasement of the female status is reversed in old age. This is a common phenomenon in societies that emphasize male dominance, the opposite of American society in which young and beautiful women are prized and older ones devalued. We suspect that the American attitude does greater violence to women.

We also learned through participant observation that the battle of the sexes is a very real thing. On the eve of large communal fish-drugging expeditions, the women gather quantities of a milky and sticky tree sap and after nightfall chase the men, smearing their victims with the liquid—we leave the psychological symbolism of this to the reader's imagination. On one such occasion, a well-daubed and thoroughly cowed Robert said to Yolanda, "These women are rough; they play for keeps." His observation went unheeded, for she had her own supply and joined the combat. This was a true "ritual of rebellion," to use anthropologist Max Gluckman's phrase, a reversal of social roles in which the modest and unaggressive Mundurucú woman became the predator. And the vigor and intensity they brought to the drama showed vividly the strength of the underlying antagonism. These are lessons that can only be learned by taking full part in the ebb and flow of daily life.

We stayed in Missão Velha for the dry season and through the planting of crops at the beginning of the rains. In December, we decided to take a badly needed vacation, during which we would get medical attention and consult with fellow anthropologists about our results, and after which we would go to one of the savannah villages. Our trip out was faster than our trip in, if only because the current was with us, and the rainy season, now in full swing, had swelled the rivers into a great flood. Arriving in Barra, we found that the company's one launch was not expected for weeks, so we decided to arrange our own transportation. We rented a large canoe and hired two men to paddle it. Chico was coming as far as Santarém, and all five of us set out in a badly overloaded canoe down the fast-running Tapajós River.

Many of the rapids that had impeded our upstream journey by motorboat were now covered by five feet of water. Our canoe raced through these narrow stretches, riding up and over the hillocks of water pushed up by the rocks. It was a breathtaking trip. During most of the time, however, we were immersed in the *New York Times*, a packet of which came with the rest of our mail at Barra; we had not read an American newspaper in six months, and nothing would deter us. We arrived at the trading post of Sai Cinza in two and a half days, after almost coming to grief in the Cachoeira (rapids) do Chacarão, only to find that no boat was expected there either. Our just-completed journey had been hair-raising, and the rapids ahead were worse; we decided to wait for the motor launch—and wait we did, for two weeks.

Our trip back in January was much faster. The new airstrip at Jacaré Acanga, only two hours from Sai Cinza by canoe, was taking FAB (Brazilian Air Force) DC-3 flights by the time of our return. We hitched a free ride on a DC-3 at the Santarém Airport and headed south in a rainstorm. The plane kept below the clouds because, lacking radio-navigation installations, the pilot's only guide was the river. The wet and muddy dirt airstrip was about a thousand feet long, and the heavily loaded plane had to come in at treetop level, flaps down, engines cut back, and set down heavily at the beginning of the strip. We didn't make it on the first try and barely cleared the trees as we lifted off again. The second attempt was successful, and the next day saw us back in Sai Cinza, our jumping-off point for a trip up the Cabitutú River to the savannah village of Cabruá.

The four-day trip up the Cabitutú was wet and hungry. We slept each night in unoccupied rubber collectors' shelters, awakening in the deep predawn mists, talking to each other in the hushed tones one uses in this liminal period between the cries and calls of the night creatures and the sounds of the day. Arriving at Cabruá's port, we found the people waiting for us, and we also found that they had just killed a tapir. We fell upon it ravenously, understanding at last the meaning of hunter's glut and protein hunger. Although it was illegal, the trader had brought a dozen bottles of cachaça, the fiery raw cane rum of the region, and our hosts became uproariously drunk. The next morning, we all set out for Cabruá, a four-hour walk that took us first through the gallery forests near the river and then uphill until we emerged from the jungle onto a grassy sun-drenched savannah and a view across wooded valleys to distant hills.

The exhilaration of being liberated from the forest darkness was heightened as we approached the village, for there we were to find a far closer adherence to traditional Mundurucú culture than we had met on the Cururú River. By this time, Robert's theoretical interest in culture change had been submerged by a search for their cultural roots. Cabruá did not disappoint us; aided by the ethnographic and linguistic experience of the first part of our trip, the second half was far more productive.

We moved immediately into the house of a person who had incurred the wrath of local forest spirits and judiciously chose to move to another community. And with us came a Mundurucú woman and her daughter who had hitched a ride with us from Sai Cinza, but who had not been invited to join our household. While we were discussing how to gently get rid of her, however, she made a broom of twigs, swept out the house, found some empty water gourds, filled them at the stream, started a fire, and made coffee. She stayed.

Our relations with the people of Cabruá were different from our Cururú ties, for they, and we, lived under different social regimes. In Cabruá, cooperatively hunted game was the protein base, and large kills were distributed throughout the four—now five—households of the village. We became part of this collective economy by making village-wide distributions of axes, scissors, and the like, rather than trading item by item, as we did in the more individuated economy of the Cururú. This did not keep individuals from asking for additional presents, however, for they had a keen appreciation of Western manufactures that has ultimately been the source of their downfall. We were continually fending off these requests, which could have left our supplies bare in a week, but they knew it and never pressed hard. In addition to all their trade needs, the Mundurucú found freely dispensed tobacco and coffee in our house. As in Missão Velha, the people liked having paying guests who also provided a constant source of diversion and bestowed upon them the ultimate compliment of respectful inquiry into their way of life.

Yolanda had found ready acceptance by the women of Missão Velha, but their primary orientation was to their nuclear families and their husbands. As will be seen, the institutions of the extended family and the men's house made Cabruá a different arena for gender relations, and both female and male solidarity were far stronger. The men still treated Robert as an outsider, for he didn't sleep in the men's house and was a burden on hunting trips. Yolanda, however, was soon absorbed into the village sisterhood, and her warmest friendships were with Cabruá women. She spent most of her days in their company and joined them in farinha-making; they looked upon her as a person with the same basic problem as theirs: men. It had been clear in Missão Velha that we should each work with members of our own sex, but Robert could ask at least a few questions of women there. Not so in Cabruá. To them he was just another man.

Our house in Cabruá was filled each night with almost everybody in the village, including infants, for we not only had a radio—totally new to most—but it was story-telling time. We told the people as much about Ameriko-be as we thought they could assimilate and sang songs, and the older men recounted myths to us and to their entire audience. We had not planned to collect myths and folktales, but the old men wanted to tell them; we soon became avid listeners, and many young Mundurucú heard them for the first time. We accumulated sixty stories, one of the largest bodies of South American mythology available, and we did it only because we had followed the direction of our informants. This is indeed what happens in most ethnographic fieldwork. It must be understood that anthropologists' informants are not specimens that we study as if under a microscope—they are our teachers.

Another attraction of our house was our medicine chest. At that time, the entire upper Tapajós population, Indian and Brazilian, was without professional medical attention. Knowing this, we brought enough medicine for ourselves and the Indians, and for any Brazilian who asked. We took care not to compete with the native curers. The shamans would extract the disease-causing objects, prescribe herbal treatments, and then send their patients to us for antibiotics. As for our credentials, we had a copy of the *Merck Manual* and a good deal of luck, for we never lost a patient.

There were two shamans in the village, both of whom were skilled healers and herbalists. Among their talents was an impressive knowledge of orthopedics; they could set broken bones and, as we discovered, treat damaged muscles. Yolanda suffered from a troublesome lower back that would "go out" occasionally, leaving her immobilized and in pain. The orthopedists treated it with strapping, heat, and pain killers, and after two or three weeks it would get better; we found out later that it would heal in the same time if left untreated. One day, she was working with the women of Cabruá, when her back went out again, leaving her unable to move. It was a real quandary, for our chairs were packing crates, our beds were hammocks, and lying on the floor was out of the question because of the things that wriggle and crawl.

In despair, we turned to Vincente, the older shaman, who told Yolanda to lie face down across her hammock; he then peered at her back intently, inhaling deeply on his cigarette as he did so. He next felt her lower lumbar area with his fingertips, said he had found the trouble, and gave instructions. Robert was ordered to grab Yolanda firmly by the shoulders, and Chico was told to pull sharply on her left leg when Vincente gave the order. The patient looked increasingly nervous. The shaman palpated the area again, then dug his two thumbs into the spastic muscle, gave the command, and Chico yanked. Yolanda got up uncertainly, walked a few steps, rotated her head, bent over a bit, and announced in wonderment that she was much better. She slept well in her hammock that night, and in two days the remaining stiffness had gone.

Our only difficulty with a shaman arose when one visited from another village and made what we thought were excessive demands for gifts. A few days later, he was called by a woman to treat her pet wild pig. It should be said parenthetically that

Mundurucú hunters often bring baby animals to their wives, who raise and often nurse them; this animal had grown into a big, mean, long-tusked boar, which sent us up to the rafters every time it got into our house. The shaman announced that Robert was to blame, for he had shot the beast with a slingshot (to which he pleads guilty, with boredom as a mitigating circumstance) and one of the fruit pits had entered its body (which was only metaphorically true). The woman demanded that Robert give her medicines, but the mixture was ineffective and the pig got worse. The lady was quite angry by now, so Robert went to the shaman and told him that he would now be happy to give him the presents he had requested. The shaman then said he didn't think the slingshot was to blame after all and told this to the pig's owner. The pig died, but the woman remained our friend, the shaman had a new knife and machete, and we had learned through participant observation two lessons: simple cultures can produce artful people, and never mess with a shaman.

Our year was finally ended, and we made preparations to leave. All our remaining trade goods and everything except items we needed on our trip were given away, leaving us with just two footlockers. The women asked Yolanda to stay, but she told them that her mother was weeping for her. This was an unassailable argument to them, but on the day of our departure, they cried. And the chief made a speech:

Before you came to live with us, our lives were as always, and we were happy. We worked, we ate, and then we slept. When you came we were glad, for you brought us many gifts. And every night, instead of going to sleep, we sat with you, drank coffee, smoked your tobacco, and listened to your radio. But now you go, and we are sorry, for all these things go with you. We now know pleasures to which we were unaccustomed, and we shall be unhappy.

The chief's words were expressive of the past century of Mundurucú history, and a prophecy of what was to come, but our contribution to the process was really minimal. As our trail wound its way toward the river, we had mixed emotions. We were deeply tired and longed for the comforts of civilization, but we were overcome by a feeling of incompleteness, a failure to possess what we had come to love. And although we had learned a great deal about Mundurucú culture, we knew that in certain respects we had only scratched the surface. We departed, then, with a lingering sense of sadness and dissatisfaction, which are the emotional residue of all fieldwork.

In the chapters that follow, we describe and analyze Mundurucú culture and the position of women in it in straightforward, positive terms, and in the standard language of cultural anthropology. Most anthropological monographs indeed are written in a style that suggests a dispassionate scientist giving a thoroughly objective account of a society, but we have tried to avoid this, for we were not dispassionate and no social science is as objective as it would like to be. To the contrary, we were deeply committed to the people, and we mourned the progressive loss of their culture. And Yolanda harbored a strong bias in favor of the women, which sometimes broke out into open advocacy in Cabruá. The reader will find traces of these sentiments throughout the book, and it would be dishonest to try to conceal them. Rather, we are freely confessing to our prejudices and warning the reader that they exist.

During the past ten years, anthropologists have come to the realization that they are not cameras; they are not free observers sitting outside the research setting, but are instead part of it. Our presence, as the chief of Cabruá said, had altered their way of life, if only temporarily. We had studied two villages—and two anthropologists, who were the center of interest in both places. It was necessary to ask, "What did you do in the evenings before we came?" Some things happened because we were there, such as the nightly narration of myths, and other things didn't, such as a delay in killing a suspected sorcerer in Missão Velha until after we left. And the people of Cabruá put off rubber-tapping, which they disliked anyhow, until after our departure because we had given them most of the trade goods they needed; besides, we were more interesting. We had unmistakably become part of the objective field of study, just as some of their attitudes and values had invaded our own consciousnesses. Subject and object inevitably merge into each other when doing fieldwork, as they do in all social life.

Anthropologists go into fieldwork with a heavy mental baggage consisting of all their own culture and its burden of categories, perceptions, meanings, and values. They also bring with them their anthropological training, and the methods and theories used to filter and organize raw observations. We had observed millions of speech and behavioral events in the course of the year, only a small percentage of which could be fitted into this book, and we accorded them significance and interpreted their meanings in terms that were a mixture of American culture, the kind of anthropology we were taught at Columbia, and the Mundurucú people's own self-image, their own view of their culture. We have no intention, in saying this, to impugn our results in particular, or anthropology's in general. Quite the contrary, for we believe that we have given as accurate a description of Mundurucú culture as possible.

We wish only to impress upon the reader that ethnography is a difficult and complex task. One does not go into the research situation, collect all the facts lying about, go home and arrange them by subject, and then write a book. The facts are hidden, imbedded in the words and acts of individuals—every one different from every other—and the headings under which we arrange them are abritrary categories taken from our own culture.

When we speak of the Mundurucú "economy," it must be understood that there is no concrete division between economy and kinship, for kin groups are the primary units of production and consumption of foods and artifacts. Family and economy are more separate in American society, and we borrow its categories only for convenience. The reader is warned, however, that culture is cut out of a whole piece of cloth that has an integrated pattern, and the divisions we make within it are done only for the sake of orderly description.

An example may serve to illustrate the ways that subjective factors intrude themselves into our analyses. In 1959, Robert published an article on the Mundurucú men's house which offered a different interpretation of gender relations than the one given herein, an interpretation that was influenced by the ideology of the Mundurucú men, and by his own male status. Yolanda was doing other things at the time, and it was only when she later turned to her own data that the female perspective—hers and that of the Mundurucú women—was introduced. Robert no longer believes in male dominance—that of the Mundurucú men, or his own. Age brings mellowness, if not wisdom.

This brings us to the final point of the chapter, which is the profound changes wrought by the Mundurucú upon us. We went to Brazil as a recently married couple, still in our twenties, and returned as time-tested veterans of the connubial state. During the entire year, we were never away from each other for more than a few hours, and for most of the time we were the only English speakers present. This is enough to break up any marriage, and some anthropological couples have indeed gone from fieldwork to divorce court, often amid bitter custody battles over the field notes. We are still not sure why this did not happen to us, but despite the mutual overexposure, we rarely quarreled. Perhaps it was because we were so far away from civilization, and relied on each other so completely, that neither could afford a breach.

Whatever the causes, we got to know each other better during that year then most married couples do in ten. And out of our mutual reliance in trying circumstances, there emerged loyalty and respect. For better or for worse, we had developed a closed marriage, a state of emotional self-sufficiency. It was not, of course, always a smooth and untroubled relationship, nor has it been since; it was just solid and unquestioned. Some of the Mundurucú view of things stayed with us, from Robert's habit, quickly broken, of going through doors first to his paper on the men's house and male dominance. That was written in only the ninth year of our marriage, a time when dominance games were still being played. Now, in our thirty-sixth year together, the games are over and each side has won and lost a bit. In a way, the relations of the sexes among the Mundurucú are reflected in our marriage, and our marriage, perhaps, has affected our description of theirs.

All these events happened over three decades ago, but they are vivid and alive to us today. We had seen things that few are privileged to witness and that will soon be lost beyond retrieval. And we remember well the evening that we stood with a shaman on a grassy hill and watched a sunset of marvelous texture. The soft, yet vivid, pastel colors rippled across the fleecy clouds, shifting, changing through the entire spectrum, taking fantastic shape, and finally shading off into the fast-approaching darkness. "Irip," said the shaman, and we replied that it was indeed beautiful.

4.

Mundurucú
/\./\./\./\./\./\./\./\./\./\. Culture

This is a book about women, but as is commonly the case, it concerns women living in a man's world. In this chapter we discuss traditional Mundurucú culture as it is recognized, conceptualized, and stated—a series of norms and standardized expectations that people have of each other, a catalogue of how the people believe their society to be organized and of what they consider to be meet and proper. Most of this kind of information was collected from the men, for much of it is male ideology and lies within the sphere of masculine activity. This does not mean, of course, that the men assiduously pursue the ideal, for as is common in societies everywhere there is a considerable gap between what people actually do and what they think they should do, or even think they are doing. However, as will become evident in later chapters, the social perspectives of the women are different, and they do not wholly identify with, nor feel bound by, that from which they are systematically excluded. The actual behavior of the men indeed does differ from the prescriptions for behavior, but not so much as does that of the women.

The ascendant role of the male in just about all human societies and the male biases of social scientists, both male and female, combine to produce one-sided ethnographies. Women's
activities are insufficiently recorded and their values and attitudes commonly neglected. They appear in the background as a
Greek chorus, but one that sings complementary parts and not
in antiphony. Because women are placed below men in the
order of things, we assume that they are submissive. Because
they are excluded from so much of what is reported by anthropologists as "the culture," we assume that they do not have one
of their own. Because they have a traditional position within
the society, we assume that the women accept it without question. And in reporting on what is conceived by men to be the
proper domain of women, we all too easily believe, with them,
that this is indeed the reality of everyday life. We seem to have
forgotten that the very essence of the relationship between the
sexes is struggle, opposition, and socially useful, however unconscious, misunderstanding. What follows, then, in our description of "Mundurucú culture" should be understood as a
point to the counterpoint of the female realm, a foil for the play
of social life.

The Mundurucú are unmistakably set off from other Indian
groups of the region by both language and culture. Their Tupian language is closely related to that of the Curuaya Indians of
the Xingú River, but we had no opportunity to determine
whether the tongues were mutually intelligible. The language
was sufficiently different from other Tupian tongues of the
region, however, to make mutual communication impossible.
But one need not be a linguist to identify a Mundurucú, for in
the past the body of every adult was adorned from head to foot
with elaborate tattoo work, applied by puncturing the skin with
thorns dipped in genipa dye. The heads of the men were totally
covered by solid blue coloring from the pate to the mouth; the

lower part of the face was decorated with geometric designs. The faces of the women were dominated by a broad band of blue that ran from ear to ear across the region of the mouth; the upper part of the face was left untattooed, but the lower part had a geometric design which, like those of the men, continued down the neck. The body tattooing of either sex was also different, though both were characterized by geometric diamond and triangle motifs. The arrangement of the designs differed somewhat, and the women's bodies, like their faces, had far less tattooing than did those of the men. The Mundurucú also painted their bodies and faces with red, blue, and white vegetable dyes for festive occasions, and sometimes because they just felt like it; it was their way of dressing up. Still, the tattooing was distinctive and the hallmark of the Mundurucú, however startling and almost eerie to an outsider. The process was part of the initiation of the young and, though conducted over a period of years, was extremely painful, often causing infection.

The young today have balked at being tattooed, and most teenagers are unmarked, while men in their twenties and thirties are only partly tattooed. It can be assumed that young people never liked being subjected to the ordeal, but the fact that modern youth can successfully refuse is a commentary on the decline of Mundurucú culture and the loosening grip of the older generation. It should be noted that older, fully tattooed Mundurucú complain continually about the younger generation. "We can't do anything with them," they say. "Kids today do what they want and have no respect for their elders or for social standards." The end of tattooing is only one example, to the elders, of general disobedience, laziness, and, to cap it, loosened sexual morality. Interestingly, we heard this complaint only from the men, never from the women. It was much like the litany of the middle-aged American male.

Today's style of male tonsure was copied from the Brazilians, but the women do no more than trim the hair below the shoulder. The men formerly shaved the front part of the head to the crown, allowing the hair in back to grow to the neck. Clothing was simple in the past, consisting of absolutely nothing for the women and of a bark-cloth belt and a palm-leaf penis sheath for the men. Nevertheless, the Mundurucú had a distinct sense of bodily modesty. Women sat on the ground with their legs stretched out in front of them and close together; such (to the European) private areas as the breasts and pubic hair could show, but not the genitalia. The men actually took greater care to conceal their penises than do Americans. Robert realized only after we had been with the Indians for months that he was embarrassing them when he took off all his clothes, jumped in the water, and then sat on a rock in the nude to dry. The Mundurucú, on the contrary, would turn their backs on their fellows, take off the penis sheath and slip quickly into the water. They would stay submerged below the waist until they were ready to come out, when they would just as covertly replace the sheath. Depressingly, most Mundurucú now wear cheap Brazilian-style cotton clothing, which they buy from the traders.

There has never been overall political unity among the Mundurucú, and each village is completely autonomous. Yet there is a strong sense of Mundurucú identity, bespoken by the fact, common among American Indians, that their self-designation can be translated as "we the people." The people, or *we dji nyö*, were distinguished from the *pariwat*, or foreigner, outsider, anybody who is not a Mundurucú, or person. Nobody is quite sure how they received the name of Mundurucú, which is not a Mundurucú word, and it can only be assumed that it was an appellation used by one of the neighboring groups at the time of the first contact. The chances are good that it was an insulting reference, but the Mundurucú are unaware of this possibility and recognize themselves also by the name by which the whites have chosen to know them.

The stable center of Mundurucú life is the village. Communities today are small, with populations ranging between 50 and 100 persons, but in times past they must have averaged about 200 persons or more. The houses of each village are set in a circle around a village plaza which is about 100 yards in diameter; the plaza is ideally kept free of weeds, but in time, clumps of undergrowth grow up, though never high enough to block the view of the other houses. The village turns in on itself and constitutes a small arena, a theater in the round, where a good deal of its life may be observed and where the individual is continually on stage.

Each of the traditional villages in the round consists of a number of dwelling houses—anywhere from three to five during the time of our visit—and a men's house. The dwellings are each about forty by twenty feet, rectangular in floor plan, and internally uncompartmented. The steep-pitched roofs are made of palm thatch over a pole framework, and the walls are of the bark of the *tawarí* tree. The houses have two doors: one in front leads out to the plaza, and the back door gives access to the edge of the village and the network of trails extending out to the forests and savannahs. The only other opening in the house is a space of about a foot and a half between the roof eave and the wall, running around all four sides of the house. Since the outside walls are over five feet high, one cannot look into the house, though older dwellings often have wide gaps between the bark sheets. Each doorway has a door made of bamboo slats, but these are rarely closed. We will discuss later the internal arrangements of the houses, but their salient feature must be mentioned at the outset—the dwellings house only females and prepubescent boys.

The men's house, or *eksa*, is the residence of all males above about thirteen years of age. Its radical social opposition to the dwellings is complemented by a physical distinction. Whereas the dwellings are walled, and the activities of their inmates sheltered from the outside, the men's house has no walls. Some forty to fifty feet long and fifteen feet wide, it is built in the form of a giant lean-to, its roof starting from the ground and rising toward the village plaza to a height of about ten feet. The men sleep in hammocks beneath the shelter of the roof, but they have little protection from winds and wind-driven rain. Adjoining the men's house is a small, completely enclosed chamber which houses the karökö, sacred musical instruments played only by the men. In contrast to the rest of the men's house, the interior of this room is totally shielded from outside eyes; one has to enter it from the back of the men's house and pass through a baffle doorway. The men's house is part of the circular house perimeter, but it is always placed on the west side, its open end facing east toward the village plaza. We never found out why this is so. The men were asked why they could not place their house on the east side of the village. They answered: "But if we did that we would look out toward the forest and would not be able to see what was happening in the village." We learned only that the men's house had to face east, toward the sunrise; the Indians could not conceive of it otherwise. And we learned, too, that it was equally necessary that they orient themselves inward, toward the activity of the village.

The world of the women is centered on the village, and within its confines their houses close them off, too. The contrast of closure versus openness may have practical reasons behind it that are easy to adduce. This is a rainy climate, and nights are cool; for people who have no blankets, walls provide warmth and protection. Insects find little difficulty entering the closed dwellings, but fires are always burning in them, and the faint smokiness of an Indian house does tend to discourage mosquitoes somewhat. Accordingly, the same advantages should argue for a different type of men's house, but perhaps its openness allows the residents to be on guard against enemy attack and less prone to being trapped by a raiding party. Such appeals to utilitarianism founder on comparative data, for we can find other groups in the Amazon that have open-sided dwellings, and most men's houses, where they exist, have walls. Whether the Mundurucú arrangement is superior, we do not know, for the other groups seem to have survived equally well.

Whatever the practical considerations, the physical layout and architecture of the Mundurucú village tell us something about their social system. Women are supposed to belong in the home, in a private sector; men are public figures, and their activities are pursued under the scrutiny of others. Village life is ideally dominated by the men and is under their purview. The women are, of course, part of this community, but they are shut out of it in a symbolic sense, though hardly in ordinary workaday activities. This distinction is not peculiar to the Mundurucú, for public places came to be frequented by unescorted women in the United States only recently, and in Latin America the man still belongs in the street or the plaza, while the woman lives in a world that can be peeped out of, but not looked into.

Immediately beyond the village perimeter lies a belt of underbrush and small trees some forty feet wide. This is an area that has been fertilized by human waste and garbage and sown by thrown-away fruit pits and seeds; one can tell how long a village has been in a certain location by the height of the brush, and abandoned village sites may be recognized as a ring of trees growing in open savannah. In time, the belt of shrubbery becomes a haven for snakes, scorpions, and other vermin—and in

days past, a cover for enemy raiders—and the Mundurucú cite
it as one of the reasons for moving their village every decade or
so. Beyond the village lies grassy savannah, broken here and
there by a grove of trees or a gallery of forest bordering a small
stream, and beyond the savannah lie large areas of forest, which
in turn give way to more savannahs. The forests and plains are
criss-crossed by trails. Some large and well-worn ones lead from
the village down to a nearby stream used for bathing and drinking water. Other large trails go out to the forests where the
Mundurucú make their gardens.

If the village is the inner circle of Mundurucú life, the region
of stream, field, and forest within a radius of some two miles of
the village constitutes a second circle. This second circle is primarily a woman's world, for it is they who draw the water,
gather the firewood, and do most of the garden work within it.
It is also a children's area, for the boys who are too young to
join the men in hunting roam through the savannahs and woods
near the village, shooting small birds, catching fish, swimming,
and, occasionally, stalking the visiting anthropologists. Beyond
this second ring is the domain of the men, the vast tract of
savannah and jungle where they roam in the hunt. Some of the
trails through this outermost circle of the village are well worn,
leading from one village to another or to a port on one of the
rivers flowing toward the Tapajós. These are the connecting
links between the village and the outer world of other villages
and, during the last century, the world of the white man. Other
trails are only faint tracks through the forest, game trails leading
to watering places or to fords in the streams. It is along these
tracks that the Mundurucú men fan out up to ten miles from
their villages in the hunting that occupies so much of their time
and which defines their masculine status. Beyond these hunting
trails there once was a network of other trails, now overgrown,

which led from Mundurucú country eastward toward the Xingú River, south toward the Serra do Cachimbo, westward across the Tapajós River and into the Madeira drainage, and north to the Amazon. These tracks were used by war parties in forays that took the Mundurucú hundreds of miles from their homeland for periods of several months, or even a year. The outer circle is, then, a male sphere, the arena of hunting and warfare, of intervillage relationships, of contacts with the Brazilians, of the outer extensions of the society.

The livelihood of the people is taken completely from their immediate habitat using a technology so simple that nature remains essentially unaltered. The Mundurucú live with their environment, exploiting its seasonal modalities in such a way that they are self-replenishing. They live off the wild life without eliminating it; they clear the jungle for gardens, but allow the land to revert to forest before the characteristics of the soil are irreversibly altered. If the people were to disappear, the country would soon revert to its primeval state, its resources available to sustain future generations.

Mundurucú subsistence is derived from four basic sources: gardening, hunting, fishing, and the collection of wild fruits and nuts (in order of their importance to the total diet). Garden products, supplemented by wild foods, provide the Mundurucú with carbohydrates, but the root crops grown in the forest region are generally low in protein. This essential part of their food supply comes almost entirely from game and fish, the relative importance of each being a function of season and village location. The cycle of rainy and dry seasons, of floods and low water, makes for cyclical variations in subsistence activities and for seasonal changes in types and amounts of food available, but we never saw prolonged hunger during our stay with them. Though lacking in many items that the average American would consider essential to the diet, the Mundurucú have a generally well-balanced and ample food supply, far superior to the diet of most lower-class Brazilians.

The Mundurucú, in common with both other Indians and whites of the Amazon drainage, practice a form of agriculture called "slash-and-burn" or "swidden." Very simply, this is a system of cultivation in which forest areas are cleared, burned over, planted, harvested, and then, after two to three years of cultivation, allowed to return to forest. At the end of every rainy season, plots of jungle land are selected by household heads as future gardens; if the house has many people, two or more of its members may initiate gardens. The gardens are each only two or three acres in size, but all the men of the village take turns in clearing each other's plots, making this task truly communal. The men first cut down all the underbrush in the future clearing and then fell the large trees; the open space is left to bake for the next three months under the dry season sun. By the time the first rains are due, the felled brush and trees are dry and brittle. The gardener then sets fire to the plot, leaving a residue of charred stumps and larger tree trunks, but reducing the rest of the vegetation completely and covering the soil with fine, nitrogen-rich ash.

Garden clearing is men's work, but the remaining agricultural chores belong to the women. The men help in the heavy work of planting manioc shoots, while all the rest of the planting, harvesting, and processing of the foods is done by the females. Their labors will be described in detail in later chapters, for it permeates, limits, and controls the entire universe of their activity. The single most onerous, time-consuming, and exhausting of their chores is the processing of the bitter manioc tubers, of which the Mundurucú grow several varieties, for the extraction of the prussic acid, which makes them "bitter," requires specialized and laborious treatment. Other crops grown by the Mundurucú include sweet manioc, yams, sweet potatoes, maize, squash, pineapples, and cotton. Beans, rice, sugar cane, and bananas are also grown in small amounts, though many Mundurucú gardeners do not bother to cultivate them. Weeding and manioc planting are done with the hoe, and a simple pointed digging stick is used for planting seeded crops such as maize and squash.

All Mundurucú gardens are made on high and dry forest ground, for the river banks are flooded every year during a critical part of the growing season and the savannah soil is either too sandy or too hard for farming. The people classify the soil into a number of types, ranging from black soil through red to clay, with minor gradations based on the amount of sand in the earth. Of the three main types, the black soil is the richest and the only one in which melons, beans, and rice can be grown. Red soil, as well as black, is good for maize, but the clay soils are used principally for manioc. Despite the luxuriant jungle vegetation, the land is not really very fertile. It lacks minerals due to the enormous leaching action of the annual rains, and only the ashes deposited when the garden is first burned provide sufficient fertilizer for farming.

The essential poverty of the soil, and the encroachment of weeds from the surrounding forests, make only two sequential plantings possible; by the third year, the garden is left to revert to forest. The rapidity of the depletion of the tropical forest soils can be judged from the fact that manioc matures in eight months in the first planting of the garden and in a year or so in the second; vegetable crops such as maize, beans, and squash can be planted only in new gardens. After the garden is abandoned, the forest quickly moves in to reclaim it, and within twenty years it is covered by thriving secondary forest; in fifty years only a forestry expert, or an Indian, would know that the jungle cover was not primeval. Two or more decades are usually allowed to pass before the land is again cleared, an interval during which all previous use rights have long since lapsed.

The gathering of wild products is not central to Mundurucú survival, but wild fruits and nuts add variety and enjoyment to the diet, especially during the sometimes lean months of the rainy season. The fruits of several species of palm are gathered for use in beverages. Brazil nuts are eaten raw or cooked into stews, and *cajú* fruit, wild cocoa, mangaba, and a variety of berries are eaten raw. The men often gather nuts and fruits on their far-flung hunting trips, especially when they have not been lucky. Parties of women also gather fruits near the village with the help of young boys, who climb the tall palms with the aid of a loop of vine passed around their ankles.

The essential male activity is hunting. The men think of themselves as hunters, not as gardeners or fishermen, the religion is oriented toward hunting, and the spirit world is closely associated with the species of game. It is the skillful hunter who is honored, not the industrious tiller of the soil. Hunting is central in Mundurucú culture because it is men's work, and not vice versa. In actuality, gardening provides a larger proportion of the sheer bulk of Mundurucú food intake and is the subject of greatest labor investment, albeit mostly female labor. In defense of the male contribution to the economy, however, it should be stated that meat is the favored food of both men and women. One can be stuffed full on root crop dishes and still feel a terrible, and almost indefinable, hunger for meat. The effects of protein insufficiency are not just felt as long-term malnutrition, but as an immediate form of starvation with a full stomach.

The savannahs are quite rich in game, though the region could be quickly hunted bare with a sharply increased human population. Among the major game animals are the tapir, the wild pig, the related but smaller *catitú*, deer, *paca*, agouti, and monkeys. Jaguars are hunted only when they roam too near the villages, but they are never eaten. Armadillos are killed when they invade the gardens, but are not eaten either, despite the fact that their tails contain tender white meat. Between one-third and one-half of the men owned firearms at the time of our visit, but the rest hunted with bow and arrow. Guns provide a certain superiority of firepower, at least in striking velocity, but the armament ranges from old-fashioned muzzle loaders through Winchester .44 carbines to fairly modern shotguns. Given the antiquity and disrepair of the guns, many of their owners frequently hunt with bow and arrow, especially during communal hunts. Group hunts usually involve all or most of the men of the village and are especially effective in pursuit of herds of wild pig. On a good day, a herd of fifty or so pigs can be ambushed and surrounded by the hunters and their dogs, and four or five animals may be killed. The Indians refrain from taking more game than can be eaten by the village, for it is considered a grievous offense against the spirit mothers of the animals to commit slaughter or to kill an animal only for its hide.

The yield of hunting varies from day to day, from week to week, and from season to season. As anybody who has hunted knows, a good part of success is pure luck. On a daily basis, however, the bad luck of one Mundurucú is balanced by the good luck of another, for the practice of sharing all food, including fish and game, tends to iron out the risk factor. If a man takes only a monkey or a couple of pigeons, the food will usually be eaten by his household alone. But if he kills a wild pig or a tapir, the animal is quartered and a share given to every house in the community. There are periods during the rainy season when heavy downpours wash out animal spoors and days pass without meat. The people become depressed, tempers are short, wives complain, and the children cry a great deal. When the weather clears, the men go out en masse, and a good kill usually results. This produces a transformation in the tempo of village life. The babricots in every household are loaded with slowly roasting meat, and the aromas waft through the village, carrying cheer and happy anticipation along with them. If enough game is taken, everybody will eat for two or three days, and the men will spend most of their time working in the men's house, talking, visiting, or just idling. The women's work goes on steadily at such times, as it seems to do always.

Fishing is a male activity, though it is not nearly so highly regarded an occupation as hunting. Fish and fishing are insignificant in the religious system, and the only honor that comes to the good fisherman is that of being a good provider. Indicative of its lower status from the male point of view, fishing is an activity in which women take a marginal part, whereas they have no role at all in the hunting economy.

The relative importance of fishing and hunting vary with season and locale. The villages of the higher savannahs are located near very small streams, and the only fish available in them are correspondingly tiny. The savannah dwellers, then, generally fish only during the dry season when they are collecting rubber along the banks of larger rivers. Those Mundurucú who live throughout the year along the major tributaries of the region depend upon fish more than game as the main source of protein. The annual floods, however, roil the streams so heavily that fishing becomes difficult, a condition aggravated by the spread of the waters, and of the fish, into low-lying forest lands. During the peak three or four months of rains, the men turn more to hunting, though the frequent heavy downpours make game hard to track.

The standard technique of fishing is by use of the bow and a harpoon-tipped arrow. This method works best during the dry season, when the fisherman, standing in the bow of his canoe, can see the fish swimming through the clear waters at depths of up to three or four feet below the surface. Giving hushed directions to his paddler in the stern, the fisherman waits for the right moment and releases the arrow, an operation that takes only seconds, but which involves calculation of the direction and speed of both the canoe and the fish and the degree of refraction of the fish's image. The Mundurucú fisherman does not, of course, consciously make such calculations—he would need a computer—and his accuracy is the result of long training and experience and finely developed hand–eye coordination.

Women often accompany their husbands on fishing trips, acting as paddlers and giving general assistance. They also occasionally fish themselves with small dip nets attached to short wooden handles. That this should be the women's instrument, whereas that of the men is the harpoon, is understandable on simple utilitarian grounds, but this should not lead one to dismiss the clear sexual symbolism involved.

Women also help in the large collective fishing expeditions that make use of drugs. These drugs, found in tropical lianas and roots known in the Amazon by the generic term *timbó*, paralyze the gills and cause the fish to suffocate; though the poisons are fatal to human beings in large dosages, the fish apparently ingest only a small amount, thus remaining edible. Timbó fishing is usually done in small streams or lagoons. A group of men gathers upstream with sheaves of timbó, which they beat into the water, dipping the shredded vines occasionally to release the milky sap into the stream. Soon the fish are swimming erratically, attempting to escape downstream, but the remainder of the men and crowds of women and children are waiting for them with nets and harpoons. During the ensuing riot of activity, huge quantities of fish are taken, some to be roasted fresh, while the remainder is dried and mixed with manioc meal.

The cardinal principle of Mundurucú economic life is that people must cooperate and share. It would perhaps be an idealization to say that the rule is "from each according to his ability and to each according to his need," but this is indeed the stated value. There is, on the other hand, strong public pressure to work, and the laggard, either female or male, finds herself or himself in the unhappy position of being an object of scorn and ridicule. In villages of under 100 people, and in a society in which almost everybody knows everybody else, or at least knows about them, this can be a powerful incentive. It is a kind of immediate and total social control, relying on face-to-face relationships and the threat of loss of the esteem of others and, therefore, self-esteem. This is the mechanism of "shame," said so often to be a characteristic of self-regulation in primitive societies, as opposed to the "guilt" feelings of modern man. Actually, the threat of self-defacement is found in complex societies, as well, and in exactly the same sort of small scale social settings of the village or the intimate group that are characteristic of the way of life of primitives. In any event, the superego twitches produced by self-accusation do not have the same power as the attacks upon the ego that can come from loss of public status. As a result, most Mundurucú work hard when there is work to be done. But the Mundurucú understand perfectly well that some workers are not as effective as others, a fact which is especially true of hunters, and the man who tries hard at hunting but never seems to have luck is not condemned. His family and household will continue to receive equal shares of the kill of others; he will not receive honor for his hunting activities, yet neither will he experience deprivation.

The same requirement of sharing extends to the products of the garden. Every household has producing fields, but, if through misjudgment a cleared garden was not fired before the rains, or if armadillos have destroyed part of a household's crop, other houses will feed the unfortunates from the yield of their own gardens. Sharing goes on even when there is no manifest need for it. A house that makes manioc flour will give at least a token gift of a calabash or so of the meal to other houses. The traditional Mundurucú do not buy and sell among themselves. If somebody is especially desirous of another's possession, he will ask for it—he may have to petition two or three times, but it is almost always given. One of the worst things that a Mundurucú can say about one of his more "civilized" fellows is that he sells food to his own brothers.

The stress on sharing is consistent with Mundurucú patterns of work and follows the rationale that that which is produced by collective effort belongs, in part, to all. Thus, men hunt in groups—the kill is not the individual achievement of the man who shot the fatal arrow. Men cooperate in the clearing of gardens, and the women of the village help each other in planting, harvesting, and processing manioc. The need for cooperation has roots in the technology of the society and in the resources being exploited, but it transcends ecological utilitarianism. People are expected to help one another whether or not the help is especially needed or, in the long run, efficient. For a person to shirk group work bespeaks alienation from others, a dangerous pose in a society that identifies sorcerers by their estrangement from their fellowman—and kills them for the crime of witchcraft. And food is shared whether or not it is the yield of collective work. The lone hunter who kills a wild pig or a deer with a shotgun is expected to share it.

Collectivization extends to the ownership of natural resources, as well as their use. There is adequate agricultural land, and that which is cleared is later allowed to revert to forest. The person who initiates a garden has use rights to the land, a function of the fact that he organized the labor that went into its cultivation, but he does not own the land while it is yielding crops, nor does he control future access to it. Similarly, there is no ownership of game or fish, or of rights to hunting or fishing locales. Houses are considered to be the communal property of their residents; it is understandable that villages which are used for only ten years or so, and are then abandoned, are unlikely to become real estate. Private property is recognized only in clothing, utensils, weapons, tools, and other portable objects.

In the early part of our field research, we were confused by the term *wat*, which we believed for a time to be roughly translatable as "owner." A person would be described to us as the owner of a house or of a garden, but it quickly became apparent that when we asked a man who was the "owner" we would be answered with a man's name; when we asked a woman, we would be told that the owner was a woman. As we became more familiar with the language, we heard the same word applied to the ownership of a village, describing the function of the chief, or of a timbó fishing trip, or of a ritual. The word, it appeared, did not mean "owner," but "person in charge," or the one who took an initiative in some undertaking. When applied to houses and gardens, the different responses that we received from men and women also indicated a basic difference of opinion as to who indeed was in charge.

Kinship among the Mundurucú, as in most primitive societies, is the anvil on which social relations are forged and the language in which they are conducted. To understand the emphasis which anthropologists have placed on ties of blood and marriage, we must go back to certain sociological premises. First, people are more than just people; they are social personages, acting in certain ways that can be anticipated by others who must live with them and cooperate with them. As such, they are social actors, playing roles assigned to them. A person is an individual to be sure, but he is also a doctor, lawyer, or Indian chief. Society thus divides people into categories and expects certain kinds of behavior from persons in these categories. Another prerequisite for any society is that its members be sorted out into groups to carry out the basic tasks of work, child-rearing, defense, and so forth. These groupings are further subdivided according to the roles their members play.

All of this is elementary, and the more interesting question is: What are the criteria that are used in various societies to make these classifications and divisions? In complex societies, the standards and criteria of social differentiation are innumerable. They are found within all the occupational specialties of the division of labor, in the intricate hierarchies of modern bureaucracies, in differences of wealth and power, in the proliferation of religious sectarianism, and in the ethnic heterogeneity of most complex communities. But what about primitive societies like the Mundurucú, which lack class stratification, have no central forms of government, are ethnically and religiously homogeneous, have no pronounced differences of individual or group wealth, and in which almost every task of work is known and practiced by everybody of the same sex? Lacking the cultural elaborations of technologically advanced societies, primitive societies make basic distinctions between people, and assign them to groupings according to characteristics that all human beings are either born into or will grow into in normal life. The most fundamental of these are sex, age, and the circumstances of birth. The attribution of certain roles according to sex is the subject of this book and we will also consider age in connection

with sex roles. But age and sex are rudimentary criteria for differentiation. Sex usually yields only two possible categories and
age but a few more; both have a strong degree of biological
inflexibility. This leaves circumstances of birth—to whom is the
individual born, what other children emerged from this union,
and with whom will the individual later form a breeding
unit—as a source of the fundamental principles by which society
is structured.

Societies require a degree of flexibility in their organization,
and kinship serves the purpose well. We are too prone to look
upon family ties as being rigid; after all, you can choose a friend
but not a relative. The truth, however, is that we are always
choosing relatives, either through marriage or through the subtle
ways in which certain family members "lose track" of each other
while keeping other kin ties intact. Kinship is not fixed by biological genealogy, but is shifting and adaptive to the requirements of both individuals and entire societies. Kinship is used in
primitive societies to provide and regulate political leadership, to
structure the principal groups of the society, and to order marriage relations. Kin groups are work groups, they are religious
cult groups, they are food-sharing units. The basic facts of procreation may be universal, but the social ties they bring into
being are malleable and wonderfully varied. The comparative
study of kinship, then, is not a curious preoccupation of the anthropologist—though they do get remarkably tangled up in the
subject—but the principal means for any understanding of how
the simpler societies are organized. And the Mundurucú are
most certainly organized along these lines. Sex roles are the
most basic form of social distinction among the Mundurucú, but
it would be impossible to understand the content of these roles
or their articulation with each other without reference to kinship.

Every Mundurucú believes himself to be linked by bonds of kinship with every other Mundurucú. These are usually not genealogically demonstrable links, however, for if such reckoning were to exist, it would call for extensive knowledge of ancestry, whether or not the knowledge is biologically accurate. The Mundurucú, on the other hand, keep no genealogies at all, and their knowledge of ties of both consanguinity and affinity—of blood and marriage—is limited to first- and second-degree links among the living and a much foreshortened calculation of ties through persons dead. The chief means by which genealogies are suppressed is through a taboo on speaking the names of the dead by their living descendants, a taboo that generates reluctance among all Mundurucú to refer to the deceased in any way. That everybody is a relative, and that one nevertheless knows how only a quite limited number of people are exactly related to him, are important facts about Mundurucú social structure, but very frustrating ones for the neophyte anthropologist. Told in graduate school that we should take down genealogies and thus build up an outline of the more extended kinship units, we queried our informants unmercifully about the names of their grandfathers, their grandfathers' brothers, and so on, only to be told by some that they could not even remember the name of their father. One middle-aged man finally became impatient with us and exclaimed: "Do you think we bandy the names of our dead around as if they were children, like you white people do?" And so we learned of the taboo and learned, in the process, that what people do not do is often quite as important as what they do do.

Given the absence of extensive genealogies, the Mundurucú do not reckon kinship by gradients of closeness and distance. Rather, each person has a category of close relatives, not formally set off in any way, however, from the rest of the kinship web, toward whom he generally shows primary loyalty and perhaps affection. The rest of the kinship network is differentiated into categories defined in the language of kinship, but which are not the result of genealogical reckoning. The most inclusive of these categories is a division of the society into two halves, called by anthropologists "moieties." All Mundurucú belong either to the "White" or the "Red" moiety, a membership which they inherit from their father through a line of male ancestry—that is, descent among the Mundurucú is patrilineal. The moiety system is basic to Mundurucú society as the primary regulator of marriage and definer of the incest taboo. It is considered to be incestuous to marry, or even have sexual relations with, a member of one's moiety. One should marry a Mundurucú, but one's opposite: Red women marry White men, and White women marry Red men.

The operation of moiety intermarriage has interesting results for kinship. A father and his sons and daughters, for example, may belong to the Red moiety, and the mother must, therefore, be from the White. The father's brother must be from the Red moiety, since he shares descent with the father, and his children, too, will belong to the Red moiety; these cousins, therefore, will be prohibited as marriage partners. On the other hand, the father's sister, also Red, must marry a man of the White moiety. By the rule of patrilineal descent, the children of the father's sister will be White and, therefore, marriageable to their Red cousins. Looking at the mother's side of the family, the mother's sister, being White, must marry a Red man; their children will also belong to the Red moiety and will be sexually taboo. The children of the mother's brother, however, will be White like their father, and they will be acceptable mates. In short, the children of the mother's brother and the father's sister, or cross-cousins, are marriageable, and those of the father's brother and mother's sister, or parallel cousins, will be of one's own moiety and thus taboo. By extension, every person in one's generation of the opposite moiety is conceptually a cross-cousin, whereas those of one's own moiety are parallel cousins. A senior man of the other moiety is in the category of mother's brother, and a senior woman of one's own moiety is a father's sister. Similarly, a senior man of one's own moiety is a father's brother and an older woman of the opposite moiety is a mother's sister. All these ties are conceptual in nature, in keeping with the total dichotomization of the society; the system of nomenclature by which people address each other, or refer to each other, consists of variations on this theme of dualism.

Moieties are conceptualized as opposites in other ways. The very color categories of red and white are seen by the Mundurucú as opposed, just as we find black and white to be antonyms. One is reserved and respectful, though cooperative and loyal, toward members of one's own moiety, but persons of the opposite group at one's generation level are potential marriage partners; the proper behavior toward them is one of joking and levity that barely covers a sense of in-law hostility. The theme of oppositeness, and even active opposition, which is so common a characteristic of moiety organizations wherever they are found, is probably best expressed in the custom by which people are buried by a member of the opposite moiety. "It is our duty," said one man; "it is our pleasure," said another. Village plans are not, however, divided into moiety halves as among the Bororo Indians to the south, and the chief physical expression of the dichotomy is the fact that men of one moiety sleep on one side of the men's house and those of the other, on the opposite side.

The moieties themselves are subdivided into clan units, membership in which is also obtained through descent from the father. Clans, as most commonly defined in anthropology, are kin groups whose members claim putative descent—that is, a bond is believed to exist, though no attempt is made to trace it—from a remote ancestor. All the members of the clan believe themselves to have a common founding ancestor and feel that they are therefore related, but they have no knowledge of the family tree that links them. Among the Mundurucú, the founders existed in the remote and hazy period of the mythic past, a time beyond exact memory during which the land, animals, people, and culture were being created. This was a time when animals had the forms of people, and man and the natural world had a greater unity than they do today. The ancestral figures, then, were not human in the sense of people as we know them now, and all of the Mundurucú clan ancestors are designated by animal and plant names; that is, the ancestors are totemic in nature, as are Mundurucú clans. Unlike many forms of totemism, however, there are no taboos against killing or eating the totemic animals among the Mundurucú. The ancestors are believed to be present still in spirit form among the Mundurucú and are housed inside the sacred musical instruments kept in the men's house. When properly propitiated, the ancestral spirits exercise a benevolent protection over the villages. When neglected, however, they may retaliate against the living.

There are thirty-eight Mundurucú clans, sixteen of which are included in the Red moiety; the remaining twenty-two belong to the White. Since membership in both moiety and clan follows the patrilineal principle, all the members of any given clan will belong to the same moiety. The clans are exogamic—one must marry outside one's own group—but this function is subsumed under the more encompassing moiety division. Nonetheless, it is considered far more improper to have sexual relations with a clanmate than with a fellow moiety member. Many of the clans are clustered into small sets of two or three clans which believe themselves to have closely related ancestry. Sexual relations or marriage within these clusters of linked clans, called phratries in anthropological terminology, are thought to be more improper than within the moiety, but still not so grievous an offense as within the clan.

Fellow clansmen are felt to be more closely related and, therefore, to have stronger ties of mutual obligation than they do toward other Mundurucú. In actuality, neighborliness and plain friendship also do much to structure interpersonal relations, but kinship is considered by the Mundurucú to impose enduring and immutable links. There is little that the clans "do." They do not own land or dwellings, there are no rituals connected exclusively with clanship, and there are no clan leaders or chiefs. The clans may have little function in the realm of activity, but they are important as a Mundurucú model of what their society is like and how it is organized, and they serve also to allocate to every individual a stable position within the Mundurucú social universe, which is predominantly a universe of kinship.

Clanship constitutes the principal statement of the ideology of patrilineal descent. It stipulates in a direct and immediate way that children belong to the kin groups of their fathers and not those of their mothers. Furthermore, clans are central to the system of personal naming, though Portuguese first names are being used increasingly. Each Mundurucú has a two-part name. The first is that of his clan, and the second, or given, name is also derived patrilineally; boys are given the name of their father's father's father, or one of the latter's brothers, and girls are named for their father's mother's mother, who was also a member of the same moiety as her namesake. It is thus possible to identify any Mundurucú by clan and moiety, and to at least know where he or she stands regarding marriageability. Clanship further segments out units from an otherwise diffuse and undifferentiated network of kinship, giving the appearance of a society that is put together of stable building blocks.

It has been stated that the clans have few manifest and corporate functions and further suggested that the neat categories posed by Mundurucú clans may well exist largely in the realm of the ideal. The reasons for this lie in Mundurucú patterns of postmarital residence. In contrast to the patrilineality of descent, the Mundurucú generally prefer that a newly married couple take up regular domicile with the family of the bride. This does not mean that the groom actually lives in the bride's family dwelling, of course, for he sleeps and spends a good deal of his time in the men's house. Though the men's house removes the young husband from the possible conflicts inherent in life among a closely knit group of in-laws, matrilocality often requires that he leave the men's house of his natal village and move to that of his bride. He thereby becomes separated from his father and from his brothers, who will, by the same rule, move away to other villages also. In time, the man will raise sons who may similarly find brides in other villages and leave. Matrilocality is not uniformly followed, but it produces a striking effect: Central links in clanship are between father and son and between brother and brother, but these kinsmen are customarily separated by marriage, and the bonds are thereby undercut and weakened through lack of continual and direct association.

The first result of the matrilocal residence rule is that despite the presence of patrilineal clanship, there are no patrilineages—that is, groups of kin sharing common descent and linked through genealogically demonstrable ties. The only exceptions to this fact are in the families of chiefs. Chiefs' sons are ordinarily exempt from the matrilocal rule, and the household of a village leader will often have three generations of men related in the male line—grandfather, sons, and grandsons, all belonging to the same clan.

The lack of genealogies and the matrilocal preference conspire, then, to rule out the lineage as a standard unit of Mundurucú society, but they do more. As we have said, people also have ties of cooperation and sharing with their fellow villagers and these, due to the factors of proximity and economic necessity, are often stronger in practice than those of clanship, whatever may be the ideal. Clan brotherhood is inevitably diluted by these crosscutting obligations. Any single clan will have its male members scattered throughout Mundurucú country, and there are no occasions when the clan, as such, has a reunion, or even occasions when a substantial number of clansmen gathers in a common enterprise. Fellow clansmen do not normally cooperate and share unless they happen to live in the same village, in which case they cooperate and share with all their other fellow villagers as well.

The dispersion of clansmen has varied consequences, aside from the weakening of clan functions. Clanship is but one of a number of institutionalized links between people, and the very fact that clans have little solidarity also means that they do not serve to isolate the individual within their ranks. The boundaries of clanship are not walls. By the same reasoning, the scattering of clansmen gives every Mundurucú ties with other villages, strengthening the solidarity of the tribe at the expense, perhaps, of the kinship units. It would appear, then, that despite the neat model of segmentation and group delineation that clans provide for both the Mundurucú and the anthropologist, kinship is indeed smoothly and diffusely spread throughout the society. Furthermore, the fact that ties of locality and of patrilineal kinship do not coincide and are indeed crosscutting provides a unique form of integration. Clans are never arrayed against clans, for this would destroy village ties. And villages do not oppose other villages, for this would pit fellow clansmen against each other. This is one of the sources of the remarkable surface peacefulness of Mundurucú social relations.

Tranquillity and cooperation are cardinal values in Mundurucú culture, and they are complemented by a strong egalitarian orientation. There are distinctions of prestige and public esteem between people, as there are in every human society, but none of these differences gives anyone the right to coerce others, except for the authority exercised by parents over their children and, perhaps, husbands over their wives. The Mundurucú honor the good hunter, the man who possesses ritual knowledge, and, in former times, the valiant warrior, but those with high status do not form a class of any kind, nor does respect bring power over others. The traditional economic system allowed no room for wealth differentials, though modern-day trade with Brazilians has allowed some industrious rubber tappers to amass manufactured articles such as guns, clothes, pots and pans, and even an occasional flashlight. But the man who sets himself off from his fellows in this way runs the risk of attracting the animosity of others and of being accused of sorcery. The Mundurucú are indeed attracted by the trader's wares, but their appetites are dampened by an aversion for rubber tapping and through fear that their acquisitions will be interpreted as a sign of alienation.

The rule that nobody should strike a superior pose or openly attempt to exercise power extends to the chiefs also. Each Mundurucú village has a chief—ideally, the oldest son of the previous chief. The ability of the chief to keep his own sons after they marry, while at the same time attracting sons-in-law, generally makes his household the largest and most cohesive of the village, a fact that automatically invests him with considerable influence. Despite the large core of kinsmen and his public position, the chief remains a "first among equals." He does not make decisions on his own, nor does he give orders to others. Instead, decisions affecting the entire community are made in the course of conversation in the men's house with most of the adult males present and the older and more prestigious men exercising the most weight. The chief acts as a manipulator of the consensus, guiding the discussion and seizing upon the moment when compromise is possible. The subtlety of the process and the unwillingness of any Mundurucú to put himself into direct public confrontation with another make the conversations long—they can continue for weeks—and the exact time and means of reaching a decision are elusive to the outsider.

Most Mundurucú claim that in past times chiefs were more powerful, a statement that is reminiscent of the "good old days when men were strong and women virtuous," a historic cliche in most societies. But beyond the attempt to idealize the past, it is quite probable that chiefs were indeed more august figures when the Mundurucú were still making war. Warfare was the predominant male occupation—one might even say obsession—in earlier times, and although the last hostilities occurred almost four decades before our visit, the men still talked about it as if it were yesterday. They had poor memories for the events of actual wars, but recounted in vivid detail the techniques and patterned activities that went into warring; one had the feeling that the entire complex could have been reactivated at any time. War was the favorite topic of all the older male informants. They became animated in the accounts, their every word and gesture followed avidly by their listeners. Permeating the narrative was a sharp and stinging sense of nostalgia for a time when life had more meaning, when what was considered good was attainable, when excitement and danger transformed consciousness and broke the flow of time.

The Mundurucú were the fiercest of all the tribes in the central Amazon. Their enemies included every other group save the neighboring Apiacá, who were subservient to the Mundurucú and sometimes joined their war parties. Forays were launched in the dry season and ended either with the rains or during the dry months of the following year. The range of their hostilities was amazing for a people who relied very little on water transportation. Their war parties were reported on the Amazon itself, along the shores of the Madeira, eastward into the Xingú River basin, and southward probably to the Planalto of Mato Grosso. From all reports, they were usually successful. After perhaps months of travel through the forests, they would surround an enemy village by night and launch an attack at dawn. Burning arrows were shot into thatched roofs, driving the bewildered occupants outside—to the lances and arrows of the Mundurucú warriors. Enemy men and women alike were slaughtered and decapitated, and the trophy heads thrown into carrying baskets. Children were captured and brought back to be raised as Mundurucú.

Whatever the importance of the young captives in maintaining population levels, the taking of trophy heads was thought by the Mundurucú to be the ultimate goal of all warfare. The heads were not shrunken, as among the Jívaro of Ecuador, but, rather, were desiccated. The brains were taken out through the foramen magnum (the socket at the base of the skull), and the head was dipped several times in boiling water and dried near a roaring fire. This was apparently sufficient to preserve the head for years; indeed, there are at least two specimens in museums to this day. The trophy head was kept in the men's house and was treasured both as a memento of Mundurucú prowess and as an object of religious ritual.

The taker of a trophy head, or *Dajeboiši*, occupied the most honored rank in Mundurucú society. During a ritual period of almost three years after his exploit, he was considered to be in a sacralized state and could not engage in ordinary social discourse, being approachable only through considerable protocol. Chiefs were also more esteemed as they were usually the leaders of the war parties; a chief might also take a head during a raid, further adding to his status. The warrior exemplified the principal values of Mundurucú culture. He was valiant without being boastful, cordial while maintaining reserve, and he was fierce while observing restraint and peaceability at home. These are still ideal traits, but they are characteristics that no longer can be given full expression.

One of the principal values of the trophy head was its beneficent effect upon the spirits of the game animals. Informants stated that the head did not contain the spirit or soul of the fallen enemy, but that it simply "pleased" the game spirits and thereby promoted the fertility of the animals and made them more vulnerable to hunting. It was customary for the Dajeboiši to take the head out to the forest with the hunting parties and wait while the charm of the trophy was felt by the game. He would not hunt, himself, but his companions would in a short time kill all the game that the village needed—or at least so said our informants.

The influence of the trophy head over the spirits of the game linked together the two major male activities, warfare and hunting. Both occupations called forth similar qualities in men, and both found a common rationale in religion. Warfare and all its attendant ceremonies have long since disappeared, but the religious emphasis on hunting is still strong. The Mundurucú believe in the existence of a host of spirits, but those of the game animals are paramount. Each species of game is said to have a spirit "mother" who exercises protection over the animals and insures their increase. The importance of the different spirit mothers to the Mundurucú is a function of the role of the animal in subsistence—the tapir and wild pig spirits are those most commonly invoked and propitiated, while those of the lesser game animals are hardly mentioned by the people. There is also a spirit mother of all game animals, serving as a symbol of the essential unity of the game and a principal intermediary between man and nature.

The game spirits were once the focus of large ceremonies involving people from many villages, but the ritual cycle had lapsed about ten years before our visit. The central purpose of the ceremonies was to make offerings to the spirits and secure their cooperation and benevolence. Though the spirits are no longer propitiated, one must still exercise caution against offending them. Killing more animals than the village can eat or killing them only for their hides is a serious offense against the spirits and can invite snake bites and other accidents or cause the loss of one's soul. This is only negative appeasement, however, and the Mundurucú believe that hunting was better when the great ceremonies were being held, just as game was even more abundant when headhunting was a way of life. The end of much of Mundurucú ceremonialism indeed removed the occasion for ritual congregation of the people and undercut social solidarity, but it also broke the conceptual links between hunting, warfare, man, and nature that gave Mundurucú culture its internal coherence and vitality.

The only rituals remaining are those that center upon the ancestral spirits and the men's house. Present-day Mundurucú religion revolves largely around the problems of evil—of illness, death, and animus. There are a variety of potentially harmful spirits inhabiting the brush and forests surrounding Mundurucú villages. Among them are the Yuruparí, a forest and water spirit that makes a thin whistling sound and attacks people who are foolish enough to wander outside the village at night. The victim is seized with fever and abdominal pain; if the spirit was close to his prey, death can be instantaneous. The Yuruparí are believed to be more prevalent now than ever before, and fear of the spirits is intense among all Mundurucú. Another class of spirits, called the Ašik, gains its recruits from the souls of girls who die just before puberty. The Ašik is particularly feared by mothers, for it steals the souls of infants, just as living prepubescent girls always want to take babies away and hold them in their arms.

There are other spirits, but the most common of all supernatural entities are those made by man. These fall into two categories, both of which are the work of malevolent shamans, or medicine men. One of the most dangerous forms of witchcraft performed by the shaman is his conversion into a supernatural jaguar that can travel to distant villages in an instant in order to consume the internal substance of his victim. The afflicted person, almost always a man and an enemy of the witch, wastes slowly away and dies. Jaguar witchcraft is considered to be the most loathsome form of supernatural practice, but its occurrence is far less frequent than is simple sorcery, or the making of harmful objects that enter the victim and cause illness. Very little happens because of simple accident or natural causes among the Mundurucú. Mishaps are usually due to an offense against the spirits of the game or against the ancestral spirits. Similarly, disease is invariably due to sorcery. The evil shaman is thought to manufacture objects, fill them with supernatural power, and waft them off into the air. The objects, or cauši, move about at random, sometimes lodging in the ground until stepped on, and sometimes floating in the air and entering the body of anybody who passes. Since they are invisible to all but the shamans, there is little that one can do to avoid them. Unlike the attack of the shaman-turned-jaguar, the effects of causi are curable. Also unlike the supernatural jaguars, the causi have no specific victims; they strike at random, and even persons close to the evil shaman can fall ill. As the Mundurucú say, "The sorcerer is angry at everybody."

Most shamans, however, are believed to be good and to practice their art for the well-being of their fellow men. The shaman's primary function today is to cure illness—that is, to undo the ravages of his evil colleagues. His power, inherited from his father, is conceived of as a diffuse energy and capacity that is inherent within him, though it must be developed and made efficacious by training. The shaman receives no recompense of any kind for his services, and he otherwise carries on all the normal work and obligations of any adult male. His techniques are much the same as those used by shamans in other parts of the Amazon basin and, indeed, throughout the New World. He blows tobacco smoke, believed to be powerful and life giving, over the sick person and sucks the intrusive object out with his mouth. The damage caused by the causi is then repaired by the prescription of various herbs, roots and leaves, some of which, like ginger root and quinine bark, are respectable items in a modern pharmacoepia. The first part of the cure, then, is supernatural in nature, though often quite effective in relieving anxiety over illness or in reducing psychosomatic symptoms. The second part is rational therapy, and the shamans often sent their patients to us to be given modern drugs, after they had extracted the causi.

One of the risks of a shamanistic practice is accusation of witchcraft or sorcery, the penalty for both of which is death. The logic is simple. If there were no sorcerers, there would be no illness and, therefore, less death. Thus, sorcerers must be killed. Generally, the people of a village do not take steps against a suspected sorcerer until deaths have occurred. An outside specialist at witch detecting is then called in, names the culprit, and cleans up and destroys all the cauši he has made. Shamans are understandably nervous every time an epidemic strikes their village, for the death rate among them is high. Several have fled in anticipation of an accusation, and others have simply gone to live among the Brazilians for fear that their turn may be next.

The seemingly tranquil life of the Mundurucú is fraught with fears of the unseen and unknown. There is little violence, or even aggressiveness, among them, but violence and aggression are indeed present in repressed and residual form. In a sense, the sorcerer is a projection, a form of symbolic expression, of these latent tendencies that simmer below the surface of Mundurucú social relations, and his destruction is a purgative of that antisocial part of the self that has been attributed to the sorcerer's person. The dangers of the supernatural world are social dangers, the fears are fears of other people and of what is intuitively perceived in the self.

The decline of Mundurucú religious ritual, of communal worship, bespeaks a decline of the entire integration of the society. The Mundurucú themselves see clearly that their traditional ways are ending and that they will not long hold out against the slow encroachment of Brazilian society. Some have already given up and have taken up life at the mission or on the Tapajós River. The holdouts in the savannah villages see themselves as fighting a delaying action against the inevitable. Their ranks are no longer as numerous, their prowess is moribund, their ties to the spirit-permeated natural world are attenuated.

One Mundurucú belief is an allegory of the present. There is an underworld that once lay below Mundurucú territory, inhabited by beings called the *Kokeriwat*. This is a remarkable place where everything is backwards: the people fish with bunches of *sipó* snakes instead of timbó, they have sexual intercourse standing up instead of lying down, and the sun rises in the west. In former times, the Kokeriwat, invisible except to shamans, went to war as allies of the Mundurucú. They occasionally played tricks on men, but they were essentially friendly, their differences serving to counterpoint the mundane order. But since the time that warfare ended, the Kokeriwat, like the Mundurucú, have been harassed by growing numbers of Yurupari, and they have moved their underworld to the forests eastward, where they no longer communicate with the Mundurucú. Even the good spirits have been displaced by the bad, just as the good times of bravery and abundance have been replaced by tedium, relieved only by ineffable fears.

5.

Women
/\\.\\.\\.\\.\\.\\.\\ in Myth
and Symbol

The status of the woman is stated clearly, unequivocally, and strongly in the formal canons of Mundurucú culture—her position is inferior to that of the man. This is a matter of official creed—male creed to be sure—reiterated at various points in the culture by elaborate symbolism and firmly held values. The women, on the other hand, do not agree with the men and, in spite of the sanctity given by tradition to their role, they neither like it, nor do they accept it. The relation between the sexes is not, then, one of simple domination and submissiveness, but one of ideological dissonance and real opposition. What follows is a description of male creed, but we enter the caution that like most ideology it bears a loose and sometimes curiously inverted relation to reality.

The entire charter and rationale of Mundurucú sex roles is contained within a single myth, which tells of the invention of the sacred musical instruments, or karökö, and of their relation to male ascendancy.

The sacred trumpets of the Mundurucú, called the karökö, are taboo to the sight of women, but the women once owned them. In fact it was the women who first discovered the trumpets.

There were once three women named Yanyonböri, Tuembirú, and Parawarö. When these women went to collect firewood, they frequently heard music from some unknown source. One day they became thirsty and went off in search of water. Deep in the forest they found a beautiful, shallow, and clear lake, of which they had no previous knowledge. This lake came to be named Karököboaptí, or "the place from which they took the karökö." The next time the women heard the music in the forest, they noted that it came from the direction of the lake and went off to investigate. But they found only *jiju* fish in the water, which they were unable to catch.

Back in the village, one of the women hit upon the idea of catching the fish with hand nets. They rubbed the mouths of the nets with a nut which had the effect of making fish sleepy, and returned to the lake properly equipped. Each woman caught one fish, and these fish turned into hollow cylindrical trumpets. The other fish fled. That is why each men's house now has a set of only three instruments. The women hid the trumpets in the forest where no one could discover them and went secretly every day to play them.

The women devoted their lives to the instruments and abandoned their husbands and housework to play them. The men grew suspicious, and Marimarebö, the brother of Yanyonböri, followed them and discovered their secret. He did not, however, actually see the instruments. Marimarebö went back to the village and told the other men. When the women returned, he asked if it was true that they had musical instruments in the forest. The women admitted this and were told, "You can play the instruments, but you have to play them in the house and not in the forest." The women agreed to this.

The women, as possessors of the trumpets, had thereby gained ascendancy over the men. The men had to carry firewood and fetch water, and they also had to make the *beijú* (manioc cakes). To this day their hands are still flat from patting the beijú into shape. But the men still hunted, and this angered Marimarebö, for it was necessary to offer meat to the trumpets, and the women were able to offer them only a drink made from sweet manioc. For this reason, Marimarebö favored taking the trumpets from the women, but the other men hesitated from fear of them.

On the day on which the women were to bring the trumpets to the village, they ordered the men out to the forest to hunt while they made the sweet manioc drink. When the men returned from the hunt, the three discoverers of the trumpets led the other women out to get the instruments. The leader of the women, Yanyonböri, sent one of the women back to tell the men that they should all shut themselves securely inside the dwelling houses. The men refused to do this and insisted upon remaining in the men's house. Finally, Yanyonböri herself went back to order the men inside the dwelling houses. Her brother, Marimarebö, replied, "We will go into the house for one night only, but no more. We want the trumpets and will take them tomorrow. If you do not give them to us, then we will not go hunting, and there will be no meat to offer them." Yanyonböri agreed, for she knew that she could not hunt the food for the trumpets or for the guests at the ceremonies.

The men entered the dwelling houses, and the women marched around and around the village playing the trumpets. They then entered the men's house for the night and installed the instruments there. Then, one by one the women went to the dwelling houses and forced the men to have coitus with them. The men could not refuse, just as the women today cannot refuse the desires of the men. This went on all night, and the women returned to the men's house all slippery inside.

The next day the men took the trumpets from the women and forced them to go back to the dwelling house. The women wept at their loss. When the men took the trumpets from the women they sang this song:

> It was I who went and hid
> I entered the house and hid
> I entered the house and almost hid
> Because I did not know I was ashamed
> Because I did not know I was ashamed
> Because I did not know
> I entered the house and hid
> I entered the house and almost hid

Like many myths, our story posits a time and a situation in which there was a reversal of the social order. The women controlled the sacred karökö and the men's house, thus enabling them to be the dominant sex. But this is far more than a simple counter-pointing and offsetting of the present, for the theme reveals a great deal about Mundurucú sexual attitudes today. The very fact that the women were believed to have once been dominant bespeaks a latent fear that they can become dominant again. The sex biases of our own society are of a different order. Our own mythology of domination and subordination in the United States, and in northern Europe, rests heavily upon a curious biological mysticism. Just as we once thought, and still murkily suspect, that character is hereditary and is passed on with the blood, so also are we prone to think, despite all evidence to the contrary, that the status, achievements, and powers of peoples and races are linked to gifts or flaws of biology. Sex attitudes in the West are cut of the same ideological cloth, sometimes masquerading as genetics. Women are observed to be anatomically different, and it is assumed that they must be mentally different. Though there are undoubtedly true psychoemotional differences between the sexes, ours is a hierarchical society, and we conceive of the differences in this way. Therefore, since women's common lot is subordination, we assume that they are submissive by heredity. In short, they are inherently inferior to men. The evidence is clear-cut: Women are in an inferior position, so they must have been made that way. This is the refrain of men who complain, paradoxically, throughout elementary school about the high grades earned by girls and throughout marriage about the domineering attitudes of their wives.

Mundurucú culture is totally free of notions of immutable heredity. People, and even animals, are the way they are because of events that happened in the past; while we may question whether the events really happened, the general rationale and method of thought is perfectly good science. The male view of the sexes is consistent with the rest of their logic. We could not find a shred of evidence to indicate that men think that women are inherently, biologically, and irredeemably inferior or submissive. Indeed, the whole key to the myth is that women once did exercise dominance, and that they had to be overthrown in a primal revolution. Women, as people, are not inferior, for otherwise the rebellion of the males would have been unnecessary. Only their status is inferior, and this is so only because the men managed to shear them of their power in the remote past.

The revolution of the men was not carried out by force or by simple physical superiority. It was made possible because the women did not hunt, and, being unable to hunt, could not make the required ritual offerings of game meat to the ancestral spirits in the karökö. The division of labor, then, is primary, and the possession by the men of culturally given hunting skills underlies their higher status. And so we come again to the common theme that manhood and hunting are inextricably linked. The women, on the other hand, made a manioc drink, which they still make today, but this is not proper food for the ancestors.

During the time when the men were under the rule of the women, there was an almost complete inversion of sex roles, except, of course, in hunting. The men carried water and firewood and made manioc cakes, activities in which no self-respecting traditional Mundurucú man would engage. And when the women actually took over the men's house, they also took the active role in sex relations. The myth is revealing in this respect, for it states plainly that the occupants of the eksa initiate sex, that their gratification is paramount, and that the role of the dwelling house residents is submissiveness. This division is true of the present, and it is believed to have been true in the mythic period when women lived in the men's house and the men in the dwellings. Not only had the men lost their active sexual role, but they also lost their position as open, public figures. The song at the end of the myth says that they "entered the house and hid," just as the women are today symbolically shut in the house while the men occupy their open eksa. The men were also "ashamed," a powerful word among the Mundurucú, connoting loss of identity and marginality of social role. But the men did not even know that they were ashamed, for the final articulation of their status came later with the control of the sacred instruments.

The instruments are key symbols in our sexual paradigm. It was their discovery that gave the women a power which they lost when the men wrested them away: they underlie sexual superiority. Each Mundurucú men's house has a set of three of the instruments, kept, as we said, in a totally enclosed chamber, secluded from the eyes of the women. The karökö is basically a hollow tube with a reed placed in its mouth. A length of the trunk of a softwood tree is cut, rounded evenly on the outside and hollowed. Those of one village were forty-three, forty-six, and fifty-two inches long, with inside diameters ranging from two and three-quarters to three and one-quarter inches. The reed consists of two strips of the wet and pliant root of the *pax-iuba* palm, placed side by side and bound together near each end. When one blows a stream of air between the wet roots, the halves of the unbound middle section vibrate against each other, making a sound reminiscent of the "Bronx cheer." When blown inside the resonant chamber of the karökö, a deep, rather mournful-sounding note issues. The middle-sized karökö of each village is played by the oldest and most experienced of the players, and it carries the basic melody. The larger and smaller ones play in harmony. All the adult males know how to play and turns are taken by most of the men.

It is believed that the ancestral spirits are pleased by the playing of the karökö, just as they are by the presentation to them of meat after a successful hunt. These are occasions when all the men gather in the men's house to take a communal meal, and when protocol requires that one of them take a gourd of the meat and place it before the mouth of each instrument, a symbolic offering of food to the totemic ancestors. After everybody has eaten, three of the men enter the chamber, and the deep sounds of the karökö are heard until late in the night. Occasionally, the men kill a great deal of game, the women make the sweet manioc drink, and the karökö are played from morning until dawn of the following day.

Special ceremonies are held when new karökö are installed in the men's house, or when old karökö are brought from their former location to the men's house of a newly constructed village. Symbolic of the division of labor expressed in the myth, the men kill a great deal of game and the women make troughs of the sweet manioc drink to feed the village, as well as guests from other communities. After a day highlighted by intermoiety joking, most of it sex play between men and women, the men form a procession to bring the karökö into the village. Three men carry the instruments, playing as they walk, and the rest crowd about them to shield the sacred karökö from the eyes of the women. The procession circles the village three times before bringing the instruments to their new home, and during this time the women shut themselves inside the dwelling houses and go through ritual wailing as an expression of their grief for having lost the sources of power.

One need not be an orthodox follower of Sigmund Freud to detect the sexual symbolism of the myth and its ritual enactments—the themes are so blatant that they come close to being a parody of psychoanalytic interpretation. The long tubular shape of the karökö is clearly a phallic symbol in the classic sense of the term. When the women controlled the phallus, they were dominant; now that the men own it, the roles are reversed. The karökö, according to the myth, originally were in the form of fish, also symbols of the male organ, and immediately evocative of the fact that bull roarers, used in other parts of South America, are commonly carved in the form of a fish. The bull roarer is a flat piece of wood which, when whirled in the air on the end of a string, gives off a whirring sound reminiscent of the karökö, and it, too, is believed to embody male power, making it taboo to the women. But fishes may be bisexual symbols; they have the external shape of a phallus, but they also have wide mouths, containing sharp teeth. Similarly, the karökö are long tubes, but they are hollow. In their cavities dwell the ancestral spirits, just as the real cavities of women contain the regenerative potential of the people and the clans.

The symbolism carries over into daily life. Mundurucú men frequently make joking references to sex as a means of subduing women. "We tame them with the banana," one man said. This is not fantasy or dream material requiring interpretation but conscious, stated thought. The penis gives power; it is how men dominate women. In the same vein, one can go beyond the toothed mouths of the fish-karökö symbols to everyday humorous metaphors such as the reference to the vagina as "the alligator's mouth." Or a man may see a woman sitting with her legs a bit apart and will call out to one of his fellows that his mouth is open. To the men, the attraction of the vagina is tempered by its dangers. The vagina, too, has power, but it must be controlled by men. And the karökö is a male possession, yet it has female characteristics as well. It is not wholly anomalous that women once owned the instruments, and every caution must be maintained to keep the karökö from even their sight. The position of the man is not given within nature, but rather within culture, and the men must defend themselves lest a counterrevolution take place.

The myth of the karökö is a parable of phallic dominance, of male superiority symbolized in, and based upon, the possession of the penis. But it is at best an uneasy overlordship, obtained only by expropriation from the original custody of the women. In one sense, the myth is an allegory of man's birth from woman, his original dependence upon the woman as the supporting, nurturant and controlling agent in his life, and of the necessity to break the shackles and assert his autonomy and manhood. The mother is the center of love and affect, but she is also an eternal threat to self-individuation, a figure of authority, a frustrater of urges, and a swallower of emergent identity; she can devour and reincorporate that which she issued, and the vagina, the avenue to life, is ambivalently conceived by the men as destructive. The role of the male, then, must be maintained by vigilance and continual self-assertion.

The men's house, its origin myth, and its ceremonies are closely involved with the Oedipal transition and the transformation of the male child to man. This does not mean that the complex of male roles springs full blown from the psychological state, however, for there are social and economic conditions for its existence as well. But Oedipal anxieties provide much of the specific content and symbolism of the myth and ritual, making it possible to see a universal human experience in the activities of a people so different from Westerners. Many anthropologists will argue about whether the Oedipus complex is general in all societies, but for our present purposes it is necessary only to demonstrate it for the Mundurucú. This can be done most succinctly by recounting another myth, this one about certain remarkable events befalling two men in the single-dimensional and timeless Mundurucú past.

Once upon a time there lived two men, named Karuetaouibö and Wakurumpö, who were married to each other's sisters. The latter was a man of normal appearance, but Karuetaouibö was very ugly. He was so ugly that his wife no longer wanted him and not only refused to accept his kill of fish and game, but had relations with another man.

One day the men of the village went to a stream far in the forest to fish with timbó. When the others returned, Karuetaouibö remained in the shelter that they had built and contemplated his unhappy situation. He was disgusted with life and reluctant to return to a wife who did not want him. As he was sitting there, the Sun came with his wife and asked him what he was doing. "Nothing," replied Karuetaouibö, "I am only sitting here because my wife has relations with another man and no longer wants me because of my ugliness."

The Sun wished to verify the truth of this and told his own wife to have coitus with Karuetaouibö in order to see if he was capable of pleasing a woman. The wife tried him out, but his penis was soft and would not enter. She went back and reported this to the Sun. To see if his wife was telling the truth, he passed his hand down the front of her body and then down her back to see if he could bring out semen. Nothing could be discovered, and he knew his wife told the truth.

The Sun then said, "Let us see what we can do for him," and he passed his hands over the body of Karuetaouibö, making him very small. He placed him inside his wife's womb, and after three days he was reborn. The Sun worked on him and fashioned him into a beautiful man of normal size. He then went to the stream and caught a basket full of fish, which he gave to Karuetaouibö, saying, "Return to your village, but do not go back to your wife. Go instead to a woman named Painun who weeps constantly for her husband, who was killed by the enemy." The Sun then brought him to the edge of the village and left him to enter by himself.

As Karuetaouibö approached the village, he signaled that he was coming. He first went to the men's house and there hung a hammock so small that there was no room for another man to climb in and bother him. Everybody gathered around him and admired his new beauty.

The men said, "Ah, I wish that I were a woman so that I could have him for myself." Karuetaouibö's wife heard this, but she did not bother to look up, thinking that he had merely painted himself. Finally, she went outside the house and saw that her husband had indeed become very beautiful. The wife was under the impression that her husband still wanted her, and she made haste to make herself appear industrious. She went to her mother-in-law, who was grating manioc and said, "Let me grate the manioc, mother-in-law." The old lady replied, "No, he does not want you to do it." In the meantime, Karuetaouibö ignored his wife and said, "Mother, go to the edge of the forest and pick up my basket full of fish." The wife offered to go, but Karuetaouibö refused.

When the mother returned with the fish, Karuetaouibö instructed her, "Go to the house there and give the woman who is weeping some fish and tell her to be consoled and cry no more." The old woman did this, and the woman in mourning said to her, "How can it be that your son wants me. I am ugly and dirty now." The mother replied, "It was he himself who sent me. He wants you." At this moment, Karuetaouibö entered the house and said to the woman, "Go to the stream and wash yourself and return to be my wife." She made herself clean and beautiful, and when she returned they started their life together.

When Karuetaouibö returned to the men's house, he got into his tiny hammock. Wakurumpö approached him and said, "Let me get into your hammock so that you can tell me how you became so beautiful." Karuetaouibö replied, "No, the hammock is too small." But Wakurumpö was extremely persistent, and after a number of days Karuetaouibö surrendered and told him the story. "But," he added, "this can mean nothing to you for you are not ugly, and your wife wants you."

The envious Wakurumpö wanted, however, to get rid of his wife and be as handsome as Karuetaouibö. He accordingly pretended that he was ugly and that his wife had rejected him for another man. Like Karuetaouibö, he went on a timbó-fishing expedition and stayed behind when the others returned to the village. Soon the Sun arrived and, pretending at first that he did not recognize Wakurumpö, eventually asked him what he was doing. Wakurumpö repeated the same story that Karuetaouibö had told, and the Sun proceeded to take the same measures. He instructed his wife to see whether Wakurumpö was capable of satisfying a woman, and the Sun's wife proceeded to have coitus with him. However, Karuetaouibö had neglected to tell this part of the story to

Wakurumpö, and the latter completed satisfactory relations with the Sun's wife. The wife told the Sun what had happened, and he verified it as he did in the case of Karuetaouibö.

The Sun then made Wakurumpö very small and inserted him into his wife's womb, whence he was reborn three days later. He proceeded to make him big again and to remodel him. But this time, he made him ugly and hunchbacked and told him, "Now go home. But go home to your wife." The Sun and his wife did not fish for him or carry his basket back to the village, and Wakurumpö had to do all this himself. When he neared the village he signaled his arrival, and all the people who came to greet him stood about and stared at his ugliness. He had to go back to his wife, who accepted him.

When Wakurumpö went to the men's house to hang up his hammock, Karuetaouibö was lying there in his hammock, playing the following song on a flute:

> It was your fault, Wakurumpö
> It was your fault, Wakurumpö
> You were curious for your mother's vagina
> You were, you were.

Wakurumpö and Karuetaouibö were killed by enemies, who cut off their heads and placed them on top of posts. A small fat boy was posted to guard the heads. This boy had inherited shamanistic powers, but neither he nor the other people knew this. One day the heads began moving and talking, but only the boy could hear them, because of his special power. He shouted to the older men. "The two heads are moving and saying to each other, 'When will we rise to the sky?' " The elders scoffed and said, "How can heads without bodies or eyes move, and how can a dry mouth talk?" This happened many times, and the men still thought that the fat boy was lying to them.

A few days later the men adorned the heads with urucú paint and feathers, and after some days the heads said to each other, "Today we ascend." The boy spread the alarm, but none of the men heeded his warning. At noon the heads were seen to start rising to the sky, accompanied by their wives. Karuetaouibö and his wife rose rapidly, but Wakurumpö ascended slowly because his wife was pregnant. The men of the village shot arrows at the heads, and all missed except one shaft sent by the fat boy, which put out the eyes of Wakurumpö.

Wakurumpö and Karuetaouibö, both children of the Sun owing to their magical rebirth from the womb of the Sun's wife, are now in the sky and appear as the visible sun. The wife of Wakurumpö is Parawabiá, the moon. When it is sunny and bright, this is because Karuetaouibö is in the sky; he is beautiful and his eyes shine a bright red. However, when it is dark and cloudy, it is because Wakurumpö is in the sky. Wakurumpö is ashamed to show his ugliness, and his eyes are dull and lifeless. For this reason he hides, and we do not see the sun.

Oedipal themes are among the most widespread of mythological motifs, but the Mundurucú version is a classic of its genre; it has almost everything. On one level it is a moral tale of envy, curiosity, and its consequences, but the envy and curiosity are quickly seen to have a sexual focus. Both men meet a woman who becomes a mother to them. One does not have intercourse with her and is made attractive to women; the other does have sexual relations with the mother figure and is made repulsive. The man who honors the incest taboo becomes virile and strong; the offender is emasculated and warped. The story is obvious enough, but the Mundurucú narrators restress the theme in Karuetaouibö's song to Wakurumpö: "You were curious for your mother's vagina." The story ends, as does Oedipus's at Colonnus, with the incestuous man blinded, the ultimate symbolic form of castration. The only major Oedipal theme missing is the killing of the father before the mother is possessed. Interestingly, although there are several fratricidal episodes in Mundurucú mythology, we could find no tales of parricide. On the other hand, in our Mundurucú tale, the Sun-father actually carries out the emasculation of Wakurumpö. There is also a homosexual theme overtly expressed in the men's desire for Karuetaouibö and their attempts to join him in his hammock. But the rest of the story has lovely parallels with the Greek version, joining with the story of the karökö to paint a broad and vivid canvas of the problematic relation between the sexes, and of the contradiction inherent in the transition from infant to man.

The castration motif appears elsewhere in Mundurucú mythology. In one story, a young man named Perisuat has coitus with a jaguar-woman, who plans to kill him and cut off his penis. In another, a man hears a female frog croaking and threatens to insert his penis in her and make her croak with pain. The frog later changes into a beautiful woman and seduces the man, but at the point of orgasm, she retransforms herself into a frog and hops away with the man's penis locked in her vagina. She stretches it out to an incredible length before she releases the penis, leaving the man immobilized. Some otters arrive on the scene, see the man's plight, and apply a preparation to reduce his penis. They reduce it too much, however, and he goes home with a penis the size of a little finger. The theme of emasculation carries over to the female role as well, for the women do indeed shut themselves inside the houses and mourn for the lost karökö when the instruments are paraded in the village. It must be noted, however, that the wailing is ceremonial and perfunctory in nature, an antiphony and chorus to a male ceremony. Any sense of loss or envy of the penis that the women may feel is not expressed with great emotion, and the observer is left with the feeling that the grief is a routine performance carried out to meet male expectations.

That the fear of emasculation is far deeper among the men than is penis envy among the women is also suggested by the secrecy of the karökö. Women cannot view the instruments under penalty of gang rape, surely a clear example of phallic power, but we never found any great curiosity among the women. Some of them must have spied on the roots of male power at some time, however, as the women can give a fairly accurate description of what they look like. And they do this with little sense of awe or fear, just as they could matter-of-factly say who was playing the instruments at any time. The women were obviously less impressed with male prowess and its props than were the men.

The karökö link male superiority and hunting, and they also tie both in with the patrilineal mode of descent because they are the repositories of the ancestral spirits of the clans. Patrilineality, although not necessarily either a result or determinant of male status, is generally correlated with a lower relative position of women than is true of matrilineal descent. In Mundurucú patrilineality, the children belong to the clan and moiety of the father, a membership that is lifelong and binding. The children of a woman, under this system, do not legally belong to her group; in a formal sense, they are alienated from her. Marriage, therefore, guarantees the status of a woman's issue, for without a father a child can have no clan and, therefore, will lack the social definition bestowed by kinship. Illegitimate children are commonly destroyed at birth, as are twins and children with serious birth defects—the latter are physical anomalies and the former are social anomalies. Those who do survive are referred to as *tun,* a word which means excrement, but can be glossed as any distasteful body product. They are not mistreated in any way, but their future marriageability is clouded by their indefinite status.

All societies intervene in the regenerative process to varying degrees. Women are indeed the bearers and nurturers of children, and only a few minutes of a male's time is required for conception, but law and custom dictate how and with whom this is to take place, setting limits in the process on the female's control over her young. Among the Mundurucú, control over the women is far more than simple domination of the opposite sex, for it involves also the social allocation of the children and the integrity of the male status of fatherhood. Marriage defines the right of access of a man to a woman, yet it also defines the right of the man's clan to the children born of his wife. Women contain the future potential of a society, and they are valued for this, but if patrilineal descent is to prevail, the formal status of the woman must be lowered to assure men the rights to the young. That patrilineality should be related so closely to the men's house and the karökö is, then, a partial function of the general need to gain power over children. The weakness of Mundurucú clans, the attenuated functions of descent in general, however, makes control of the disposition of children less than critical. And the general tendency to matrilocality makes the alienation of the child from the mother a formal matter at best. This suggests that male control over the women is less complete than the ideology requires, a supposition that will be borne out in later chapters.

The Mundurucú believe that the substance of the fetus is formed from the seminal fluid. It follows from this assumption that a woman must have several sexual contacts with a man to amass the necessary material. The man, by this reasoning, is essential to procreation; he provides the raw material for the child, which then grows in the mother's uterus. And, because several acts of coitus are necessary to the process, the biological genitor of the child will generally be its legal father. Extramarital affairs are common enough among the Mundurucú, but most are not of long duration; thus, it is the husband who usually has the continuing access to his wife that is necessary for conception. Faulty embryology and ideology are one among the Mundurucú, just as ideology often unites with bad genetics in our own society.

There are interesting mythological ideas on the origin of women. In an early part of the Mundurucú creation cycle, human beings are already present in the world. The culture hero and creator, named Karusakaibö, lived among the people with a handsome young son, named Korumtau. Despite Karusakaibö's prohibition, the women all seduced his son, leading the angry father to turn him into a tapir. Undaunted, the women copulated with the tapir until one day the men found out and killed the animal. The enraged women then marched single file to the river, where they turned into fish. The world was left without women. Later, Karusakaibö and his trickster friend, Daiiru the armadillo, found an underworld and pulled out of it the people from whom the Mundurucú are sprung. But there were only men among these human beings, and Karusakaibö proceeded to make women out of clay. The various animals of the forest copulated with the women, and the different sizes and shapes of their penises account for the differences now found in the vagina. The armadillo finished the work by smearing a bit of rotten Brazil nut on the mouth of each vagina, which is why the female organ smells the way it does today.

Women, then, were created on one occasion by a male god, but in another part of the cycle they turned into fish; it should be remembered that the karökö were once fish, too. The stories also tell us that not even the culture hero could control the women. When he did take revenge for their infractions it was against his son. And when the women were finally frustrated by the killing of the tapir-son, they threw themselves into the water. There are passages in other myths that also tell of seductions by females and the inability of the men to control them.

Women occupy a lower status than men in Mundurucú myth, but they are also portrayed as ungovernable. This is much the way the contemporary men look on their women. As an end note to these comments on mythology, the Biblical story of Adam's rib undergoes a curious inversion when told by the Mundurucú. According to their version of Genesis, when Karusakaibö made the women out of clay, he gave one to each man. He had, however, made one too many, and, to make a husband for the extra woman, he took one of her ribs when she slept and made it into a man; their names were Adjun and Eva. Man is indeed born of woman, and there's the rub.

The superior status of the male is manifest in the rituals of everyday life. Women occupy no formal positions of leadership of any kind, a situation that finds parallels in most primitive societies. Among the Mundurucú, this male monopoly extends to all religious offices as well, an exclusion that is not at all as prevalent cross-culturally as is political domination. Some Mundurucú said that women did, however, inherit shamanistic powers, though they never used them. Other men claimed that in the remote past women actually practiced shamanism, but in view of the rest of the culture this seems dubious. Whatever the female potential for shamanism, no women are considered capable of curing, clairvoyance, or communication with the spirits, and, luckily for them, none are believed able to practice sorcery. Their only connection with shamanism is in the role of patient, a rather passive situation in most societies.

The formal position of women in ceremonies has the same element of passivity; they serve as a chorus and not as instrumental figures. During the ceremonies for the spirit mothers of the animals, women sing songs about the peccary and, at a signal, rush upon the men, capturing some to be "singed," just as they would a slain wild pig. There were no puberty ceremonies of any kind at the time of our visit, but informants told us that rites used to be held for young boys. The children were taken into the men's house when they were only four or five years of age and kept there for a period of two years. At the end of their seclusion, a ceremony was held in which the boys, equipped with sharp wooden beaks, played the role of *jacamím* birds and chased after the women, pecking at them. Again, the symbolism of the beaks and the pecking of the women has clear phallic components, and the rite is a statement of the partial separation of the boys from the women and an augury of their future relations with them. There were no comparable rites for girls. Women did, however, occupy a special, and sacralized, ritual status during the old ceremonies for the trophy heads. Both the successful headhunter and his wife were accorded highly special treatment and were prohibited from sex or other mundane activities. The headhunter's wife could not look directly at another person because of the possibility that he or she might have had recent sexual relations. She was also expected to remain in her hammock until late in the morning when hunting parties left the village, and she could not bathe in the stream. And she could not work, leaving all her chores to be performed by a woman of the opposite moiety.

A woman is supposed to be retiring and demure, at least during her child-bearing years. And she does not seek the company of males. Both women and men gathered in large groups every evening in our house, but these were about the only occasions when this occurred. But even in our house, the men sat in front, occupying the packing crates which were our only chairs, while the women sat on the floor in the background. Significantly, all these strictures are suspended in the case of postmenopausal women. An old woman will sit where she pleases, and men will actually defer by making room for her. She may talk on whatever subject interests her, and if this requires that she interrupt the men, then so be it. Her opinions are freely given—and listened to—on matters of community concern, and they are shown marked respect. By graduating from sex and child-bearing, she has graduated from the female role and, in a legal sense, has become a man, albeit an old one.

Backseat status is standard for younger women; they sit in the rear, walk in the rear of a file, and eat after the men do. A woman is retiring in other ways as well. If something amuses her, she is supposed to cover her mouth when she laughs. An open mouth is like an open vagina to the Mundurucú men. And a proper woman does not look directly at a man, nor would she ever engage his eyes. This is considered to be a rank and blatant invitation by the men, and, of course, by the women as well. Demureness calls for a closing off of the active communication zones of eye and mouth, a setting of symbolic distance. By the same reasoning, men and women do not touch, except as a tentative prelude to sex.

Women who violate these rules, and some indeed do, are considered to be *yapö*, a word that can be translated by anything from "wanton" to "nymphomaniac." In actuality, women who "accidentally" touch men, laugh openly at their sallies, or eye them do so for the purpose of initiating sexual relations, and the assumption that they are promiscuous is well taken. The problem of the yapö is, however, not a moral issue but a medical one. Yapös are created by unethical shamans who bewitch a woman, making her insatiably desirous of men. Unlike many forms of love magic, however, the woman desires any and all men, not just the guilty shaman, and the best that he can usually expect is to get there first. There is a special cure for the condition, and the yapö can retrieve her reputation by undergoing the treatment. The yapö role is of interest for two reasons. First, the fact that the shaman's magic cannot give him exclusive access to her is consistent with the general collectivization of Mundurucú life—she belongs to all the men, just as sorcery, once spread, can kill anybody. And it is also noteworthy that though the yapö is the aggressor in sexual liaisons, it is a man, in the first instance, who makes her this way. Thus, even in the case of the promiscuous female, it is the men who control her sexuality.

The delinquent woman poses a problem to the ideology of the men. On one hand, they pursue such women with expectable enthusiasm, but, on the other, she constitutes a threat to their superiority. Men, as in most things, are supposed to be the aggressors in sexuality, exactly as expressed in the myth of the karökö. The loose woman who seduces men takes this initiative from them, intruding upon the separation between the sex roles. When a woman persists in this behavior to the point of public scandal, and when the available cure is either unsuccessful or refused, the men, as a group, retaliate. The punishment is exactly that meted out for spying on the sacred musical instruments: gang rape. On these occasions, up to twenty or more men will drag the woman outside the village and violate her. Rules of moiety exogamy are suspended, and we even heard of cases in which first degree parallel cousins participated in the rape. The punishment is as interesting as the crime. After all, the woman could be just as easily beaten or subjected to some other physical abuse, but it will be remembered that the men consciously state that they use the penis to dominate their women. This is a textbook instance of phallic sadism.

One of the dilemmas created by the yapö, or any aggressive woman, is that she has stepped beyond male control. One Mundurucú myth tells of the gang rape of a woman who was said to "have no owner," again a word that can be translated also as "director." Every woman must have an adult male who will protect her and vouch for her, on condition that she conform to the standards set for women. A woman who lived in our house was a yapö, but she was not assaulted by the men because she took the prescribed cure. And when the cure did not work, she remained under our protection—we were her "owners." The custody of a woman can be held by her father or brother, but that of most mature females is held by their husbands, a reaffirmation of the right of the men, and their patrilineal clans, to the sexuality of the women. But that the sanctions extend beyond the question of children into a general defensiveness against self-assertive females is illustrated by the gang rape of a girl who ran away from the mission school. Here, the concern was not with promiscuity or spying on men's secrets. Nor were the Mundurucú upholding the rights of the missionaries to educate their children, for at best they are unenthusiastic about losing their young to the school. The girl's sole crime was the flouting of male authority and the pursuit of her own inclinations.

Any woman who sets out on her own is a mark for the men, and the women guarantee each other's propriety by constantly being in the company of other females. Every morning and evening when the women go to fetch water and bathe, they leave the village in groups, And when they work in their gardens it is always in the company of at least one other woman, and preferably more. The woman who leaves the village by herself is always considered to be heading for a tryst and, even if she is not, any male has the right to accost her and demand that she have intercourse. These events sometimes approximate rape, but force is never involved. The woman has left herself defenseless and has no choice but to comply. A fourteen-year-old boy in a Cururú River village took advantage of this rule with remarkable success. He would each morning climb a tall tree near the village and patiently sit in its upper branches surveying the entire village. Occasionally a woman would slip furtively out into the underbrush and meet her lover, all under the boy's unerring scrutiny. When the tryst had ended, he would intercept the woman on her way back to the village and demand the same. The men knew of his activities and viewed the situation with high humor, though they knew that he was taking a second turn with their lovers and, perhaps, their wives. But, then, boys had few restrictions placed on their behavior, and sex was hardly considered immoral. "He spends a lot of time in that tree," said the men, "but he sure gets a lot of women."

The rules governing female conduct testify to their lower jural status, but they also guarantee the separation of the sexes. It is this theme, more than subordination, which pervades the relation between the sexes and permeates all institutions of Mundurucú society. With but few exceptions, men and women make different contributions to the economy, and even when they work together it is often on separate chores. It was only after we had been among the people for some time that we discovered that the excursions taken by a man and wife for the stated purpose of gathering or gardening were usually subterfuges for some private connubial love. This separation of activities and of formal social roles is expressed in most complete form in the men's house. There is separation of the sexes in all societies, and among South American Indians it is generally quite sharp; however, few groups go so far as to provide separate sleeping facilities.

The degree of segregation of sex roles is paralleled by actual separation of the sexes, a fact which will become manifest in chapter 5, but the separation juxtaposes the sexes as groups and not as individuals. This may well be the reason why the Mundurucú men do not regard individual women as somehow polluting, contaminating, and ritually unclean, as is the case in many societies. In some societies taboos on women are expressed in a revulsion for menstruation and in beliefs and rites that require a woman to undergo special treatment during or after her menses. The restrictions might involve seclusion during her period, a taboo on her own body so strong that she has to scratch herself with a special stick and not her fingers, postmenstrual baths, and a variety of other limitations. But none of these customs can be found among the Mundurucú, except for an injunction that prohibited women of child-bearing age from making the ritual sweet manioc drink prepared for the now lapsed ceremonies for the trophy heads. Only old women or prepubescent girls could make the drink, for fear that it could be contaminated by menstrual blood or semen; the drink could also be defiled by a man who had recently had sexual intercourse. Today, however, the menstruating woman has practically no restrictions. She does not engage in sex during her period, but she cooks, associates with other people in a routine way, and bathes in the stream. It is worth noting that the men always bathe upstream from the women, however, though we could find no evidence that this was due to fear of contamination. But, aside from these instances, women were not looked upon as unclean, impure, or debased in terms of attributes inhering to their persons.

This returns us to a theme expressed in the beginning of this chapter: Women are not intrinsically, personally, and naturally inferior—their roles are inferior. Similarly, the separation between the sexes and the domination by the males is less an interpersonal matter than an intergroup question. The sexes among the Mundurucú indeed constitute a division of the population along lines of anatomical difference and function, just like everywhere else. But the split is more than that. Each sex is a social entity, each has its own internal organization, and each has a sense of solidarity and a consciousness of its own unity and its opposition to the other. The battle of the sexes is not carried on by individual gladiators, as in our society, but by armies.

6.

The
/\\/\\/\\ Woman's World

Women are indeed inferior in the ideology of Mundurucú men, but they are also threatening. Male status is not secure and immutable, fixed in nature and beyond challenge, for women once held power and can regain it if male vigilance is relaxed. Women are governed by men, but they are still regarded as unpredictable and difficult to manage. They are denied formal authority, but it is conceded that they have potential power. Men are dominant in sex and reproduction, but it is women who bear and nurture the children. The dogma of male dominance is thus pervaded with doubt and contradiction. It must be regarded less as a statement of what things are really like than as the posing of a riddle, the expression of a dilemma, and an ideological device for its resolution.

The contradictions of Mundurucú social life become even more pronounced when we compare the ongoing, day-by-day, practical realities of female activity with the beliefs of the males on the proper status of women, as we do in this and the next chapter. This will take us away from the formal culture to an examination of how the women work, where they live and with whom, how they raise their children and manage their marriages. This is the sphere of pragmatic life, which is not lived in rigid accordance with the guidelines of the culture but, rather, uses the culture as a backdrop and sometimes as a counterfoil. It is in this practical realm that people maximize their positions by mundane and daily strategies and in which they group themselves in subtly defined coalitions. And it is on this level of everyday activity and grouping of people that the role of the Mundurucú woman is transformed from one of symbolic abasement into a position of real strength. All cultures are, to a large extent, collective illusions, and so also are Mundurucú standards of womanhood. They are, however, the illusions, or self-delusions, of the men, for the women are firmly grounded in social reality—they are masters of the practical.

The Mundurucú house is the center of female life in the traditional community, the stronghold, and liability, of her status. It is at once the place where the woman sleeps, where she bears and raises her children, where she cooks, weaves, relaxes, plays, loves. Its architecture and interior design are adapted to the role of the woman, fitting her needs and expressing her values and activities. Like homes everywhere, its very shape and layout tell us a great deal about the relations among the inhabitants themselves and between them and the outside world.

In just this way, a typical contemporary California house opens on a patio bounded by a high wooden fence that belies the easy affability with which the residents treat their neighbors; and the openness of the house to this palisaded exterior, and of its common rooms to each other, is again counterpointed by the closed-in, small-windowed, locked-door motif of its sleeping areas. It is a study in private lives, of a nuclear family that curls in on itself and finally fractionates into its individualities. The Mundurucú house is almost an exact opposite of its California counterpart. Its interior is dark, opening to the outside only through two narrow doors, but once beyond the doorsill one is in a public plaza and instantly visible from the other dwellings and the men's house. And within the interior of the house there are no private areas. It is totally uncompartmented, and every corner of the house is visible from every point within it. There are no hiding places for nuclear families or individuals, for the residents of the household are a single social unit, just as the village is also a unity.

The house is some twenty by forty feet in size, with a thatched roof and bark walls. There is an open space of some eighteen inches between the wall and the roof for circulation of air, but the height of the vent and the overhang of the roof make it a poor window—the residents, instead, keep abreast of village happenings by peeking through spaces in the wall or looking through the door. The design of the house frame is quite simple. Two large center poles, some fifteen feet high and spaced about twenty feet apart, support a ridge pole. Lateral roof poles extend from this ridgepole down to the walls on all four sides to form eaves. The framework of the roof is then covered by a thatch that remains reasonably watertight in the winter rains, yet permits the filtration of air at other times. The house is well adapted to the tropical climate. Its high roof allows the hot air to rise and slowly work through the thatch, keeping it reasonably cool during the day, and the looseness and venting of the walls allows for constant cross-circulation. What it lacks in insulation is compensated by ventilation.

The interior of the house falls into two major zones, demarcated by the two poles supporting the roof. In the center, between the poles, is a commons area, where a good deal of housework and ordinary relaxation takes place. The ends of the house are used for sleeping. Across each center pole is tied a long horizontal pole that runs from one side of the house to the other, attached at either end to an upright post of the wall. This pole, which runs parallel to the ground and some five feet above it, serves to brace the house frame, but is also used as a place from which to suspend the hammocks in which the Mundurucú sleep; the other end of the hammock is tied to a similar horizontal pole running along each end wall. The residents thus sleep dormitory style, their hammocks hung parallel to each other and only a few feet apart. The hammocks are usually hung three or four feet above the ground, where they are reasonably safe from the fleas that infest the dirt floor and which have a remarkable jumping ability.

The sleeping zone is also used for storage of personal possessions. On one side of the house, not too far from the door, a large forked branch is usually planted in the ground and is used as a hanger for the women's carrying baskets. At the other end of the dwelling, a raised platform serves as the storage area for cheap suitcases bought from the trader and which contain clothing and other personal possessions. The platform also contains the household's supply of manioc flour and a few staples such as salt and sugar. Personal possessions are also kept along the walls near each woman's hammock. The men, too, keep most of their personal property in the house, either on the platform or near the hammocks of their wives.

The middle part of the dwelling, between the two rows of hammocks, is the equivalent of the American living room. With a doorway at either end, it is the natural route of traffic through the house, and it is also the principal work area. Near the back door are kept some hollow gourds, each with a hole in the top, which are the family water bottles. Also near the back door, and a bit to the side of it, is the hearth. There is only one fireplace in each house, a highly significant fact for, though a number of nuclear families may occupy a single dwelling, the kitchen is communal. The rest of the center area is kept clear, except for an occasional log or empty packing crate on one side which serve as seats.

The household is a busy place. Its women, and their neighbors, are constantly going in and out on one chore or another, and a few are always either sitting near the fire, resting in their hammocks or working off to one side. In most houses at least one woman is usually making a hammock, fabricated on a vertical loom kept close to her sleeping area. Others may be stirring the cooking pot or adding wood to the fire, and still others may be nursing babies. The scene is usually enlivened by the little children, who are continually dashing in and out of the house, playing with one of the puppies, or looking for attention from their mothers. The dogs occasionally wander in—only to be chased out when they get too near the food—tame parrots waddle around the house squawking at nothing in particular, and every now and then one of the tamed peccaries kept by the women gets loose and rampages through the house searching for food. Somebody's baby always seems to be crying, adding to the hubbub of the other children and the conversation of the women. Men generally visit the houses in the morning and in late afternoon to evening, but if there is no hunting they may drop in at any time. Sometimes they come for a drink of water or a bit of food, or they may be in search of a bow and arrow or gun. The men also sit and talk to their wives, though these conversations are rarely prolonged, and they are often seen playing with the little children. Some men even keep an extra hammock in the dwelling to lounge in during their visits, but they sleep in the house only when they are ill and need the care of their wives. Despite these visits, most of a man's time is spent in the men's house, a far more quiet and tranquil place.

Through their wives or mothers, the men are considered to belong to one or another household, and the males frequently refer to a house as being under the direction of the senior male. Thus, if the senior couple in a house are named José and Maria, following Brazilian usage, the men will refer to the dwelling as "José's house." The women, however, look upon this as just one more male pretension and will be quite emphatic in saying that the house is Maria's. After all, they point out, it is Maria who lives in it and directs its activities, and not José, who just comes there for sex and water. Faced with this objection, most of the male informants back off and admit that the house probably is the woman's, but qualify the concession by saying that the distinction is not very important. The women's position is, however, valid and accurate, for the men, as we will see, have little to do with the direction of the internal affairs of the household and, though members, remain marginal to it.

Each house is the dwelling of a number of nuclear families. In former, more populous, times, say the Mundurucú, a household could well number fifty or more people in ten or twelve nuclear families. Today, village population has shrunk to between fifty and one hundred persons, the number of dwellings to between two and five, and the average household population to between twenty and twenty-five—the latter figure includes the attached males.

The women are the residential core of the household, and they also form into clusters of kinswomen. According to the matrilocal residence preference, it will be remembered, men join the households of their wives after marriage, and the women stay in place. The tendency, then, is for households to be centered around a core of related women. The preference should not, however, be interpreted as a rigid rule. Informants say this is the ideal arrangement, but, as in everything else in Mundurucú life, there are situational exceptions. And, given the very deep change and dislocation being experienced by the Mundurucú, the exceptions are much more common now than they were in the past.

At the time we lived in the village of Cabruá, a total population of about eighty people lived in four houses. There was a fifth house, but it was abandoned at the time of our visit and became the residence of ourselves, our field assistant, a Mundurucú woman who helped in the household chores, and her daughter. Numbering the other houses as roman numerals I to IV for convenience of reference, we can review their residential composition for clues to the operation of Mundurucú society. House I was the dwelling of the chief's family. He and his wife were the senior members of the household, and she was understood to be its leader. One of the chief's sons resided in the house with his wife and two sons. The wife's two children by a previous marriage also lived in the household, as did a parentless young girl who had been adopted by the chief's son. Another son resided matrilocally in House IV with his wife and her mother. Despite the matrilocality of the household, the son remained in the same village as his father, whom he eventually succeeded in the chieftainship. Such succession would have been a problem had he resided in another village.

Thus far, House I has a patrilocal slant, as is expected in a chief's family, but there were matrilocal arrangements as well. The Cabruá chief's wife had been married, and widowed, twice before she married him, and her three daughters remained with her. One married, bringing her husband to Cabruá, where they had three children. The other two were unmarried, though mature. The two girls were thought to be ugly and malicious by most of the villagers, and their single status made them a threat to the other women, who accused them of trying to seduce their husbands and of rumor mongering. Whatever the pecadilloes of the chief's stepdaughters, their presence in his house illustrates the enduring ties between mothers and daughters, sisters and sisters.

It should be noted that, though traditional Mundurucú culture accorded the right of polygyny to chiefs, this Cabruá headman had always been monogamous. A case in a distant village came to our attention, however, which tells us much about female status and why polygyny has disappeared. The village chief, whom we will call by the pseudonym Tomé, had acquired his position through pressure exercised by a trader. The villagers were irate at this departure from custom, and Tomé tried to consolidate his position by marrying a woman of the village who was older than him and less than attractive. His marriage helped his position a bit, and Tomé, now overconfident, decided to exercise the traditional chiefly right to polygyny, forgetting, however, that the custom had lapsed. The new bride, a young and pretty girl, was brought to his house, where the outraged first wife tried to kill her. Also, the very people with whom Tomé sought closer relations, the kinsmen of the first wife, turned on him. He brought the new bride to the safety of a kinsman in another village, visiting her occasionally, only to find that he was being cuckolded by all the men during his absences. He shuttled unhappily between his village and that of his new wife for months.

The story is instructive for a number of reasons. Tomé misunderstood the present status of Mundurucú marriage rules—they are monogamous, and the women enforce the monogamy. Also, he was not able to coerce the first wife into accepting a rival. To the contrary, supported by a nucleus of kin, she succeeded in driving the young girl from the village. One would think that the second wife, living now in his kinsman's house in another village, young and unsupported by relatives, would be an easy mark for husbandly domination. But she seemed to do whatever she pleased; and what pleased her most was other men. Tomé started by using marriage and a woman to gain power; he then sought to enhance his position through the control of a second woman. This action, after all, corresponded to Mundurucú ideology. He did not reckon, however, on the vagaries of ideology and the vast gulfs that are common between theory and practice. Instead of being a strong chief who accumulated women, he ended by being henpecked at one end of the trail between the two villages and cuckolded at the other. Mundurucú women, we will see, are not easily victimized.

Continuing our review of household composition, House II had twenty-five inhabitants, again including men. The core of the group was formed by three sisters, one of whom was dead, and their husbands and children. The three children of the dead woman stayed on with their maternal aunts, whom they addressed, according to normal kinship usage, as "mother." Another sister, Maria, had one child, but the daughters of her husband's dead sister also lived in the household. One of the daughters was unmarried, another was married and had one child, and the third had been divorced and left with a daughter. The other of the two core sisters, Catarina, had four children, one of whom, a daughter, was married and living in the house. The daughter of Catarina's husband's dead sister was also a member of the household, as was the girl's husband.

House III was unusual, for the core of its membership was three men who were related to each other as father's brother's sons, or patrilateral parallel cousins. The principal woman of the household, Louisa, was not, however, without near kin; she was a native of Cabruá, and her sister and mother's brother lived in House II. How this particular arrangement arose could not be discovered. We asked, of course, but our inquiries were rather vaguely answered by: "They just wanted to live together." The actual histories of their residential movements proved to be equally elusive, for most informants had a difficult time reconstructing such chains of events. It was not really significant information to them—the Mundurucú live very much in the present.

House IV exhibits predominant matrilocality. The senior woman of the house, Zabelina, was the center of a network of kinship strands that linked the residents to one another. Two of her three young children were with her, as was her stepdaughter, Amelia. Amelia's husband formed part of the household, as did her younger brother and his wife. The younger brother was also Zabelina's stepchild, and she was rearing the son of a third stepchild who had died. The fact that Zabelina's stepchildren had stayed with her is noteworthy, for their father was still very much alive. He had merely divorced Zabelina and moved away to another village to remarry. Despite their patrilineality, the Mundurucú saw nothing unusual in this situation. Women and children stay fixed in residence; men move about. The tie between mother and children is paramount, and the fact that Zabelina had reared the children established her as their adopted mother. It was, therefore, quite proper to the villagers that the biological father should move away and leave the children with the stepmother. Zabelina had also had a daughter by each of two deceased husbands. One of the daughters was dead, but her husband and child remained in the household. The other daughter lived in Zabelina's household with her husband, the son of the chief, and their three children. Thus, the preferred patrilocal residence of the chief's sons is not a firm rule either.

The Mundurucú household is a rather eclectic grouping, at least from the perspective of kinship. About 65% of Cabruá's marriages were matrilocal and 35% were patrilocal. There are many reasons for this variability. The Mundurucú have a high death rate, and a high divorce rate as well, and most adults have been married at least twice. Children usually stay with their mothers when a marriage is terminated, but when the mother dies the children may stay with the father or in the late mother's household. The preference for mothers and daughters or for sisters to stay together is indeed strong, but the bride's mother may be dead and she may have no living sisters. Under these circumstances, residence with her husband's people may be the logical alternative. Some marriages begin in a matrilocal setting but end patrilocally, or even neolocally. There may be difficulties between the groom and his in-laws that will cause the couple to move, though in the early years of marriage such frictions more commonly result in divorce. Families today do not necessarily move from one Mundurucú village to another, for they have the additional option of life at their rubber-gathering home, where they may live in the isolation of the nuclear family or in proximity to one or two other families. One of Cabruá's men, for example, was planning to move with his wife and children the following year, a shift that would break up the integrity of one of the matrilocal extended families. His reasons had little to do with kinship, for he was a shaman and feared that he would be accused some day of sorcery.

The Mundurucú household does not yield a neat and uniform matrilocality, but the practice is nonetheless dominant. Men do tend to be isolated from their close kin, and women more commonly have first degree relatives living in either the same house or nearby. And in a society that phrases solidarity in the idiom of kinship, this means that the women are surrounded by larger groups of supporters than are the men. A simple indicator of the perspectives on kinship of men and women may be seen in the fact that the men never asked Robert about his brothers, his father, or indeed any of his relatives. They were interested in *Ameriko be* (there in America), but never thought to ask about kin. In contrast, Yolanda received continual inquiries from the Mundurucú women about her female relatives. "Do you have sisters, Iolantá?" they would say; or "Don't you miss your mother? Doesn't she weep for you when you are so far away from her?" When we finally left the Mundurucú, the men took their parting from Robert with some regret for the departure of a bearer of gifts and an object of interest, but they were accustomed to men leaving their midst; that is what men do. But the women began wailing, perhaps only ceremonially, for Yolanda, telling her that she should stay among them forever. Women remain in place, and together.

There are ties of cooperation, friendship, and mutual loyalty among men, to be sure, but the ties are diffuse, and one man may substitute for another. One gains the impression, though it must remain an impression, that the bonds between males do not have the same immediacy and affective quality as those between females. The pivotal link in a patrilineal society should be that between father and son, for this is the line of both authority and transmission of group membership. But among the Mundurucú, both men and women agree that the truly enduring bond is between mother and daughter, and this is how they phrase their matrilocal preferences: "Mothers don't want to lose their daughters"; or "How would a girl manage without her mother to help her?" The tie is indeed close. Mothers and daughters work together, they relax in each other's company, they are seemingly inseparable. This same unity carries over to the relations between sisters, who are expected to form enduring residential groups. Sisters must be loyal to one another, they must share, they are a unit. One of the two cases of suicide that we heard of among the Mundurucú was of a woman who lived in an extended family centered on three sisters. The people are very reluctant to talk about suicide, looking upon it as the worst of all crimes, a lethal blow to society itself, and we were not able to gather much detail beyond the simple statement that "her sisters began talking about her." This is classic phraseology among the Mundurucú for being frozen out, isolated, and either ignored or gossiped against, and it was clear that the woman preferred death to continued estrangement from her sisters. If the same thing had happened among brothers, the disaffected one would simply have moved.

The solidarity of the mother–daughter and sister–sister dyads extends itself in diminished degree to a union of all the women of a household and, ultimately, of the village. One of the chief sources of this cohesiveness is, very simply, the work process. The work of the men tends to be sporadic. They expend enormous physical energy in spurts of hunting, fishing, or garden clearing, with intervals of rest that may last two or three days. The women, on the other hand, work far more steadily on more days per week and for longer hours. Some of their labors are light and pleasant, but other tasks involve drudgery. The most important and time-consuming of the latter is farinha processing.

Bitter manioc is a remarkable food. It can grow in poor sandy soil, and it has the useful property of being harvestable at any time within the span of a year. The tubers ripen in about eight months, but keep growing bigger for another year, after which they turn woody and inedible. Nevertheless, although a supply is always available, the tubers contain sufficient prussic acid to make them inedible if simply boiled or roasted. Manioc is an im-

portant staple food, which unfortunately requires a great deal of
effort to convert it into a dry, storable, and nonpoisonous form.

The manioc plant grows to a height of six to nine feet, and at
the base of its long stalk, tuberous roots spread like fingers from
a hand. Tubers are usually harvested when about a foot long,
though tubers two feet in length are sometimes dug up. The
harvesting is done by the women of the household, occasionally
aided by neighbors, who work in groups. The work actually can
be done by one, but the women like company, and company,
after all, is their chief protection from men on the prowl. The
earth around the plant is loosened, and the clump of tubers ex-
cavated with the blade of an old steel machete. The dirt is
knocked away from them, and they are placed in carrying baskets. If it is near the beginning of the rainy season, the stalks are
saved, to be cut into six-inch shoots for later planting. The carrying baskets fill up rapidly, and the harvesters carry them off
on their backs hung by tumplines of bark cloth passed across the
forehead—men, it might be added, have similar baskets, but
pass the lines across their chests and shoulders.

Depending on the processing method, the women carry their
twenty- to thirty-pound burdens from the garden either to the
village or to a stream near the village. If it is directly to the
village, it is for the purpose of making what is called *farinha seca*
(dry manioc flour) in Portuguese; if the tubers are placed in the
stream for soaking, *farinha d'agua* (manioc flour from water) is
being manufactured. Making farinha seca is the more laborious
of the two methods. The tubers are brought to the farinha shed,
an open-sided, thatch-roofed structure measuring about fifteen
feet on each side, located in the village plaza. There they are
peeled with knives in quick chopping motions by another group
of women. After being peeled, the tubers are grated into a long
hollowed-out log that serves as a tub. One or two women are

usually bent over the trough, grating the tubers on a flat piece of sheet metal, commonly the side of a five-gallon can, which has had holes punched in it. This is the nastiest job of all, for it gives backaches, grated fingers and knuckles, and it is hard work besides. The workers, however, trade off chores frequently, giving everybody a turn and allowing rest periods for the weary.

Peeling and grating reduces the manioc to a wet pulp, which is then placed in large metal basins to which water is added. This soaking process leaches a good deal of the prussic acid from the pulp, and it also requires that some women make frequent trips to the stream to fetch water. The pulp is scooped from the pan by hand, the excess water squeezed out and it is then stuffed in the tipití for further extraction of liquid. The pulp, now slightly damp, is then put through a basketry sieve, the larger chunks mashed with a mortar and pestle, and the portion is ready for toasting. In the meantime, the water in which the pulp was first washed is allowed to sit for two days, after which the pan is carefully decanted of its liquid content, leaving behind a residue on the bottom of pure tapioca starch. The tapioca is converted into granular form through the sieve and is toasted separately.

Much of the prussic acid is washed and squeezed out by the time the product is ready for toasting, but, if eaten in this state, it would still produce severe gastritis. The acid is, however, highly volatile, and the toasting drives out what remains, while at the same time drying the flour into a preservable state. The farinha seca process has the merit of preserving most of the starch content of the tuber, both in the form of tapioca and in the farinha itself. It is, however, a tedious and back-breaking affair, and Mundurucú women usually choose instead to make farinha d'agua. The tubers are placed in a stream and left there from three to eight days, by which time they are thoroughly softened, the fibrous structure broken down, and much of the prussic acid released. The manioc is then simply broken open, the skins thrown away, and the wet interiors carried to the farinha shed and dumped in the trough. A few of the women tread it into a wet pulp, and it is then processed through the tipití and the toasting pan. The labor of peeling and grating, surely the most time-consuming parts of farinha making, are avoided, but the resultant food product is not nearly so nutritious as farinha seca because much of the starch is leached out in the stream.

It would be possible for one woman to manufacture farinha by herself, going through each of the many steps in turn, but it would take her days to make just twenty pounds. To complicate matters, she would tie up the village farinha-making facilities, rendering it impossible for others to work; one way out of this dilemma would be for each woman to have her own oven, pans, trough, toasting pan, and so on, an extravagance beyond Mundurucú means. Hence, the only answer to the problem is communal use of facilities, which the Mundurucú do through joint ownership and use of the equipment, and collective labor.

In order to process the greatest amount of farinha in the shortest possible time, all phases of the work go on at once. Some women are fetching firewood from an old garden, others are going back and forth to the stream for water; one or two may be peeling the tubers while two more are grating; a couple of women may be taking a rest by sitting on the end of the tipití lever; another will be washing out pulp; and if the process is far enough along, one or two will be toasting the flour. The farinha shed is not allowed to sit idle for very long. By the time one household has finished all the early stages of work and has nothing left but the toasting process, another is already bringing tubers from the garden and peeling them.

The fundamental unit in manioc processing is composed of

the women of the household. The senior female of the house initiates and directs the work, and the others carry the burden of the labor, especially of the more onerous tasks. But in Cabruá, no single house had enough adult women to do the job expeditiously; two of Cabruá's four houses, for example, had six women, one had four, and the fourth had only two. It is necessary, then, for women from other houses to join in the work, especially during the middle part of the cycle, when all tasks are being done at once. The need for labor also draws young girls into farinha production, usually to draw water and peel tubers. Not all of the village women would work at one time, but it was quite common for over half of them to be involved at a given moment and for all of them to help during the course of a day. Each household in Cabruá had to make farinha at average intervals of ten days. It took almost two days for a house to make a supply and, since there were four houses, farinha was being made on most days. Cooperation among the women was an almost daily affair.

Women do most of the garden work. The men clear the fields, but the women usually go along on these occasions to watch, gather palm fruits, and prepare food for the workers. As in most collective ventures among the Mundurucú, there is a somewhat festive atmosphere, and productivity is often sacrificed for conviviality. But in the hard work of planting, there is little fun. The men dig holes for the manioc shoots with hoes, and the women follow, planting and covering the shoots with earth. The men are almost invariably absent during the planting of minor crops, and the women are also left to do all of the weeding. These chores are usually done by the women of the household that initiated the garden; there is little need for large-scale cooperation, but two or three women usually work together for the sake of both company and propriety. Gardens are not carefully tended by the Mundurucú, however, and except for the planting and harvesting of manioc, the average woman will work no more than a few hours per week in the fields.

Housework in the European or American sense of the word is not very heavy in Cabruá. There are no wood or tile floors to be cleaned, nor are there rugs to be guarded against spillage or periodically shampooed. Furniture consists of hammocks and some boxes, leaving nothing to be dusted and polished, and the kitchen is a hearth on the ground. Chores do include sweeping the floor every day, a job that is done by one woman in fifteen minutes with a bunch of leaves. If a child urinates on the floor, the nearest woman will kick a little dirt over the wet spot; if one defecates, one of the dogs will soon come along and eat the leavings and then follow the child to lick his backside clean. Dish and pot washing is simple enough, as a house may use only one or two large pots to feed everybody, and each person has one small metal plate from which he eats and a metal cup. Utensils generally consist of a knife that can be wiped clean on the ground and then on the trousers before being resheathed.

Cooking is the chief household chore, but the fires are tended by every woman in the house, making it unnecessary for any one "to spend hours over a hot stove." In any event, Mundurucú cuisine is not elaborate. Every meal is accompanied by farinha, which is eaten without further preparation. Yams are cut up and boiled, plantains are put into the hot embers of the fireplace and palm fruits are made into a drink. Meat and fish are either boiled or roasted slowly on a babricot above the fire and are eaten with salt and, of course, manioc flour. Occasionally a stew is made of meat and yams, sometimes with grated Brazil nuts added for flavor. This is about the most venturesome creation of the Mundurucú chef. Everything else is eaten plain—cookery does not occupy the undivided and prolonged attention of Mundurucú women.

Women spend a good deal of time in small, intermittent chores such as cotton spinning, dress mending, and weaving. Cotton bushes grow around the village and in old gardens, where they have matured after earlier planting, and a woman who is weaving a hammock will wander about and pick cotton wherever she finds it. She carefully forms several balls of cotton into a long roll, which she spins into a heavy thread with a simple spindle whorl, joining it onto previously manufactured thread as she works. When sufficient thread has been accumulated, she strings it lengthwise on a vertical loom to form the warp pieces of the future hammock. Weft sections are twined across at intervals of about an inch, making not so much a true woven product as a string hammock. Usually only one loom is found in any house, and women take turns working at it. It is a one-person job, but the weaver is seldom alone, and hammock making is an occasion for relaxed conversation and idle watching. Like mending and patching, it is also a spare-time job, and hammocks are generally months in the making.

The main work of house building is done by men, but women make the floors and carry the thatch. Villages are built every ten years or so, and the circumstances of the move require that all houses be built during the same wet season. The men cut the timber, set up the framework, and carry most of the heavy materials, but the women bring in roof thatch and clay for the floors. The men place the thatch on the roof, yet the women lay the floors, a job that involves carrying baskets of wet and heavy clay and the dirty work of spreading it and smoothing it down. Everybody works on each house in rotation while all continue to sleep in the old village.

House building, timbó fishing, and garden clearing are the only occasions when all the men and women of a village work together—cooperative activities abound in this society, but they almost always take account of the strict division between the sexes. The division of labor is rigorously observed by the Mundurucú—or at least by the men—and very few tasks overlap. Husbands and wives rarely engage in joint work of any kind, and the nuclear family can in no way be considered a production unit. Indeed, the family is not even the point where the division of labor between the sexes meets, in terms of women doing women's work for the family unit and men doing men's work for it. Rather, the division of labor poses all the women of the household and the village in complementarity to the productive efforts of the men.

Except for minor household chores, women's work is always done in cooperation, or in companionship, with other women. That women work together in manioc processing can be explained by productive efficiency and technology, but it has other dimensions as well. Mundurucú women enjoy each other's company, and the congregation of women in the farinha shed turns the tedium of a grinding chore into a chatty sort of sewing circle. They switch tasks, allowing each other to rest or wander off, and keep the workers amused with constant conversation. They do engage in rather malicious gossip about one another, of which more will be said later, but the general tenor of their interaction is amiable. Though the men cooperate with each other as much as do the women, the women appear to be more sociable and outgoing, more dependent upon others. And just as they do not work with the men, neither do they seek their company. Men associate with men in this society and women with women.

The core of the woman's world is her household and her close female relatives within it. The house, and not the nuclear family, is the fundamental unit of consumption and it is also a primary unit in production. Its facilities are shared by all of its women, even hearth and utensils, and only the arrangement of hammocks bespeaks the presence of familial subdivisions. In the house, the woman finds a number of females to whom she is bound by kinship and with whom she has been reared. These ties allow them to function together smoothly in work and to make sharing and commensality a lifelong habit. The kin ties of the men tend to be scattered; those of the women are localized. It matters little that a mother and her daughter belong to different clans and moieties, for here we are not talking about formal affiliations and marriage regulations, but about the development of emotional attachments and loyalties.

In a sense, the village is an extension of the household, from the female's point of view. Beyond the house, her kin ties are attenuated, but, to the extent that matrilocality has been operative, the other women may be persons with whom she has been raised, with whom she played as a child, and whom she has known intimately throughout most of her life. In her adult years, these are also the women with whom she makes farinha, washes clothes, bathes, and amuses herself. They have moments of tension with each other, of course, but these animosities are tempered by the fact that there is strong inter-dependence among all women in the village. The village, too, is an arena for sharing and for the distribution of food. When women help in farinha making, they are always given a share of the product. And if a household runs short, others will give it enough farinha to tide its women over until they can make more. If a garden fails and a house is left short of food for a season, they will be allowed to harvest from the gardens of others. The distribution of farinha, it must be emphasized, is handled completely by the women. It is a woman's product, and women control its disposition. But even the distribution of game eventually falls under female control. The man brings his kill to his wife, or his closest female relative if he is unmarried, and she and her housemates butcher it. They send pieces to other houses, but they determine who gets which parts. And if the take has been small, the food may be shared with only one household—the choice is the woman's and she generally opts for the one housing her closest relatives. Thus, within the network of pan-village sharing, there exist smaller networks that are structured by kin ties between women. Women, then, have effective control over the economy of food distribution by virtue of their roles in food processing.

It has been said that even the men grudgingly attribute leadership of the household to its senior woman, a recognition on their part of a reality. The oldest woman, reinforced by kinship bonds with her own resident daughters, her younger sisters and their daughters, is the undisputed director of all the internal affairs of the house. Because of these maternal and sororal ties, the structure of authority is mild and benevolent, consistent with the even-handed egalitarianism of the value system. The oldest woman does not rule alien and antagonistic daughters-in-law, as did the tyrannical traditional Chinese mother-in-law, but rather women with whom she has close emotional ties. Moreover, she is coordinating the activities of a group of women who have been cooperating with her, and each other, for most of their lives. As a result, the direction of household affairs is a subtle and delicate matter. Orders are seldom given, because they would be unnecessary. What has to be done is generally anticipated, and, if it is not, the senior woman merely has to mention the matter. She need only say, "We need more water," or, "We have almost finished peeling the tubers," and a younger woman will soon call a companion and go off to the stream or the garden.

The main responsibility of the older women is the initiation and direction of manioc processing, but they are consulted on other matters as well. They serve as midwives, give advice on making hammocks, and are an active presence in the maintenance of the life of the house. Theirs is an easy and gentle kind of authority, but it is an undisputed one—perhaps this is why it is so mild.

The man's position, including that of the senior male, is rather ambivalent. Men do not intrude upon the economic sphere and work activities of the house, for this is the province of the eldest woman. Moreover, the house is outside their orbit, for they live in the men's house. Men are the public figures in Mundurucú society, however, and the outsider can quite easily receive the impression that they run the households because they speak to outsiders for the women. When a trader visits the village to buy farinha, it is the men who deal with him, a reflection of both male status and the inability of the women to speak Portuguese. But throughout the bargaining, the older women remain in the immediate background, voicing their demands to the men, who relay them to the trader. They do not do this when rubber is being traded; however, farinha is the woman's product and the men are their intermediaries in this transaction. In almost all other matters, the women of the house maintain autonomy, directed loosely by the senior woman, but working together on the basis of smoothly adjusted and long-established modes of behavior and with a strong sense of solidarity. Men are respected in household decisions, yet they, too, respect the integrity of the female members.

A remarkable amount of gossip is relayed by the women about the men and, especially, about each other. Now gossip is not inherently malevolent or spiteful, though we commonly think of it as such. Much of the female gossip consists of exchange of valuable information about people. They speak of possible marriage prospects in other villages, which leads inevitably, and necessarily, to a discussion of the personal characteristics of the boy or girl. And they exchange harmless information on the activities of kinsmen, the visits of the trader, events in other communities, and nearly every other subject conceivable in their restricted worlds. Indeed, one may well wonder how there could be so much to talk about in such a small society, and in such a humdrum life, but one should keep in mind that every Mundurucú knows about every other and each has an enormous circle of relatives, friends, and acquaintances. In a society of this scale, everybody is famous—and everybody is significant to everybody else. Gossip, in short, is an expression of the relevance that gossipers and gossipees have for each other. One does not talk about people who have no significance, and gossip effectively defines the boundaries and integrity of the social group, as Max Gluckman (1963) has so lucidly argued. It is understandable, then, that the women of any village talk mostly about their fellow villagers and, among them, mostly about other women. It may be worrisome for a Mundurucú woman to know she is being talked about, but it would be a disaster if she were to discover that nobody was talking about her.

Gossip does, however, become quite negative at times. The women exchange notes about the sexual escapades of others, they discuss traits of sloth and laziness that they find in somebody, and they cast aspersions on each other's physical appearance or characteristics ("they say that her vagina is so big because of all the men who entered it," and so forth). Although some of the information is false and malicious, a venting of personal animosity or jealousy, some of it is quite true. A woman who has loose sexual morals becomes an immediate butt of gossip. She is, after all, a threat to all the other women as a potential husband stealer, and she is a threat to womankind as well. The errant woman breaches the moral solidarity of the females, as a group, and invites the intervention of the men. In this way, she is akin to the member of an oppressed group whose behavior augurs the intrusion of the police; such communities usually attempt to control the deviant before this occurs. They thus find protection in morality.

Gossip, then, serves as a negative sanction exercised by women over their wayward member to bring her back into line before the men stage a gang rape. And a gang rape, by its collective nature, must be understood as directed against all women as a form of exemplary punishment. But gang rapes are rare, largely due to the timely intervention of the women, and the promiscuous woman usually ends with nothing more than a tarnished, but redeemable, reputation, and perhaps a divorce. Indeed, gossip is often said to be the reason for a divorce ("he left her because people were talking about her"). This is rather interesting, for malicious gossip, though it goes on largely among women and about women, actually reinforces their solidarity. On the other hand, it often breaks up ties between men and women.

Talk among the women continues whenever they are together, but the place par excellence for gossip is the farinha shed. The farinha shed is the female equivalent of the men's house, and women sometimes gather there to talk even when there is no work. But when work is in process, conversation is continuous, and it ranges from talking about what is being done through neutral bits of information to outright character assassination. Obviously, the women do not gossip about others in their presence, but when one of their number leaves they wait only until she is out of earshot. Robert often watched the eyes of the women train upon Yolanda as she returned to the house, and then waited for the animated conversation to break out behind her. Little snatches of laughter would follow her back to the house, leaving her with the uneasy feeling that "people are talking about me," as the Mundurucú say. The Mundurucú women liked to be talked about even less than she, and their solution was to stay and work. Gossip keeps the women together in a very direct and pragmatic way—it reinforces economic cooperation.

The division of labor and residential arrangements impose a deep separation between the sexes, and the preference for matrilocality and the rule of female cooperation beget an unusual degree of solidarity among the women. The separation and solidarity are increased, however, by the very ideology of the men about women. Women may need to cooperate in farming and farinha making, but there is no such necessity in drawing water, fetching firewood, or in doing some of the lighter garden chores. Rather, they join together for company and also to obtain protection against men. The lone woman is a legitimate sexual mark for a male; her loneness announces her availability and states that she is operating outside custody. The men are thus seen as potentially threatening in a very real, direct, and physical way. They force the women together, make them travel in bands, and actually increase their dependence on each other. The men do enforce the propriety of the women, but they do so at the expense of heightening female antagonism toward them and strengthening female cohesion.

The propriety of the women costs the men something else, too. Male sanctions are exercised only in cases of flagrant promiscuity; the woman who engages in an occasional dalliance in which she at least feigns being passive and acts as the victim of a seduction is subject only to female gossip, not gang rape. But the social setting for seduction is hard to find among the Mundurucú. All of the men would like to have an occasional paramour, or at least they say so, but the problem is to find a woman alone. Women always travel either in groups or with one other female, if only a daughter, and the "chance" encounter leading to sex does not happen often. For extramarital sex to occur, the woman must contrive somehow to sneak out of the village, hopefully unobserved, and this is not an easy maneuver in small tightly knit communities. She must plan the occasion with intent and forethought; consequently, there is not at all as much casual sex available as the men would like to have. Even more to the point, trysts require very considerable initiative on the part of the woman, and this does not fit into the passive role that the men have allocated to them.

The women, of course, are well aware of their secondary status in the official scheme of things and make little open challenge to the ideology. They recognize it, and they actively resent it, but they cope with it as a fact of life. One way of coping is through the minor etiquette of female demeanor. We have said that the woman averts her eyes from men, does not laugh openly at, or with, them, and keeps a physical distance between herself and males. In one sense, this behavior can be interpreted as submissive, although at another level it is a primary form of defense. Women guard their emotions before men, communicate as little as possible of their subjective states, set themselves off with reserve. The woman who casts down her eyes when near men is not really saying that she is inferior, but that she is apart and distant, that she is not to be interfered with. She becomes symbolically impenetrable.

The antagonisms between the sexes are very real and evident, ritualized by the men and verbalized by the women. Mundurucú women are visibly annoyed and perturbed at the very mention of gang rapes. They may not approve of the behavior of the victim, but they regard the punishment as oppressive, cruel, and arbitrary, a threat to each of them, as it is meant to be. The separation of the men in the men's house is also a sore subject. The women know very well that the Brazilians and the Mundurucú of the Cururú River do not have men's houses but live in nuclear family domiciles. This they regard as a better way of life, and they are often active instigators of moves from the traditional villages. The division of labor is another point of contention. The women frequently complain that the men do not help them. They hunt or fish for a while and then lie in the men's house, while they, the women, are working hard in the farinha shed.

Mundurucú women are quite cognizant of the fact that their share of the work is often dull drudgery and that they work longer hours than do the men. Their attitude is sometimes expressed in sniping remarks—on one occasion, however, it erupted fully into the open. The women one day were making farinha while a number of men were lounging in the men's house. Yolanda jokingly suggested to the women that the men should help them, bringing the usual retort that the men were too lazy. Encouraged, one of the older women called out to the men to help, a cry that was echoed by Yolanda and the others. The demands became rather insistent, and two of the men shuffled over to help grate tubers halfheartedly and with great embarrassment, until the laughter of their comrades made them give up. The women then began to shout at the men in earnest, to be greeted with hostile and stony silence from the men's house. The confrontation reached a peak of open hostility, at which point it was swiftly dampened. Neither men nor women can abide open conflict, and both sides had backed away. But it was a standoff.

Intersexual hostility comes out clearly in the joking relationship. Joking occurs between the moieties, and ideally without regard to sex. In most instances of playful banter, however, the antagonists are men versus women, and this sometimes occurs without reference to moiety differences. Women and men would ritually capture each other in the old ceremonies or throw water on each other; sexual banter was common. Like most joking between the sexes, however, there was a mixture of sex and antagonism, as in the instance of the initiated boys who assumed the role of birds and pecked at the women with long "beaks." During our stay, our assistant introduced the men to the wonders of the slingshot, which they promptly used to pepper the women with palm fruit kernels. The women were not amused.

These are all relationships between men and women as groups, separate collectivities, opposed entities. Relationships between individual men and women will be the subject of chapter 6, but it should be stated here that Mundurucú women are not servile toward men in either a real or a symbolic sense. The men are regarded as exploitative and dominant; not as superior. We never heard a woman state that her lack of knowledge about one thing or another was because she was "only a woman," nor did they speak of the men as having a superior position in the way an American woman will claim, often hypocritically, that "my husband wears the pants in our family." Women do, however, think of themselves as separate from the men, and they have a strong sense of their identity as women. The Mundurucú woman does not confront the male world as a lone individual, in open competition with other females, but as a woman among women.

Given this sense of belonging and cohesiveness, one should perhaps ask: Why do not the women have rites and myths that validate their position and express their opposition to the men?

Perhaps it is that the women have fewer anxieties, less of a feeling that they have a vested interest which can be lost. But beyond this consideration, it must be remembered that the women have no mythology or rites of their own whatever. This is due in part, of course, to the fact that they are either wholly excluded from the religious life or play only restricted roles in it. But are they kept out of something to which they avidly want access? Not at all—the women look on religious rites as something the men do, which only partially concerns them and which is not of great interest to them. Rituals are social affairs to both sexes, yet to the women they are mainly social affairs. They like to listen to myths, although they are far less absorbed in their content than are the men and usually keep up a subdued conversation among themselves during the narration. And they never tell myths themselves. They are, however, deeply afraid of sorcery, the Yuruparí and similar supernatural threats, and are constant visitors to the shaman—their primary religious concern is with threat, evil, and personal affliction, whereas they are apathetic to the positive and reaffirmative aspects of religion.

The women are secular and pragmatic in their orientation to life. There is a matter-of-factness and straightforward earthiness in their manner and world view that contradict forever our popular notions of the awe-stricken savage. They believe the myths, they credit the efficacy of ritual, they are sure that there are spirits—they believe all these things, but they do not think too much about them. None of the Mundurucú seemed to be deeply concerned about the afterlife, but the men at least treated the subject with some seriousness. The women, on the other hand, just looked rather surprised when they were asked about the hereafter, for it was clear that the question seldom arose. One laughed and said, "I'm going to live in a termite hill"; another said, "I'm going to live in your village, Katiwat (white man), where everybody has a lot of wonderful things." As for the men's house, they seemed largely indifferent to it except as a living arrangement. They knew all about its ritual paraphernalia, though none would admit peeking, and they were neither mystified nor cowed. It is as if they had investigated the secret sources of the men's power—and had found absolutely nothing.

7.

Women
/\/\/\/\/\/\/\ and
Married Life

Marriage is a remarkable institution. It serves in every society to trap both males and females, locking them into a relationship that is exclusive and, presumably, enduring. It usually does endure well beyond the original impulse to marry, enmeshing people in a series of relationships which, like those with in-laws, are sometimes difficult and always limiting. The disadvantages of marriage are so manifest that one can well wonder why it exists in any society—yet it is a social universal. Usually, we rationalize marriage as a convenient, even necessary, means for providing an elementary division of labor between the sexes, each mate contributing her or his talents and capabilities to the economy of the family. The family is by this reasoning an economic essential, providing for the sustenance of the dependent young and forming at the same time the setting for their socialization. Being rather ethnocentric, we may well reason out from our own lives to see the family as the bulwark of society, the protector of the young, and the provider for the weak, meaning women and children.

It is true that in many societies the family is the integral group, primary in the domestic economy and paramount in child-rearing—but not among the Mundurucú, a society that leaves one wondering why the people marry at all. It should be clear from our description of the household and the economy that the nuclear family is not the principal unit of production and sharing. The family, it would be fair to say, is the irreducible consumption unit; if a man kills two pigeons, he, his wife, and his children eat them, but this is not the typical situation. Rather, the extended family occupying the household is the junction point for the economic contributions of either sex, and it keeps a common table and larder—in actuality, the wife of the man who killed the two pigeons would surely end by doling small portions out to her sister and to the children of the house. Under these circumstances, it is not necessary that a woman be married for her children to eat. Other men of the household—whether husbands, brothers, or fathers—would bring meat and fish home, and she would receive a full share for herself and her family. And food would always be given to her household by women of other houses. Women and children simply do not go hungry among the Mundurucú for lack of a husband and father. The nuclear family is not even a domestic unit in the strict sense of the term. The man is attached to the house of his wife, but he does not live in it, thus occupying a curious marginal role between that of member and that of constant visitor. It would be erroneous to say that the man is master in his own house, for his proper house is the eksa—and the household of his wife is led by its senior woman. The man is indeed the head of his nuclear family, but it is a family that has few functions.

Marriage among the Mundurucú may seem a relatively unimportant institution from the practical and pragmatic point of view, but it provides the entire framework of interpersonal relationships and is essential to the formation, as well as the connectedness, of social groups. The division of the society into two parts which are internally exogamous and intermarry with one another indeed begets cross-cousin marriage, but the moieties may also be looked upon as a logical outcome of consistent intermarriage between cross-cousins. Similarly, clan membership derives from patrilineal descent, but this identification provides the individual with only one part of his total kinship universe. The marriage of one's mother and father, on the other hand, gives the individual a rounded and full spectrum of kinsmen, extending beyond the patrilineal clan through the mother's relatives, then those of the person's husband or wife, and, later, those of the children of the union. Marriage, more than "blood," is the great social glue of Mundurucú society. Marriage and the corollary prohibition of incest are among the Mundurucú, as in every society, the means by which social units break their barriers, overcome isolation, assert their dependence upon other groups, and weld discrete entities into a broader social fabric. This is all elementary to the anthropologist, but the Mundurucú help to remind us that marriage and kinship are more than conventional means of reaching useful ends; they are also the basic criteria and conceptual bases for the division of society into its parts and for the reamalgamation of these parts into a unity. Larger units among the Mundurucú do carry out most of the "functions" usually attributed to the family, but there would be no such larger units were it not for the legal and stable ties produced by marriage.

Marriage is considered the normal estate for all adults, except for the old and widowed. There is no role for the bachelor or spinster in Mundurucú society, and, though we encountered persons who were widowed or divorced, as well as a couple of girls of marriageable age who had not yet found mates, we heard of no cases in which a person went permanently unmarried. Marriage, of course, is the approved outlet for sex, but it also serves to stabilize a person's position as a fully adult member of the community. A person without a mate, and in-laws, and so forth, is an anomaly. The unmarried are also considered a threat to existing marriages because of potential mate stealing. Adultery, of course, is common enough; yet adultery is only mate borrowing and not, therefore, a grievous matter. It is assumed, on the other hand, that younger persons without a mate are by necessity looking for one.

Monogamy is the norm among the Mundurucú, as the case of Tomé illustrates. Informants claim that in times past chiefs were able to have more than one wife, but even they usually confined their marital acquisitions to two or three women. Today, however, no chief, except for the ill-advised Tomé, who brought disaster on himself through polygyny, exercises this prerogative. Actually, polygyny is always difficult to manage in a matrilocal society, for it would require a man to join the household of his first bride and then bring her to that of the second wife, thus contradicting the rule while observing it. In addition to this problem, co-wives never did get along among the Mundurucú. One chief formerly had two wives, but they fought so hard that he could not keep them under the same roof. One died, and he never tried polygyny again. The women of a household form a tight corporate unit, and a new, intrusive second wife is descended upon by the residents like white cells on a virus. The men may style themselves as polygynous, but the women have a different conception of the system. The only way that polygyny could be handled under these circumstances is through marriage with two sisters, or sororal polygyny, a common form of plural marriage in both matrilocal and patrilocal societies. The Mundurucú, however, did not take this alternative, and marriage is

uniformly monogamous, one result being that there is a fairly
equal distribution of available marriage partners in the society as
a whole. Some imbalance was noted, however, in the villages of
the savannahs as compared to those of the Cururú River. The
general drift of migration has for years been from the traditional villages to those of the river banks, frequently taking the
form of young savannah men marrying women on the Cururú
River and remaining there in matrilocal residence. On the other
hand, few Cururú men wish to move to the savannah villages,
and the result is a slight shortage of available men in the savannahs and of women on the Cururú.

The only true rule in Mundurucú marriage is that one must
find a mate outside his or her moiety. Moiety exogamy goes
beyond marriage and prohibits sexual relations with a fellow
moiety member, too. It was difficult to ascertain whether the
latter rule was broken often, though it sometimes was, but
breaches of the marriage ban were very rare. No cases were
known to us in the traditional savannah villages, and only one
came to our attention on the Cururú River. In times past, say
the Mundurucú, the preferred marital choice was between first
degree cross-cousins, and marriages were frequently arranged
for their children by brothers and sisters. We were able to find
only two true cross-cousin marriages during our research, although all intermoiety marriages are, of course, with cross-
cousins by extension. This follows from the fact that a woman
must marry a man who belongs to the same patrilineal moiety as
her mother's brother or her father's sister. The same logic of
exchange between two groups makes both the sororate (marriage
with a deceased sister's husband) and the levirate (marriage with
the deceased husband's brother) permissible; we encountered
only one case of each, and they were clearly the outcome of personal preference rather than norm. There is, then, great latitude

in Mundurucú marriage choices; one need only marry within the complementary moiety of the tribe.

Older Mundurucú complain that the elders used to control the choice of mates but that today's young people marry whomever they wish. Like most such nostalgic reminiscences, this is part truth and part fond fabrication. One man claimed that his wife was chosen for him when he was only two years old, though others said that the arrangements were made when the children were four to seven. Such arrangements were made only for the first marriage, however, and subsequent unions were left more or less to the discretion of the principals as long as no incest taboos were violated. Nowadays, marriages involve a subtle compromise between the old and the young; this is a familiar situation to Americans, but Mundurucú parents still have far greater authority than do their "civilized" counterparts.

If one asks a Mundurucú man who has proper custody of a woman and the right to dispose of her in marriage, he will reply that it is her father. If you ask a Mundurucú woman who has the right of either choice or approval of a woman's husband, she will reply that it is her mother. According to the norms officially enshrined in Mundurucú culture, or at least male values, a woman must be under the jurisdiction of a man, ideally either her father or her husband. "Nobody is in charge of her," say the men in one Mundurucú myth, just before they gang rape a delinquent woman. But the reality of the situation is more complex, and if a man indeed has formal custody of a woman, it is her mother or her sisters who surround, chaperone, and protect her. In effect, women are vouched for and their marriages are approved, to a large extent, by other women.

Unions may be negotiated in a number of ways. The parents of a young man or woman may receive information about the availability of a mate for their offspring and will speak directly with the parents of the prospect; the mother of the young woman would be included in the deliberations either directly or through the mediation of her husband. If the discussions go well, the prospective son-in-law may come to the village for a prolonged visit. The initiative of the parents is not necessary, however, for young men in search of a mate often wander about to different villages, or to some particular community where a young woman or two are said to be available. And some men find young women in their own villages. Wife-finding and courtship are greatly facilitated by the men's house, for the visiting male need only hang his hammock among the men and participate in their hunting activities. People are continually visiting back and forth, and his arrival is not especially noteworthy, though of course everybody knows why he is there. But he is nonetheless spared the embarrassment—and to a Mundurucú it is indeed embarrassing—of residing with possible in-laws.

It is during this time, when the young man is under the direct scrutiny of the young woman and her family, that her wishes and those of her mother become most important. Prearrangement sets up the possibility of marriage, but if either of the young people is adamantly opposed, the outcome is in doubt. Great pressure may be exercised on either the girl or the boy to go through with the marriage, but the young sometimes win. It is at this time, too, that the mother's wishes are most strongly felt. Her first question is whether the youth will agree to live in the village matrilocally, for, otherwise, who will help her make farinha? She would be unhappy and lonely without her daughter, and the daughter would be left without the guidance and aid of her mother. The mother is also concerned with the industry of the future husband, a concern about his prospects as a food provider, and also as a rubber tapper. His ability to buy things for her daughter, and maybe even for herself, are important considerations, as they are for the future bride.

Needless to say, sexual attraction enters into the marriage decision, too. An important element of courtship is the young woman's willingness to accept the sexual advances of the suitor, and, as in the case of extramarital love affairs, she has a fair degree of control over the course of the romance. If she finds the young man to be to her liking, she can easily steal out of the house to meet him in the forest. Her mother and the other women of the house may know very well where she is going, but they also know that this is how one gets a man. As for her father, the chances are excellent that he will not have even an inkling of her whereabouts. In any event, premarital love is not especially threatening to the men, and they reserve their suspicions for their wives. But the prospective bride can also refuse the young man by the simple expedient of staying close to the other women. She thus maintains a strong degree of control over her sexuality, despite male ideology. The true guarantor of her integrity and inviolability is, therefore, the congregation of females.

The Mundurucú drift into marriage in a series of steps that finally become ratified by simple public recognition of the union. There are no gift exchanges, bride prices, or even ceremonies connected with marriage. Rather, a final agreement that the couple should wed is reached by the consent of all the concerned parties, including the bride and groom and their parents, and the bond is recognized to exist. In the case of second or third marriages of more mature adults, only the acceptance of the status by the man and woman themselves is necessary. Since sexual relations already have started between the couple, and since the man does not move from his place in the men's house, it is often difficult to tell exactly when the marriage is considered to have become official. The chief symbolic act establishing the union, and thereafter restating its continuity, is the bringing of the day's kill to the bride, and the women of the village watch anxiously to see whether a courting man brings game to his nearest female relative or to the young woman. After the initial presentation of food, the newlywed couple—for that is what they now are—go through a three-day period of avoidance of others. The man will either stay close to his hammock in the men's house or go off hunting by himself. The woman keeps busy inside her house, talking as little as possible to the other women, and they to her. This is the period of transitional status, of ambiguity in social identity, as the couple moves into their new roles. The Mundurucú, in common with many other peoples, resolve the ambivalence by withdrawal. Or as they say, "Newlyweds are ashamed."

Marriage does not entail a series of radical changes and reaccommodations, as it does in our own society. Matrilocality is the ideal, and it is commonly followed, at least during the early years of marriage. But it is a rather strange form of residence, for the groom does not actually move into the bride's house. Rather, he stays in the men's house, which, after all, is where he may have been living for some time. His new bond is expressed, however, in the presentation of food and in openly visiting his wife in her house, a place that he had previously shunned. He will also visit at night, after everybody is presumably asleep, to crawl into his wife's hammock for love-making.

Sex between husband and wife is not restricted to the house and hammock by any means, and even long-married couples go to the forest or to secluded grassy areas for intercourse. The Mundurucú do not have the acute sense of embarrassment about sex that is characteristic of our own society, and they do not insist on total privacy. The other residents of the house usually know when a husband visits his wife at night, for it only takes one waking child to spread the news. This does not bother them much, but they are somewhat inhibited when a good part of the household is restless. The sorties to the forest thus give the couple minimal privacy and take care of daytime urges also. Almost any trip by a married couple, whether for the announced purpose of gardening, bathing, or gathering, is interpreted by the Mundurucú as being for sex. In fact, our own trips to measure gardens, survey old village sites, or just to get away from the village for a while were widely regarded as amorous. In the transition to the married state, then, not even the locale of sex need change; the former fiances simply walk out of the village together, where they used to sneak away separately.

Sex is one of the most difficult areas of investigation among the Mundurucú, as it is in most South American groups. They are not prudish about sex, and the men openly engage in sexual joking among themselves and in mixed audiences of women and children. Women, too, find sex an excellent source of humor, but they never joke in front of the men as this would be a provocative act. A male anthropologist does not count quite the same, however, and Robert's inquiries to them were always greeted with howls of laughter. Even the most veiled, but leading, question would be picked up by the women and turned on him in such repartee as: "I hear that you men in Ameriko bé have big penises, Katiwat." This discouraged serious interviewing, to say the least, and only Yolanda could ask the women personal questions. As for the men, Yolanda could not interview them on sexual subjects, and Robert's questions were simply occasions for jokes, like: "That woman screws so much that the sides of her vagina flap together when she walks—suk, suk, suk, they go." Our questions were not greeted with disdain or stony silence, but, rather, they were continually diverted; the effects were the same.

In spite of these difficulties, information was slowly gathered, revealing an active preoccupation with sex but little of a colorful nature. Intercourse, whether in a hammock or on the ground, is customarily in the "missionary position," with the woman lying on her back, legs spread, and the man mounting between them. Orgasm is sometimes reached by women, but it is our impression that in most cases climax is experienced only by the male. The sexual approach of the Mundurucú men reflects ideology. Women are subservient to men in sex, the wife has no choice but to accept her husband's advances, and male satisfaction is the goal. There is little foreplay, and sexual encounters are brief in consummation. The only obstacle to sex between mates is the menstrual period; we found no evidence of prolonged postpartum sex taboos. The woman, then, usually derives far less satisfaction from the sex act than does the man, but she also understands that sex is the means by which one gets a husband and then holds him.

Adultery presents certain difficulties due to the pressures toward female bonding and the high degree of visibility of everybody in the society. There are no private rooms, there are no motels, there are no places where one can be anonymous, there is hardly any refuge from the observation of others. But there are occasional chances for escape, and people are quick to spot them and take advantage. The Mundurucú say that most men and women occasionally have adulterous relations, making lifelong marital fidelity the exception, rather than the norm. The men enter on them for variety, adventure, and plain sex, but the motivations of the women are probably more complex. In the case of Tomé's wife, it was clear that her sexual desires were mixed with some antipathy for her husband and a wish to abase him in the eyes of others. It would be difficult to say how strongly such retaliation motivates adultery, but one woman stated that this indeed is how one gets revenge on an adulterous husband; it is certainly the woman's ultimate weapon in a society that places such strong emphasis on male dominance. Whatever the reason, adultery is rife and a common source of family squabbles and divorce.

Most Mundurucú have had two or three husbands or wives by the time they reach middle age. This is in part due to a high death rate, but most people also experience at least one divorce. Divorces happen for a variety of reasons. The new husband may turn out to be lazy or inept and sufficiently irritating to his in-laws to be sent off. Or he may experience personal difficulties in the household, leaving him with the alternative of taking his wife away with him or divorcing her; the kin ties of the wife in such cases usually turn out to be stronger than the conjugal bond. The man may leave a woman because she is lazy, or he may discover her in an adulterous relationship and walk out in outrage. Similarly, the wife may become angered with the extramarital affairs of her husband and seek backing from her housemates to divorce him. The man is mobile and can leave at will. The woman must have support, due not only to her lower female status but also because her decision affects the entire house.

Whatever the cause, divorce is a simple matter. Just as marriage entails no public ceremony or observation, so also is divorce effected by the simple departure of the man and his announced intent to leave the wife—or by the recognition of the woman's household that the marriage is ended. If the man is from another village, he simply goes home. If he is from the same village, or chooses to remain in his ex-wife's village, the only sign of the change of status is that he no longer brings game to her. During our stay, one man had an on-again-off-again relation with his wife. Their marriage was experiencing problems, and they fought and made up in a cyclical fashion that saw him one day bringing meat to his maternal aunt and the next to his wife. His itinerary, as he reentered the village each day, was eagerly followed by everybody as the only clear sign of the status of the marriage. Another man was married to a woman of the village but spent little time in her house. As the women said, "He is married to her only at night." Marriages, especially in their early phases, often go through such marginal periods, indicating a certain frailty in the relationship. This, however, is a weakness in a tie between two people and not an institutional weakness, for the Mundurucú still believe that everybody should marry, and the divorced usually find a new mate in due time.

There is a lot of passion and little trust in the early phases of a Mundurucú marriage. Some marriages last only weeks or months, but as time wears on the unions that last become more stable. This is, of course, a tautology in one sense, yet on another level it can be shown that most divorces occur during the first two years of marriage, after which mutual confidence grows and open affection becomes more manifest. With the addition of children, the marriage has a good chance of lasting until broken by the death of one of the partners.

Broken marriages leave behind little economic dislocation, but ex-wives are commonly bitter and cynical about men. One who had been abandoned said that she would never remarry, and another was hesitant about entering a new relationship for fear that the man would walk out on her as soon as she became pregnant. This attitude is most common among women in their twenties, but even the older ones with settled marriages look upon men in general and their husbands in particular with some distrust. Most of them complain over the fact that they are kept pregnant much of the time and blame the men for the series of children, miscarriages, and stillbirths which are their common experience. Distrust of the philandering activities of their husbands and their lot as constant child-bearers is mixed with an underlying resentment of the female work role. The laziness of husbands is a common complaint, and the women particularly resent men who collect little rubber during the dry season and, consequently, can buy few things for their wives. This is a special bone of contention, for the rest of the economy is heavily oriented toward household and village sharing and cooperation. Rubber tapping, on the contrary, is the occupation of individual males, who deal with the traders as individuals; it is the one part of the economy that is organized around the nuclear family unit. A woman with a lazy husband or none at all eats as well as any other, but her wardrobe is usually scant and ragged, the cast-offs of a sister or the largesse of a male relative.

The primary loyalty of the woman and the source of her real security rests in her female housemates and not in her husband. She knows from experience that husbands come and go, that men are not to be trusted, and that whatever happens to her marriage she must find her home in the extended family. This dilutes husband–wife ties to a very thin consistency and promotes marriage instability, which in circular fashion pushes the woman into deeper dependence on her household. Given these circumstances, and the male–female antagonisms that are so manifest in group relations and symbolism, one would expect marriages to be rather stormy—but they are not. We heard stories about fights between husbands and wives over adultery, and women were reported to occasionally chase their errant husbands with a burning firebrand. The men, of course, claimed the right to beat a delinquent wife. During the entire period of almost a year of fieldwork, however, no physical violence ever occurred between husband and wife—no wife ever raised her hand to a husband and no man struck his wife either in our presence or within our very efficient information network. Perhaps the people were "on good behavior" due to our presence, but it is most doubtful whether we could dampen connubial antagonisms for months on end. We even sat through an all-night drinking party when a trader brought rum to a village, yet saw no violent episodes between the sexes—this would be remarkable in any society. To go beyond physical aggression to simple argument and open, loud verbal antagonism, we never witnessed an overt violent loss of temper between husband and wife during all our stay. This is a quite striking fact.

Part of the surface tranquility between men and women on the individual level is a matter of Mundurucú style. Displeasure is expressed in quiet undertones or in brusqueness and avoidance, not in open aggression. The Mundurucú do not strike each other—that is a trait of white men, in their view—nor do they raise their voices. All discourse is calm and measured; violent displays are shunned and one's emotions should at all times be kept under control. To a degree, the nonviolence carries over into husband–wife relations.

We should also ask what exactly is there to fight about among the Mundurucú. Most fights in American families are ultimately about money, which is reminiscent to a degree of the Mundurucú woman's demands for trade goods, but only to a very slight degree. Otherwise, the economic activities of the sexes do not overlap greatly and the industriousness of the individual female is more a matter of concern to the other women than to her husband; the converse is, of course, also true. Most marital fights among the Mundurucú center on adultery. If the husband is known to be having relations with another woman, his wife may upbraid him, although she just as often retaliates against the woman, either by gossip or, rarely, by physical attack. Or, again, she may take revenge by committing adultery herself. If the wife is discovered in adultery, the husband does not assail his rival, for this would break the code of nonviolence among Mundurucú men. He can attempt to chastise his wife, of course, but this too requires caution. He, after all, may well be from another village and without close support, but his wife is surrounded by a whole group of kin. He can divorce the woman, and this is common if the marriage is a new one; however, if he has been married a long time, he may well find that the easiest way out is to turn his back and smolder in silence. And smolder he does, leaving an undercurrent of resentments beneath the calm flow of Mundurucú daily life and etiquette.

Mundurucú women defer to their husbands in many ways. The correct wife waits on her husband, serving him food or water when he wishes, washing his clothes, weaving his hammock, and performing other small services. But the area of personal service is not heavy. She does not cook specifically for her husband, who, in any event, takes most of his large meals at the men's house. When she cooks, it is as part of a team and for a household. This is a service to the husband, but only an indirect one.

A husband seldom gives orders to his wife, for his sphere of interest and hers do not intersect deeply. The conduct of the household is the ultimate responsibility of the senior woman, and the husband of a younger wife would not interfere with her prerogatives. The senior woman is also usually an older woman who enjoys enough status by virtue of age to be able to deal with any man, including her own husband. In one of the houses of the village of Cabruá, for example, the oldest woman was a widow, and the ranking male member was her son-in-law. He treated her with the respect and deference due a mother-in-law and an older woman and listened quietly whenever she had anything to say—and she had something to say quite often.

The authority role of the husband is further undercut by the communal nature of much of woman's work. It is one thing to tell an individual woman what to do, but no Mundurucú man would be so incautious as to try to organize the activities of a houseful of women or those of an entire village. And the division of labor, which relegates certain tasks to females, is also a tacit statement that men should stay out of women's affairs. Senior women organize and direct female work, and not men. The prudent male goes about his own business, satisfying himself with the gestures of respect that he receives from his wife, looking the other way when it is wise to do so.

The surface appearances of marital relations are subdued. By American standards, the Mundurucú are not demonstratively affectionate, and one also has the feeling that husbands and wives are not emotionally as close. The hothouse quality of American marriage is cultivated by the economic and social isolation of the couple and by the near totality of their dependence on each other. This produces both love and homicides. The seemingly cool and aloof tone of Mundurucú marriages is in part a cultural matter, a style of expression, but it also bespeaks the separation of the sexes, the looseness of the interdependency of the individual man and woman, and the overall tone of antagonism between the sexes. There is more a sense of intimacy and closeness in the behavior of long-married couples, a demonstrativeness that sometimes goes so far as putting an arm across a wife's shoulder in public. However, this is unusual. The same factors that keep Mundurucú mates from fighting with one another also keep them from the kind of close-knit ties that are the ideal in American marriage. The Mundurucú watched us in bemusement whenever we had an argument. They knew about it immediately, even though the dialogue was conducted in English, and we suspect that they somehow even knew what the argument was about. And our solicitude for each other, the small shows of affection that go unnoticed at home as part of the ritual of the wedded life, were a source of comment and conversation. In retrospect, we probably appeared quite exotic to them—as we were.

The ideology of dominance of male over female runs through rite and myth, but it is not so evident in daily life. If we were struck by one feature of relations between husbands and wives as individuals, it was by the evenly modulated egalitarianism of their interaction. But it was an equality born of disarticulation of roles, based not on dogma but on the simple fact that men and women are separated from one another. Coercion and obedience had no subject matter, and the men expressed their maleness, their need for ascendancy, their fears that perhaps their power was not real after all, in the public fantasy of ritual.

The two activities that occupy most of the woman's time are farinha making and child-rearing. The casual visitor to a Mundurucú village cannot help being struck by the large proportion of adult women who are pregnant. If his observations are too casual, he may well mistake a few cases of abdominal distension due to worms and dietary factors for pregnancy, but he would indeed be largely correct in surmising that any woman can expect to become pregnant many times during her life. Spontaneous and induced abortion, along with occasional infanticide, account in part for the fact that the population level is more or less stable. Nevertheless, most of the wastage of children comes about through diseases during infancy. During our stay, an epidemic of whooping cough traveled through the Brazilian population of the Tapajós River and then hit the Mundurucú of the Cururú villages, killing most of the population below the age of two. Measles and the common cold also take their toll, as do several other diseases to which the Indian population has poor resistance. Given the conditions of public health, then, it requires a high conception rate for the Mundurucú to just hold their own.

Women, it has been noted, are resentful of the continued cycle of pregnancy and birth, regarding it as an encumbrance and physical handicap and the source of their principal preoccupations and labors. Most of them are quite affectionate mothers after the child is born, and they usually want children during the early years of marriage. After three or four live births, however, their desire for more children declines markedly. Men want children more than do women, they say, and men also favor boys over girls, a sentiment which is not shared by the mothers. The women were impressed by our lack of children at the time of our research and eagerly asked Yolanda what she did to prevent conception. Their own contraceptive techniques, they complained, had only variable success. There are several birth control remedies used by Mundurucú women, the chief of which are ginger root and another, unidentified, root. Either root may be grated into water to make a strong solution, which is then drunk for three consecutive days after birth; it is said to prevent pregnancy for a year. If taken over a period of a month, the women claim, permanent sterility results. The same drugs may be used to induce abortion during early pregnancy; a strong infusion is prepared, and abortion ensues four days later. We had no opportunity to verify the efficacy of the medicines due to the secrecy surrounding their use. The men know very well that the women use the roots for this purpose, but they do not know who is using them and when. The attitude of the women toward the male disapproval of contraception and abortion was quite simply that it was not their business.

The fetus, it will be remembered, is formed of the raw material of semen, requiring repeated intercourse over a several day period for the accumulation of a sufficient amount. At this time, informants say, the culture hero Karusakaibö enters the woman's womb and forms the child into exactly the shape it will have at birth, only much smaller; the fetus simply grows to birth size during the intrauterine period. Women who had been influenced more by missionary teaching often said that it was Tupanyö, as the priests translate "God," who forms the baby from the semen, but other women expressed doubt that any supernatural being was responsible. Pregnancy is recognized by the interruption of the menstrual cycle and by the onset of morning sickness, described by the women as nausea at certain smells. They know that the gestation period is ten moons, but most do not bother to keep close count beyond the rough calculation that a pregnancy begun at the end of the dry season, for example, will come to term early in the next dry season.

The woman goes about her normal business during pregnancy, performing the usual female tasks until the onset of labor pains. A number of taboos on food and other forms of contact with certain objects are observed. For example, during pregnancy, a woman should not see a jaguar, fresh-water porpoise, or snake as she will become ill and the child will die. The capibara and the turtle cannot be looked at, lest the child become wan and pallid, and if a monkey is seen the baby will be fearful for life. Animals that live in the water, such as the alligator, should not be looked at either, as the child will not be able to walk properly. Most of the sight taboos are based upon simple association of characteristics and do not impose a great burden upon the woman. She need only keep her eyes down when out of the village to avoid most of the tabooed creatures, a small problem as most women keep their eyes down when on the trail anyhow.

Dietary restrictions impose more hardship than the sight prohibitions, but not enough to endanger proper nutrition. Yam and pineapple cannot be eaten for two weeks after birth as the child's skin will peel and itch. Brazil nuts must be avoided, too, during the immediate postpartum period for fear that the child will be afflicted with chronic vomiting. A number of smooth-skinned fish are believed to cause dysentery for the child if eaten by the mother during pregnancy and for several months after birth, and the consumption of one fish called *wöi* must be avoided until the child is a toddler lest he become a clay eater—clay eating is quite common among Mundurucú women on the Cururú River, where fish is the principal protein source. Red pepper must be avoided for a week or two after birth to prevent redness in the child's eyes, and honey eaten during this time will cause suffocation. Even foods of Brazilian origin, rarely eaten by the Mundurucú, have fallen into the taboo system, as in the cases of duck and domestic pig, both of which cause dysentery in the child. The sight taboos apply only to the women, but the food restrictions apply to the men also; however, most female informants mention this as an afterthought.

The period of labor appears to be shorter among Mundurucú women than among Europeans and the pains less intense, though our opportunities for direct observation were limited to two births. For a period of two or three months before the birth, the woman drinks an infusion made of the bark of the *biribo* tree or another prepared from the leaves of the *puwo* tree. These help ease the birth of the child, but in difficult cases, in which great pain is felt in the terminal period of pregnancy, the nose of a paca, a river-dwelling rodent, is burned to ash, mixed in water, and drunk. This procedure is believed to be efficacious because the paca gives birth with notable ease. When labor pains reach climax, the woman squats on the floor of the house in an area where the clay floor is broken and soft. An older woman, pref-erably her mother, sits behind her in a hammock, and as birth approaches she grabs the pregnant woman under the shoulders and holds her in the squatting posture a few inches from the floor. If there is difficulty another woman may gently press down on her abdomen to encourage birth; in unusual cases, such as a breech birth, a helping woman will slip her hand into the canal and aid the delivery. The shaman is sometimes called in if there is a fear of causi, the malignant objects of the sorcerer, which can cause miscarriage or stillbirth. Occasionally, the shaman will help in abdominal massage, but this is usually done by the women.

At birth, the child falls to the ground, a short distance but usually enough to help breathing begin. If this is not sufficient shock, the child is patted gently on the body. With the baby still lying on the ground, the umbilical cord is cut by the mother with a sharpened sliver of arrow cane, she washes off the child with cold water, wraps it in cloth, and places it in a nearby hammock. She then washes her own body and takes the baby to her hammock. The attending women dig a hole in the floor, into which they carefully put the afterbirth and umbilical cord. One must take care, they say, to keep the dogs from eating the umbilical cord, for it would surely ruin their hunting abilities.

The birth of a baby is an occasion of great interest in a Mundurucú village, not solely because of a heavy emphasis on children but because so little else happens. At one birth all the women of the household were assembled, the shaman was standing by to remove any malignant objects that might be near, and the men of the house were sitting around eating and talking to each other. Children wandered in and out of the scene, as they always do no matter what is happening. The woman was having a difficult delivery, and her groans of pain alarmed her youngest child, who was in a hammock a few feet away, but the men did not even look up from their food. After the birth, the father gave the mother a piece of cane sliver that he had prepared, barely glanced at the newborn baby, and returned to his companions. The squalls of the infant drew women from the other houses to see it; most simply remarked on its sex and stood by chatting to one another. Little attention was paid to the mother.

The atmosphere was curious, and one received the ineluctible feeling that the occasion was loaded with tension. The people were obviously happy at the birth of the baby but reluctant to express their joy fully. Women from other houses stayed away until after the child was born, and the men of the household played cool and aloof throughout the period of labor. But the remarkable fact was that, despite their almost bored air, they had all gathered in the dwelling instead of in the men's house, something that rarely happened at night. Very little solicitude was shown toward the mother, reflecting semiavoidance rather than lack of sentiment. What we were watching was a *rite de passage* without ritual, a crisis that was not ceremonialized but which elicited behavior that followed the general scheme of birth rites. The immediate community of the woman had gathered, and the onset of labor pains placed her in a situation of social marginality which was resolved by casual aloofness, except for those immediately waiting on her. Not even the birth resolved the anxiety, for children are often stillborn or deformed, and they sometimes die after only a few hours of life. The woman and the baby cannot be fully reincorporated into the community for a few days, and this is a side function of her two- to three-day period of hammock rest.

Infanticide is infrequent, yet it does happen often enough to affect population size. Although the missionaries have made very strenuous efforts to eliminate the practice, they have been more successful among their Cururú River parishioners than in the traditional savannah villages. The destruction of illegitimate children has been noted, but it should be added that if the mother is determined to keep the baby, she is usually able to do so. One infanticide occurred during our fieldwork. A young woman had married a youth a few years younger than herself and came to live in the household of the new husband, who resided with his sister. It soon became evident that the bride was pregnant and even the rude arithmetic of the Mundurucú showed that the husband could not be the father. Though she had been pregnant when he married her, the groom was fond of the wife and decided to rear the baby. Unfortunately, the biological father, who resided in another village, boasted that he was the father and made a joke of the matter. This was too much for the groom's sister, and she urged her brother to send the girl away. He refused, but all agreed that the child should be smothered and buried immediately after birth. The bride had no choice but to consent. Infanticide also occurs in the case of children born with serious birth defects, and, in common with many primitive peoples, the Mundurucú also destroy twins. Only one woman would tell us of this, for they know very well that outsiders do not approve of infanticide. Multiple births, however, are an especially terrible anomaly to the Mundurucú, and we did not know of a single case of living twins in the society, though one did indeed find an occasional illegitimate child or a person with a congenital abnormality. Most informants claimed that it was impossible for human beings to have multiple births. Only *animals* do this, they said, which is what they also say about incest with a first degree relative. And therein lies the reason for the danger of twins—they are a reversal of man's differentiation from nature.

The mother provides an almost complete environment for the newborn baby, just as the baby is the mother's constant and total concern. During the first three months or so after birth, she is rarely absent from her baby. If she is working in the house, the infant either rests in her arms or is put to sleep in a small hammock next to her. When the baby is restless, she soothes it; when it is hungry, she puts it to her breast. This intimate connection between mother and child carries over into the use of the carrying sling, which we have described as a six-inch-wide loop of soft pounded bark cloth that is passed over one shoulder and across the opposite hip, bandolier-style. The child is placed in the sling facing the mother's front and side, its body resting on the sling and the mother's hip, and held gently by her arm. When the child gets a bit older it can cling to the mother's dress, thus freeing both her hands, but even with an infant the woman maintains considerable ability to go about her normal tasks. She can sit, for example, in the farinha shed peeling tubers while the child rests on her lap and upper arm, or she can carry loads of wood or water without great difficulty. The baby is not only near her, but in physical contact with her body. The position of the child in the sling is such that its face is no more than a couple of inches from the mother's breast. When the infant whimpers, the woman need only pull her dress aside a bit to feed it, and the older baby soon learns to pull the dress down itself. The intimate contact of the day is, if anything, increased at night, for the women sleep with the babies against their breasts, occupying the same hammock until the child is about two years old.

Feeding is wholly scheduled by the child's demands, and infants are breast-fed whenever they show signs of hunger. No attempt is made to wean children until about three years of age, and, even then, the process is slow and gentle. Some mothers allow the child himself to relinquish the breast, often because of teasing by other children, but it is possible to find an occasional four-year-old child suckling briefly as a placebo. After the age of about four months, the child is fed gruels of tapioca and yam and somewhat later he is given meat, premasticated by the mother. The frequency of nursing decreases as the solid food diet grows in importance, and the final relinquishment of the breast is gradual and unmomentous.

This open, free, and unrestricted treatment of feeding and weaning appears conducive to the formation of oral-receptive type personalities—warm, outgoing, generous, dependent, and so forth—but there is a catch. When a younger sibling is born, the unweaned child is sharply and suddenly denied the breast in favor of the newcomer. The Mundurucú mother makes little attempt to prepare her child for the birth of an infant, and the child may continue to suckle until immediately before the event. He is then told, bluntly and directly, that the breast is for the new baby and is sometimes physically shoved away when he seeks to nurse. He is also given his own hammock. The child reacts by emotional squalls, temper tantrums, continual crying, moodiness, and acute manifestations of sibling rivalry. We saw little ones try to hurt infant siblings, and the exquisite cruelties commonly visited on household pets by Mundurucú children probably have the same source. Mundurucú mythology, too, is rife with themes of fraternal conflict, scenes that would be unimaginably horrible in real life. Sibling rivalry seems to afflict the unweaned child most severely, but it is not restricted to them. A Mundurucú mother devotes much of her time and affection to infants, and, when a baby is born, her attention is immediately transferred to it, to the loss of her older children. From being the center of the maternal universe, the child is instantly put on its periphery, and the career of childhood is in part a history of coping with this problem.

This pattern is characteristic of many primitive societies. In an excellent study of socialization among the Mescalero Apache of New Mexico, Ruth M. Boyer (1962) noted an abrupt and total displacement of maternal attention to the newborn, with similarly traumatic results for the older child. Due to the smaller size of the Apache household, however, the child is frequently deprived even of mother surrogates, and the emotional distress is probably considerably more acute. The Apache situation is further aggravated by heavy alcohol use on the reservation, resulting in cases of actual physical neglect. This does not happen among the Mundurucú.

The extended family organization of the Mundurucú household, and particularly the strength of its female linkages, provides the mother with help and support in child rearing. For the first few months after the baby's birth, the mother is responsible for almost all the care of the child. However, as it emerges from early infancy other women of the house increasingly share the burden. If the mother is working at a task in which she will be encumbered by the baby, her own mother may put it in the sling and carry it about. Similarly, her sisters or other household women may tend the child for periods of up to an hour or two, allowing the mother freedom to go to the stream or the fields; if one of them is lactating, she may even feed the child. By the time the baby is six months old, the little girls of the household are pressed into service, and seven-year-old girls are often given the care of their year-old siblings or cousins for hours on end. The ease of the mutual baby-sitting arrangements is such that children are continually being passed back and forth from one woman to another and to the girls between seven and twelve years of age.

Ideally, it would seem that the extended family allows for the development of diffuse emotional attachments, and so it does. And, ideally again, it would seem that the availability of a wide range of mother surrogates acts to provide the child with a sense of security that is impossible to achieve in the American nuclear family, in which all affect becomes focused upon the mother— but this is not true. Mundurucú children are indeed cared for by a number of women and girls, but the baby knows very well which one is its mother and it unmistakably wants the mother. A child passed from the mother to another woman will commonly cry, and it is not unusual for it to continue crying until restored to the mother's baby sling and arms. Indeed, Mundurucú children do not have happy dispositions, and there is a heavy frequency of chronic crying and emotional upsets. Moreover, the women are not very demonstrative with their babies. There is very little playing or display of affection, they do not talk to the babies much or exchange gurgling noises, nor are they dandlers and fondlers. It is true that the infant is in close physical proximity to the mother or another woman most of the time, but the women relate to them passively, fulfilling their wishes and needs, but otherwise carrying them about as if they were parts of their own bodies.

There is considerable individual variation, of course, but the average mother is not unrestrained and open in affect, however free she may be with the breast. Still, mothers are much more affectionate to their own babies than to those they happen to be tending, and the baby is quick to recognize this difference. The child over the age of six months actually spends less time with the mother than does a baby of comparable age in our own society, and the loss distresses them. It may be quite impossible to empathize with a baby, but the early life of the Mundurucú child must be blighted by unfulfilled strivings, interrupted and frustrated yearnings for the mother, constant shifts from person to person, and an external world that is largely passive, though readily nurturant. The psychological tensions of childhood are only one component of the struggle to survive and grow up among the Mundurucú, for the babies are not usually very healthy. Although our ability to gather medically useful information was limited, the thinness of most infants and the distension of their stomachs suggested malnutrition, with early infestation by the worms and parasites endemic to the population. The ambience, both physical and emotional, of the Mundurucú baby is not, then, as friendly as it first appears. He learns early of physical discomfort and suffering, and he also learns early of that curious kind of emotional isolation that can thrive in a close-knit household of many people.

"Toilet-training" is relatively simple compared to our own society, in part for the obvious reason that there are no toilets or other narrowly specified places for elimination, nor are there rugs and other finery to be dirtied. At about the age of a year and one-half to two years, he is brought out of the house when it is apparent to one of the women that he is about to have a bowel movement. If nobody sees the child on time, however, no fuss is made nor is the child reprimanded. Most children are trained by three years of age, though they often eliminate inside the village, and by the age of five the child knows that he is supposed to go beyond the village.

The lack of any strict training regimen is also characteristic of the Mundurucú attitude toward children, which is indulgent and nonauthoritarian. In keeping with this laissez-faire orientation, children are not strongly encouraged to walk and are allowed to proceed at their own pace. When a little one does struggle to his feet and makes his first tentative steps, however, adults and older children guide him and save him from tumbles. But he is not urged, goaded, or pushed to walk, or for that matter, to do anything else. In the same vein, children are almost never given corporal punishment. An irritated parent may swat a child gently to stop it from doing something, but punishment as such or severe thrashings never occurred during our field-work.

Fathers have little to do with their children, boys and girls alike, until they are at the walking stage. This disinvolvement from the very young is so pronounced that we cannot remember ever seeing a man holding or carrying an infant in any of the traditional villages, though fathers often pick up toddlers. But after the child starts to walk and venture out into the village, the father often drops into the dwelling to play with the child or simply to watch him. Youngsters' also wander out to the men's house, where they lie with their fathers in the hammock. The growing interest of the man in his child often coincides roughly with the arrival of a newborn, given an average spacing of two or three years, and the father serves as a refuge from the mother's rejection, as she turns her attention to the infant. This cycle of total dependence upon the mother followed by a period of care by several women, displacement by the new sibling and an awakened interest in the father has all the ingredients for producing the Oedipal complex. The cycle affects both boys and girls, for, although the men express a preference for boys and show them special attention, fathers are nonetheless demon-stratively affectionate toward their little daughters. But the fa-ther's attentions come relatively late, and the central figure of both dependence and ambivalent attachment is the mother.

Until the age of about four, the lives of little boys and girls are not strongly differentiated. Most of their play is in or near the house and their wanderings through the village are brief. Boys and girls play with each other in small groups of three or so children which generally center on the household. Most, by this time, have younger siblings and they have already learned to seek help and comfort from others in the house aside from the preoccupied mother, though at times when they are hurt or sorely frustrated they still go to her for solace. Grandparents, if still alive, play an important role in the life of the child during this transition which sees them lose the constant attention of the mother. Grandfathers, especially, play with the little ones, dote upon them, give approval for almost anything they do, and, in general, play the benevolent role that we have come to expect of grandparents in most societies.

By the age of five or six, the watershed between boys and girls is reached. The little girls maintain a focus on the household, but the boys begin to range throughout the village and out into the nearby savannahs. This is the start of the classic pattern in primitive societies, which sees the sexes divide into separate play groups, the boys striking out from the home and the girls staying behind. Future sex roles are forged in the activities of the children, and child play is both the template of adult life and the reflection of it.

Boys between about five and seven years form into a loosely defined play group, and those between eight and thirteen another. The younger children wander about the village and its periphery, drifting in and out of the houses, playing in unoccupied hammocks in the men's house, hunting crickets with small bows and arrows, stalking mice in the underbrush, bathing in the nearby stream, and occasionally touching home base for food. But the attachment of the boys to the household loosens during this period. They go where they please, eat where there is food, and generally confuse visiting anthropologists who are trying to make an accurate house census. Whatever the problem created for the anthropologists, the boys at this age are far less of a problem and concern for their mothers.

This progressive separation from the household and the world of the women is even more pronounced among the boys in the older age group. Their orbit has already shifted from the village itself to the savannahs and forests of the vicinity. Armed with small bows and arrows, they shoot fish in the stream and kill small birds from the seclusion of blinds built near fruit trees. They eat their take in the forests, rounding out the repasts with fruits and whatever they can gather from old gardens. Their evening meals are taken in the village, the very youngest eating in the house and those ten years and over at the men's house, where they wait second turn at the communal meal. By the age of eleven or twelve, they are already sleeping in the men's house, hanging their hammocks in the outermost positions, where they are occasionally drenched by the rains. But these discomforts are more than compensated for by the mark of maturity that comes with leaving the women and the dwelling house.

The older boys maintain a loose sort of attachment to the household. They still depend upon the women for water, for the mending of clothes and for some of their food, but it is a tenuous link at best, held together by sentiment, not by the practical needs of life. In this sense, they are already beginning to approximate adult male status. The proper stance for the prepubescent boy is one of independence. They have little to do with girls, and they take a chary view of the adult world in general. The five or six-year-olds were our constant visitors and companions, but the older boys spent little time in our house. When they did drop in, it was usually to take some tobacco, a luxury for all the boys yet one seldom indulged, not so much because their elders disapproved as because the men kept it for themselves. When our own supplies began to run low, Robert had to limit the boys, much to their outrage. "You're a passive pederast, white man," was among the pleasantries they would cast back as they left, which he would respond to with something equally ribald, but in English. In any event, by the time a boy is eight years old or so, it is difficult to speak any more of "child-rearing," for they have departed from the orbit of the household and operate without substantial adult supervision or interference. Only after they are about fourteen years old and enter into the hunting activities of the men are they reincorporated into the core of the society. In the interim period of boyhood, they have been marginals, albeit very happy ones.

The lot of the girls is wholly different. At five or so, their playmates come to include most of the prepubescent village girls, and their range expands to the entire village. Unlike the boys, however, they do not go beyond the village except when in the company of their mothers or other older women. Girls also become economically active at a much earlier age. By the time they are seven, they are helping to care for the babies of the household and they assist in some of the lighter chores of farinha making. Like their mothers, they gravitate around the house and the farinha shed, learning to keep close to other females and learning to take part in cooperative work. As they grow older, and stronger, they are brought more completely into the labor force, and, by the time they are ready for marriage, they are fully productive members of the village. Girls are under adult supervision and in adult company to a far greater extent than boys. Childhood, for the girls, is a period during which ties to the mother and other women of the house are being reinforced and strengthened, but to the boys it is a time of estrangement from their elders. Boys indeed become men, but by the time they do, they may very well be leaving the village for marriage. Girls, on the contrary, are expected to remain and maintain the bonds formed in childhood.

There are, we have noted, no communal rituals observed at the time of puberty for either boys or girls, and the past practice of tattooing was the closest approximation to a female coming-of-age rite. When a girl has her first menses, she is prohibited from bathing for three days, as a certain kind of bird may drink the blood, causing the girl to turn yellow and die. She is also sent to fetch firewood, and to do it speedily, for now, the older women tell her, she is a woman and must become strong. With the passage through puberty, the girl is now considered to be sexually available and goes through a period of courtship and liaisons. By fourteen she is ready for marriage, and the cycle of mature womanhood begins.

The typical woman will, in all probability, have three or more husbands during her lifetime, from two to four surviving children, and a series of miscarriages. The age of thirty-five may well find her a grandmother, her breasts and abdomen fallen, most of her front teeth missing, and well into middle age. But there will be some compensation in her gradual increase in status until the point in her forties when she passes through menopause and becomes established as a leader in her household and among the village women—a personality in her own right, whom not even her husband will challenge in haste.

Marriage and motherhood are of a different order in Mundurucú society than in our own. That a woman should be married is even more compelling among them than with us, but it is an investment in a status rather than in a particular mate. Husbands and wives may indeed love each other and depend upon each other, but they have other loves and other dependencies. The experience of childhood does not dispose them to deep and particular attachments, for they learn at their mother's breast that the Mundurucú style is one of giving and relating while remaining somewhat aloof and detached. They also learn from the mother that they are easily displaced and that their desires for the original love object are unattainable. They find that they must seek their satisfactions from a number of other people, a compromise which, while perhaps not wholly fulfilling, does allow them to get along. Their attachments are indeed more spread out and more diffuse, but they are correspondingly shallower. It is this residue that they carry over into adult life and proceed to perpetuate through their relations with their children.

The ultimate severance of the male children from the mother is complete on the surface level: they resolve the mother's rejection through the play groups and the final separation from their natal house. That it is not complete on the psychic level, however, is documented by the men's house and the mythology; they are fighting the Oedipal battle all their lives. Daughters seem to resolve the loss by a final reidentification with the mother. The social system permits this through matrilocality and the organization of the extended family. Girls are not forced into the same degree of autonomy as are boys, nor do they have the same requirement for differentiation from their mothers. Indeed, this very lack of self-differentiation is one of the bases of female solidarity in Mundurucú society. It also produces more rapid maturation. Mundurucú boys are a species unto themselves; Mundurucú girls are little women.

The very imbeddedness of the conjugal unit in the extended family is the condition for Mundurucú-style socialization. Women are able to concentrate attention upon their infants because they are backed up by a cadre of other women and girls who will care for the older children. The household is a collective nursery of sorts, but it is one in which the children react against the early removal of the mother and the shift of her concern to the most recently born. The older ones fend for themselves and find their needs within the household at large. In a very real sense, one can speak of the individual mother taking care of her own particular child only for the first four years or so of the child's life. After that time, the mother–child tie endures, of course, but it is attenuated by the collectivization of relationships characteristic of the household and of the society itself. As in marriage and all other things Mundurucú, individual bonds are softened and diluted by the tightness of the social matrix. It is a bit paradoxical, perhaps, but wholly understandable, that in the midst of the strong communal arrangements of Mundurucú society, interpersonal links seem to be based on so little affect. If emotional bonds between women are more enduring, it may well be the result of a reawakening and reinstatement in later life of the mother-child tie. We may well ask, in this light, whether the males have really been freed and the females fettered. Perhaps the boys have been cast out.

8.

Women
/\.\/\.\/\.\/\.\/\.\/\.\/\ and
Social Change

Women have often been considered to be stumbling blocks to
progress, conservative elements in social change. Lodged within
the household and the matrix of the family, the female is insu-
lated, according to this view, from the economic and political
currents that move societies. The great anthropologist Julian
Steward, for example, once pointed out that the process of
change hits first at those social institutions that are of widest
scope in a society, institutions such as regional markets, state
religions, kingships, and paramount chieftaincies (Steward,
1955; pp. 43–63). He saw change as working down from this
level to that of the community and finally to the household, a
last stronghold for those mundane and early-learned patterns
of behavior that are inherited from the past. It would follow
from Steward's quite valid generalization that the woman will be
the last and least affected by the transformations of culture.
After all, it is the men who usually operate in the larger sphere
of politics and the market and who must cope with the shifting
exigencies of this outside world. The life of the woman, revolv-

ing around child-raising and the hearth, seems to remain relatively unaffected.

All of this would apparently be true of the Mundurucú. It is the men who conduct most of the dealings with the traders and who, therefore, have greater knowledge of outside commodities, their values, and their uses. In the process, the males also pick up enough facility in Portuguese to enable them to trade and communicate on a few basic matters with their Brazilian neighbors. They also come to learn quite a lot about Brazilian culture. Much of this knowledge is poorly perceived and assimilated, but it is nonetheless fuller than that of the women. As part of their commerce with the whites, the men have also been forced to modify many of their activities. They are the rubber collectors, and it is they who occasionally perform wage labor for the whites. Women may help in rubber tapping, and a few have even worked as domestic servants for traders, but the involvement of the men is more complete, their degree of estrangement from traditional activities greater.

The situation is not, however, quite as simple and transparent as would first appear, a theme with which the reader should by now be familiar. The Mundurucú woman, like women in most other societies, has indeed been less affected by social change, but this does not in any way mean that she is either resistant to it or even indifferent. It is her circumstance—her role of childbearer, nurturer, and custodian of the household—that accounts for her manifest traditionalism and not any deep emotional adherence to tradition. What appears to be conservatism is really a result of being left out of something, an exclusion which is not necessarily a form of deprivation considering the tainted and dubious benefits of Western civilization. The clue to this can perhaps be found in expressions of nostalgia. Mundurucú men reveled in the recall of the past, of times of valor and strength, of a more abundant life, of a period when the benevolent spirits were still vital and active in the affairs of man. The women, on the other hand, never had anything to say within our hearing about the "good old days"; in fact, they hardly ever talked about times past. It was men who mourned the end of the ceremonial cycle, the forgetting of myths and of lore, and the passage to a future dominated by outside forces. Many accepted it as inevitable, few as desirable. The women, to the contrary, never expressed to us even a hint of grief for the death of the old.

The difference in attitudes of the sexes toward change was striking, but we were to encounter it again a year later during research among North American Indians. And now, musing upon the matter, one can ask whether these differences are not present in our own society. Is it not the male American who acts as guardian of the traditional virtues, who looks upon his past with tenderness and longing, who spins out and devoutly believes nonsense about a frontier America in which people labored hard, won by dint of sheer individualism and carved out an empire by honest effort? Women engage in these reveries also, but not to the same extent, nor in the same way.

Men are the true cultural conservatives, and there are good reasons for this. If men yearn for a stable past and cherish their traditions, it is because the traditions and the past belonged to them. Just as there is little cause for American women to hark back to a largely mythic rugged individualism from which they were systematically excluded, so also is there little reason for Mundurucú women to recall fondly wars fought by the men or ceremonies at which they were mere spectators. The valued activities of traditional Mundurucú life were male activities—almost by definition—the women had small emotional stake in them, and what they did have was sometimes negative. The world of symbols, of stable and fixed things, is largely a male world, and it defines and encompasses life to the male. The woman, however, is the producer of life, and her life is endowed with meaning by life itself, in all its evanescence. Life indeed goes on and on for the Mundurucú woman, no matter how it falls apart for the man.

Beyond their lack of active conservatism, the Mundurucú women have actually done much to promote culture change. The chief dynamic toward transformation during the last century has been trade with the whites, especially in wild rubber, and the sole motivation has been the acquisition of manufactured items. The men have been avid consumers of the traders' wares, eagerly seeking knives, axes, machetes, guns, and a variety of other objects which they obtained first as luxuries and now rely upon as necessities. But the women have been even more desirous of Western goods than the men. They absolutely need metal pots and pans, having almost forgotten how to make them of pottery; they, too, use knives and axes; and they also have an insatiable desire for clothing, ornaments, perfumes, and other such attractions. Since rubber tapping is the chief means of obtaining these things, and since this is male work, the women depend upon their husbands to buy for them. Thus, when a woman says that a man is "a good worker," she means that he collects lots of rubber, not that he is a skilled hunter or fisherman. A good worker is a desirable husband, and if a man is not an especially industrious rubber tapper, then his wife will urge him on to greater effort. Wives cajole, nag, and even help their husbands—and, in the process, help to get them more deeply into debt. But of greater importance, more complete involvement in rubber tapping requires an entire change in locale and life style.

It was noted in chapter 2 that the savannah villagers generally work a foreshortened rubber collecting season lasting only about three months. This limitation is imposed by the agricultural cycle, for garden clearing ends in May or early June, and the fields must be burned over and planted by late September. Rubber can be collected, however, during most of the low water season, or from about May to November. Thus, if a family's needs or desires for manufactured items pass a certain point, the only solution is to relocate near the large rivers, where one can collect rubber and attend to agricultural chores at the same time. Most of the Mundurucú have already made this choice—really a Hobson's choice—and the bulk of the population now lives along the streams near the rubber trees.

Rubber tapping is the work of individuals who trade as individuals, and the consumption unit of Western goods is the nuclear family. When the decision to leave the traditional villages of the savannahs is made, it is, therefore, made by the group involved in the rubber economy—again, the family. The migration to the Cururú River, then, was not carried out by whole villages, or even by extended families, but rather by nuclear families or small clusters consisting of one or two closely related families and a scattering of near relatives. The first settlers simply lived according to the dry season pattern. Wattle and daub houses, the residences of one or two nuclear families, were built in small clearings, but no men's houses were constructed. As other families arrived, the clearings were expanded and the settlements grew into small villages. The residents cleared gardens in the forests, and they went out each day by path or by canoe to their rubber "avenues," the trails that connect a man's rubber trees to each other.

People gravitated to these new villages, for village life was, and still is, considered to be the desirable mode of existence, but their composition was more eclectic. One commonly moved to be near his rubber avenue, not to relocate with former housemates or fellow villagers, and whatever residential uniformity prevailed under the matrilocal preference was totally disrupted. And as the villages grew in size, some outstripped the availability of nearby rubber avenues. People began to locate their permanent homes in the villages and to establish secondary residences near their rubber-tapping activities. The availability of water transportation, however, made it easy for these migrants to return to the village when garden work demanded and then to resume rubber tapping until the floods finally forced them back to the village. The end result of the process was a series of villages and scattered dwellings along the Cururú River. The villages range in size from a couple of dozen to one hundred people and consist of from two to a dozen adobe houses scattered about a clearing. The houses are not arranged in the usual circle, and there is not a single men's house to be found.

The total disappearance of the men's house outside the traditional savannah villages is one of the more striking, and profound, changes that have occurred in Mundurucú society. The piecemeal nature of the migration to the river banks, the development of the villages as extensions of dry season residence, and the historic lack of the men's house during these periods account in large part for the failure to reinstitutionalize them. But along the Cururú River, another dimension appears. This is that trade along the stream has been controlled since the 1920s by the Catholic mission. The priests followed an astute policy in their catechization program. Their goal, of course, was the conversion of the Indians, but they understood quite well that religion has strong social bases. They sought to reinforce the nuclear family through the imposition of the marriage sacrament and the accompanying ban upon divorce. And they exerted every effort to discourage the building of men's houses on the Cururú River. It may be assumed that their chief opposition to the men's house arose from its being a ritual center, but their efforts also did much to undercut the division between the sexes and to assert the primacy of the family unit. The sanctity of the marriage tie, the fundamental importance of the nuclear family, and the enduring nature of the ties within it were hardly Mundurucú doctrine, but the priests pressed the ideology with vigor. Whether or not the Mundurucú of the Cururú River have incorporated the teachings as part of their own values is another question, but they know very well that departures from it will bring the displeasure of the priests upon them.

The Mundurucú men really only wanted knives, guns, axes, and the like, but, as is always the case in culture change, they got very much more. Their desires started them down a road, along which their women have relentlessly pushed them, that has seen the disappearance of the men's house and a good deal of the social organization that went with it.

A description of one of the Cururú River villages will perhaps show the extent of these changes. We lived for about five months in a community located about two hours by canoe from the mission. It was situated some 500 feet from the shores of the Cururú during the dry season, but the annual floods brought the river to the edge of the village. The path to the river led southward across a strip of grassy flood plain to the port, where the canoes were kept; unlike the savannah people, those of the Cururú are water travelers, and most households had at least one canoe. The Cururú is, however, a muddy stream, and we know by personal experience that it harbors several strains of dysentery as well. For this reason, the people went to a small stream east of the village for drinking water, bathing, and clothes washing.

The village itself had a depressing aspect. The country along the river is flat in most places, and the village was hemmed in on most sides by tall trees that cut off the breezes and whatever view there may have been. There were eleven dwellings at the time of our visit, and their only uniformity was that all faced in the direction of the river, blocked off though it was by a fringe of trees and shrubbery. Three of the houses were located in a little pocket at one end of the village, and the remaining eight were scattered about a large clearing. This section also had a quite large farinha-making shed, which was used by all the people of the village.

The houses of each savannah village are generally of the same style and size, all having been built at the same time by all the people, but those of the Cururú village are variegated. Some are quite large, and others are small; some have open sides, and others are walled; some have mud walls, others have walls made of vertical slats of wood, and still others have a mixture of the two. One village house even represented an attempt to perpetuate old styles: it had a steeply pitched roof and was oval in ground plan, but its small size and mud walls belied its authenticity. Most roofs have shallow pitches, in the Brazilian fashion, and the adobe walls and open-sided cook sheds in the back complete the caboclo appearance of the dwellings. Only the absence of windows distinguish them from the forlorn houses of the Amazon region.

The rather eclectic nature of the architecture and the form-lessness of the village bespeak a certain eclecticism and form-lessness of the social order on the Cururú. Each house is built by its residents, with perhaps a bit of help from one or two other families, and each residence unit has its own ideas of what a house should be like. Lacking the tawari bark of the savan-nahs, the Mundurucú build of pole and adobe, and lacking the unity of the savannah villages, they build as they please. The houses are also built at different times, for the villages grow by accretion, not by concerted plan. The ordered circular village layout is lost, the men's house is lost, the central plaza is lost, the focus of community life is lost. Walled in by trees, baking under the sun, the Cururú villages stand as tropical growths, bleak and sad.

Forlorn as they may be to the anthropologist, and as unfulfilling as they may be to the Mundurucú men, the women like life in the Cururú villages and prefer them greatly over the savannah communities. The women are not given to involved theorizing on the question of their status, and their reasons for this preference are simple and direct: savannah men are lazy, they do not help their wives, nor do they buy things for them. We already know that the men of the Cururú River are able to work a longer season in rubber collection and are thus able to buy more trade items for their families, but the question of their helping the women introduces a new topic. This, very briefly, is that the traditional organization of labor has largely broken down in the new communities, and the nuclear family has become the primary unit in the subsistence economy, as well as in the trade economy.

The houses of the Cururú River, it has been noted, are smaller than those of the savannahs. Moreover, unlike the open interiors of the latter dwellings, most of the Cururú houses are partitioned into three parts. Each has a front and back door, as in the savannah houses, but in place of the horizontal poles for hanging hammocks that run across the house at either side of the doorways, there is a wall. Each end of the house is, therefore, an enclosed room used for sleeping purposes, and the central section either is a common area or can be used for sleeping. Most of the houses have an open-sided roofed extension on the back which serves as the common kitchen and gathering place. The Cururú River household still keeps a communal hearth, but it is the fireplace of a much abbreviated social unit.

What has happened can best be shown by a few basic statistics. At the time of our residence in the Cururú River village, the population consisted of some ninety people living in eleven houses, an average of about eight people per household as compared to twenty in the savannah community of Cabruá. And whereas the average savannah dwelling housed four nuclear families, the figure for the Cururú village was just under two. Six of the eleven houses were inhabited by one nuclear family, two houses had two conjugal units, and three houses had three married couples. In many of the houses there were also one or two unmarried adults in addition to the children; these were often widowed mothers or fathers, and five of the houses included three generations. There was, however, no pronounced tendency toward unilocality, and cases of joint residence were about evenly split between patrilocal and matrilocal options. The tradition of matrilocality is well known to the Cururú River people, and they are also aware of the fact that it still prevails in the savannah communities, but their own preferences are variable and weakly stated. In terms of actual choices of postmarital residence, they can best be described as either bilocal or neolocal; that is, a couple can reside with either the bride's or groom's family, or with neither.

The household, then, often consists of small extended families composed in some cases of a couple and a married son or daughter, or in other cases, of two siblings, their mates, and children. But there are just as many houses that have but one conjugal pair, their children, and perhaps a widowed parent or sibling of one of the spouses. If there are two or three families in the house, each will usually live in one of its rooms, sharing the cooking facilities with the others. And, of greatest importance, the men live in the same dwelling as the women and children. Nuclear family life is not attenuated by the duality of residence we found on the savannahs, and the men are not marginal to the household. They live within its confines, relax and sleep there, eat in the house with their families, and socialize in it as well. As far as the women are concerned, this is the way things should be. They want the men in the house, not in a men's house, and are just as earnest champions of the nuclear family as the priests.

The pattern of household life is indeed different on the Cururú River, and many of the changes derive from a shift in work patterns. With the exception of communal fish-drugging expeditions, there are no enterprises that involve all the men or women of a village. Residence by a large stream rich in fish has resulted in a changeover to fish as the basic protein source. Men still hunt, especially in the rainy season when the rivers are high and roiled and there is no rubber collecting, but a good deal of the hunting is done by individual men armed with rifles or shotguns. The large-scale collective hunts using dogs and bows and arrows are rare, and most game is taken by lone men or small parties of two or three hunters. Fishing, on the other hand, is possible for about eight months a year and may even be profitably pursued during the rainy season with a hook and line. A timbó fishing trip will bring together all the people of a village, or even of two neighboring villages, to drug a small stream or an oxbow lake left behind by a shift in the river course, but these ventures take place only a few times a year. Most Mundurucú fishing is done by the individual or by a pair of fishermen. The most common technique is with bow and harpoon-tipped arrow from a canoe, requiring only the fisherman and one person to paddle for him. This may be a male friend or relative, or it may be his wife; in the case of the former, the scope of cooperation remains narrow, whereas in the latter instance the male–female separation in subsistence activities has broken down.

Fishing has other implications for social structure. First, it is far more steady and reliable a source of food than is hunting. An individual may hunt for a week without raising any game at all and will depend during this period on his luckier fellows for food. On the other hand, the rivers teem with fish, and the outside traveler can spot them with ease; the Indians, of course, are much more experienced and astute at locating fish, and even the most inept manage somehow to catch enough for their families. A man will often collect rubber until noon, smoke the latex afterward, go off fishing in mid-afternoon, and return with a large enough catch for dinner that night, and breakfast the next morning. Or, he may work in the garden until mid-day—few people do so in the hot afternoons—and still find time to go fishing. Hunting, on the contrary, is an all-day affair, and a chancy one at that. Another distinction between fishing and hunting is that of gross size of the catch. A tapir yields well over 100 pounds of meat, more than any family, or even household, can eat before it spoils; sharing it is more than common sense, it is a necessity. But if a hunter takes only a pigeon or a small monkey, it will be remembered, the meat usually stays within his household, sometimes to be eaten only by his wife and children. Similarly, the average fish taken in the local rivers ranges from one to five pounds, hardly a fit subject for sectioning and sharing, and the catch, by the same logic, stays in the family larder. A man could spend the entire day fishing, of course, and bring home enough to be shared, but since his fellows can take fish so readily themselves, this would hardly be productive. Besides, the time remaining for fishing after the day's other activities have ended is usually only enough to take a sufficient catch for the household. Finally, the Mundurucú do not fish like Americans on a party boat—they take what they need and quit, secure in the knowledge that there will be a next time. The very nature of fishing—

the individuality of the activity, the ease of the catch, the time available and necessary, and the size of the fish itself—all militate against collectivization of the catch. And, being a family or household matter, fishing, unlike hunting, does little to promote broader social cohesion.

Farming follows much the same cycle and technology as it does on the savannahs, but the patterning of work differs. Whereas garden clearing and some of the manioc planting is done for each garden by all-village work parties in the traditional communities, the household is the work unit on the Cururú. Depending on the size of the household unit, from one to three men will usually make the clearing. In the houses having but a single nuclear family, the wife often helps clear the underbrush with a machete. Sons are pressed into service from about the age of eleven, no matter what size the household. They cut the smaller underbrush, run errands, and make themselves useful in a variety of ways. The same units are also involved in planting, harvesting, and processing manioc. The men do the heavy work of digging holes for the manioc shoots, while the women follow them, planting and covering the cuttings. Men occasionally help their wives in harvesting the tubers and carrying them back to the village, though this is less common in the larger households, where the women have help. There is no doubt that gardening strains the resources of the nuclear family households, requiring the joint efforts in most phases of production of men, women, and children. The problem can be alleviated somewhat by developing cooperative relationships with other small households, but the work teams are still far smaller than on the savannahs.

The reduction in scope of cooperation on the Cururú River has contributed to the breakdown of rigidity of the sexual division of labor. Garden clearing and manioc planting do not really need the combined effort of an entire village—the large work parties of the savannahs tended to invest as much time in play as in toil—but they cannot be effectively done by single individuals within the time available. Husbands, wives, and older children have to join in most phases of the agricultural cycle by force of circumstance. But this is a two-way process, and it can also be argued that the blurring of lines in the sexual division of labor has made the smaller household a viable farming unit. Certainly both things have been happening at once and have been reinforcing each other; the result is that the major production and consumption units are comprised of one to three nuclear families, rather than large extended families or entire villages.

Nowhere is this change in the division of labor more striking than in farinha making. The farinha shed in our Cururú River village had most of the same equipment as had the one in Cabruá. There was a long trough, the oven and toasting pan, large metal basins and the tipití, but there was also a hand-operated mechanical grater. This instrument, bought through the mission, was a relatively primitive affair by modern standards, but it helped accomplish a sexual revolution. The most onerous and time-consuming of all manioc processing chores became reduced to a simple task in which the man turns a crank and the woman drops the peeled tubers into a hopper—but the man indeed does turn the crank. This is not the man's only task, for, if his wife is unaided, he may lend a hand in peeling the tubers, and some men can even be seen loading pulp into the tipití. Another task that has increasingly fallen to the men, unthinkable though it may be to a savannah dweller, is hauling water for farinha processing. No Cururú man will fetch household water, and none carry water in gourds, but they commonly bring water to the farinha shed in two five-gallon cans suspended from the ends of poles borne on their shoulders. As the women say, the men indeed help them on the Cururú River, but it could be added that they help them only because there is often nobody else available; the women still do most of the work. The manioc-grating machine helps make it possible for two or three people to process farinha, and therefore for the men to become involved, but it is not the critical element, for men in Cururú River villages without the implement work with their wives, too. The small work teams do not, of course, make as much manioc flour at one time as do large groups, but they are not feeding as many people, nor are they sharing it extensively with other households.

The ultimate individualization of the economic life takes place in rubber collection, and the degree of involvement of a family in trade is usually a good index of its isolation from the communal life. The individual rubber tapper has rights to collect raw latex from the trees of a certain area. In the early morning, he makes a round of the trees and cuts a short incision, sloping diagonally downward, in the bark of each. He places a small metal cup at the base of the incision and allows the milky sap to drip into it, returning later in the day to collect the latex. When his rounds are over he returns to the village, or his rubber avenue house, and pours the liquid latex over a pole that is slowly revolved over a smoky fire. As the latex congeals into raw rubber, it forms a ball, which is added to in subsequent days until it is almost two feet in diameter. It is then slipped off the pole and brought to the trader, or, along the Cururú River, to the mission.

The man's wife or a son may help him, but rubber collecting from start to finish is really a one-man job. In times past, say the Mundurucú, the chiefs used to trade on behalf of their followers, and whole villages were credited or debited as a unit with the chief acting as a middleman. Today, this system is nowhere in force and, though traders often attempt to coerce chiefs into encouraging increased rubber production, all accounts are in the names of individual men; women, to the best of our knowledge, always rely upon men to represent them in trade and do not deal on their own account. This form of individual holding of an economic resource, of individual production, and family-oriented consumption has acted to diminish wider dependencies in all sectors of the Mundurucú population, but it is strongest on the Cururú River. The family unit has emerged supreme, and the old social system is moribund.

Distribution of food follows the same lines as its production. There is no pattern of village-wide sharing, although close kinswomen in neighboring households occasionally give food to one another. Large game is distributed more extensively, reaching all houses in smaller villages and closely linked ones in larger communities. Fish, however, is far more basic to the diet than is meat, and it generally stays within the household of the fisherman. The communal unit, then, is the household, in contrast to the savannahs, where, though the household is also the basic unit of sharing, many foods are distributed throughout the village. And the Cururú household is but a vestige of the old matrilocal extended family, shrunken in many cases down to the bare nuclear family level.

The locus and nature of sociability in the Cururú River villages differ as well, centering on the house rather than on village-wide institutions. There are no all-male or all-female gatherings. Lacking the men's house, the male stays close to home. If he wishes to rest, his hammock is hanging in the dwelling, and he retires there for a nap or just to swing slowly back and forth. This is also the place where he takes all his meals, for there are no more sacred instruments to be ritually fed, nor is there a congregation of men to partake of a common meal. His wife, or one or two other female residents, prepares the food, and the entire family—men, women, and children—eats at the same time.

The center of household activity is the open-sided cook shed at the back of the house. Sheltered from the sun but open to the breezes, it is also a good vantage point for watching the movements of other villagers, for the Cururú River residents have not at all given up their lively interest in people. This is where food is eaten and where people gather during slack hours of the day and at evening for conversation or just idling.

The cook shed is also where visitors are received. Visiting between households is frequent, but it does not produce large gatherings. During our stay, sizable groups would appear at our house every evening to listen to the radio or to talk to the exotic strangers, but this is not the usual pattern. Generally, visits are made by nuclear families or individuals and are hosted by a family or household. Women do not retire from the scene if a man arrives by himself, though they may not have much to say to him, and, if he brings his wife, the women will hold a separate conversation from the men.

In gatherings of three or four families, the women usually occupy their customary position in the background, but this is not always the case. Actually, the separation of the sexes on these occasions is not radically different from what one would find in a similar collection of married couples in the United States. Like food-giving, visiting often follows kinship lines, indifferent to line of descent, and families interact with others in varying degrees. Other factors enter into sociability, and one household of three families had little to do with the rest of the village because one of its members was suspected of witchcraft.

The farinha shed, the gathering place of the savannah women, does not have this function on the Cururú River. People occasionally stop by to chat with families working at manioc processing, and they might even help a little, but it is not a day-long gathering place, nor do many people collect there at a given time. To the extent that the women congregate at all, they do so in the cook shed of one of their number. The reasons for this are simple enough. The farinha shed was traditionally a female place, the site of a specifically female activity, but this exclusiveness is now absent. It was traditionally an arena for cooperation, too, attracting women for the purpose of work as well as amiability, but this element also is missing in the modern scene. The men now help the women, but at the cost of the vital center of female life.

The failure of communal institutions on the Cururú River and the proximity of the mission have stripped Mundurucú religion down to its basic elements. There is no more men's house or sacred instruments, and the entire cult of the clan spirits has effectively disappeared. Many of the older men still remember extinct ceremonies and some are repositories of myth, but traditional lore is much better preserved on the savannahs, where it remains relevant to social life.

The main occasions for festive gatherings are now provided by the mission. Most Sundays will find a number of visitors from various villages who come to trade, and also to attend services. Religious holidays draw larger numbers of Mundurucú, attracted by the food, evening dances, and the opportunity to meet with their fellows from other villages. The extent and effectiveness of Christian indoctrination has been discussed in Robert Murphy's book, *Mundurucú Religion* (1958), and it need only be said here that conversion was far from complete. One aspect of native religious practice that has remained strong has been shamanism, and its attendant belief in sorcery and witchcraft. As in the savannahs, it would seem that the benevolent spirits have departed, leaving a residue of evil.

The missionaries have been quite successful in the administration of the sacraments of baptism and marriage. Children are usually brought to the mission for baptism within the first few months after birth, and the priests baptize most of the others during their travels up and down the river. Most marriages are first entered into according to the traditional Mundurucú format, though the young women seem to have more latitude of choice than on the savannahs. In the eyes of the missionaries, however, the newlyweds are living in sin, and they bring every pressure to bear upon the couple and their families to persuade them to marry at the mission.

Marriage, we have said, is a time of social withdrawal for the Mundurucú, a time when one feels "shame," and a public wedding is, for most of them, a painful experience. On one occasion, we watched a church marriage conclude with the bride and groom walking down the aisle, eyes cast down in desperate embarrassment, and as they left the church they quickly separated, the bride to join her family and the man to lose himself among his friends. But married they were, in the eyes of the church, and married they would stay as far as the priests were concerned.

Divorces, or abandonments, do occur, but their frequency is far lower than among the savannah people. Whether this is due to the vigorous intervention of the priests, or to the increased importance of the nuclear family, is difficult to sort out, but both factors are probably operative. The influence of the priests is strong, but it is not limitless. In most cases, history has been on their side: the men's house and large extended family are indeed absent on the Cururú River, but so also are they on the Tapajós and other areas to which the Mundurucú have migrated.

The increased strength and stability of the nuclear family

have had far-ranging results. Just as the small household or the nuclear family is now the center of the individual's social life, so also is it the center of child-rearing. The household, harboring only one to three adult women, does not provide the back-up for child care that we found in the traditional communities. Another woman, or a young girl of the house, may tend the baby, but the child is not passed around as much; usually its own mother takes care of it. Fathers are also available for baby tending. Mundurucú fathers, no matter where they live, are very affectionate toward their children, but the men's house reduces their interaction with them. On the Cururú, the father is in the house, and the children often climb into the hammock with him or make other demands on his attention. It was mentioned that savannah men rarely, if ever, carry infants in the prewalking stage, but this is a common sight in the Cururú villages. The woman is busy and needs both hands free, and the only person available to hold the baby may be the husband. He understands necessity even better than tradition, so he holds the baby. This, after all, is what happens in social change—necessity erodes custom and eventually becomes it.

On the Cururú, children are more closely attached to the nuclear family from their very infancies. They receive greater attention from their mothers, more care from the fathers, and grow up in a smaller social unit. But children are also an economic asset at an earlier age. The life of the girls is much like that of their savannah counterparts, but that of the boys is quite different. A boy of eleven or twelve may be called on to help in the garden, aid in manioc peeling, paddle the canoe while his father fishes, and indeed to perform a host of services once carried out by adults through cooperative arrangements. Their utility calls for a higher degree of control over their activities, and the free and easy life of the savannah boys is largely missing. They do not play in the same large groups, nor do they play as much. Correspondingly, their parents exercise a tighter control over their movements, for the boys are not always willingly available workers. This increased discipline extends down to earlier child training as well, and Cururú parents scold their children more often and swat them with greater frequency than do those of the savannahs. Perhaps the parents are testier with their children because they can escape them less, but, whatever the importance of sheer irritation level in the disciplining of the young, it anticipates future roles. The boys of the Cururú do not make a break from the household as do those of the savannahs—but then neither do their fathers.

The changes in Mundurucú society have been profound and irreversible. The structure of kin groups has been altered; the men's house is gone, changing the very nature of living arrangements; the sexual division of labor, though still separating particular tasks, has shifted to bring men and women into cooperative, side-by-side work; the nuclear family, or small clusters of such units, is the basic element in both production and consumption; and the cohesion of the sexes as social groups in themselves has been lost. These changes are not restricted to the larger, outside social orbit, but have impinged upon family life, marriage, and child-rearing. They have, in the process, transformed the female role.

Is the woman of the Cururú River better off? Superficially it would seem so, as the men's house and all the ritual and mythic apparatus of male dominance have disappeared. The Mundurucú men no longer hold a ritual monopoly. Instead, it is held by foreign priests—males, but totally outside the system—and the Indian men, just as much as the women, are now mere spectators. The men are no longer arrayed against the women as a unitary force; they are fractionated into family units and now depend more upon their wives than their fellows for economic cooperation. And the change in the division of labor has caused the men to assist their wives directly in the heaviest task in the subsistence economy. It is true that the women still work harder at farinha making than the men, but the relative positions of the sexes have shifted subtly in the process of male involvement. It is doubtful that women on the Cururú work less as a result, for the help of men is no more effective than that of women. But the status of the sexes is a relative thing; if male status falls, then female status must be said to have risen. Finally, one might argue that the very fact that the men now live with the women and share with them in decisions affecting the family bespeaks an improved position of the women.

Let us now look at the other side of the picture. The symbols of male domination are indeed gone, but it has been shown that there was more symbol than substance to the tyranny of the men in Mundurucú society. The woman is still seen by the men as occupying a passive position; they no longer are gang raped for spying on sacred trumpets, but they still are for serious impingements on the male role. The woman still has to travel with an escort. It is true that the men of the villages have lost their solidarity, but so also have the women. The attenuation of cooperative work patterns has radically diminished the cohesion of the women, and it has also undercut the leadership role of the senior women of households. Men have emerged as the clear heads of the dwellings, and on the Cururú it is rare to hear a person refer to a house as being that of a woman. The latter process has been furthered by the dissolution of the matrilocal tendencies. The leadership role of the senior woman in the savannahs derives in good part from her being the eldest of a group of women related in the female line; this is also a source of the solidarity of the household, a form of cohesion that the men lacked. Moreover, the expectation that most Cururú River daughters will leave home in marriage does much to reduce the strength of the mother–daughter and sister–sister bonds.

The women of the savannah villages, we have stressed, confront the men as a bloc. On the Cururú River, however, relations between the sexes do not have this group quality but are largely dyadic relations. So also is it within the household. Husbands and wives do join in decision-making, but the decisions are generally ones that affect only the nuclear family. If women have a greater say in their individual destinies, then men also have a greater say in household matters. As for community-wide decisions, there are even fewer to be made in the new villages than in the traditional ones. It can be said that everybody has less to say in collective planning, because the collectivity is now so weak.

Our question of whether or not the status of the woman in the Cururú River villages is better has not really been answered. One reason why this is so is that we really do not possess the criteria for evaluating the relative status of the sexes; when we talk about "the position of women," we often are not asking the right questions. One might surmise that the Cururú woman has an improved position, but perhaps only because the prestige of the male has declined there. It is, we have said, a relative matter, but it is also a very complex one.

Instead of asking ourselves who has it best, perhaps we should be asking the Mundurucú woman. The answer here is quite unequivocal; with but few exceptions they prefer the nuclear family arrangements of the new communities. They do so because trade goods are more readily available, and they prefer their men to help them. On one level, this is exactly what the women want—they seek aid and relief in the drudge work of manioc growing and processing. They do not like the work, and they resent the fact that the men, as a class, leave it to them, as a class. But beyond the surface response, "helping" is a metaphor for the autonomy of the nuclear family and its co-residence in a single dwelling. Under the new arrangements, the woman is more bedeviled by her children, more subject to the demands of her husband, and more isolated from other women, yet she prefers it to the traditional institutions of the men's house and the extended family. She wants her husband living with her, not in a house across the village, and she wants her husband to stay with her and not to pack up and leave under the easy conditions of Mundurucú divorce.

What makes the women want to lock into marriage and the family? We do not think this question can be answered easily, but we also do not think that the sentiment is restricted to the Mundurucú. Perhaps it can be better phrased as: Why do the women want to lock the men into marriage and the family? Here, we should stress that whatever we may think the relative status of the woman to be in the traditional, as opposed to the new, communities, the Mundurucú women think it is better in the latter. And though there may have been little absolute improvement in their situation, the gap between them and the men is perceived by them to have narrowed. The women may not have been elevated, but the men surely have been reduced.

The woman, then, is an active factor in social change. She has seen another way of life, and she has opted for it. It is for this reason that a Cururú woman will rarely marry a savannah man and move to his village, though the reverse is quite acceptable. And it is for this reason that, if a savannah man contemplates a move to the Cururú River, his wife will often encourage him, torn though she may be by an equal desire to maintain ties with her female relatives. In the restless drift that has seen the savannahs slowly become depopulated and a whole way of life disappear, the women have been powerful agents. The drift of migration has affected family after family, and it is within the family that the woman has her primary influence. It is doubtful that she can be said to have found liberation. In the long run, she may, in common with other seekers of freedom the world over, have found a new form of oppression. As for the men, they have given up their sacred trumpets without a struggle, finding that the women did not regain dominance after all, only association.

9.

Women
∿∿∿∿∿ and Men

The myth of archaic female dominance is not at all unique to the Mundurucú, for variations on the idea are found throughout South America. The ancient Greeks, too, believed in a race of Amazons and threads of the story were spun into the fabric of European folklore. This gave rise to the misapprehension of the Spanish explorers of South America that the great river of the forests was peopled by female warriors—thus giving the Amazon River its name. It was this theme, only a leitmotif in the European tradition, that was developed by the nineteenth-century social evolutionists, fortified by similar myths from around the world, into the idea of the primeval matriarchy. According to this notion, women were once the dominant sex; both the reckoning of descent and the tenure of authority were passed through a line of females until a time in human history when the men wrested control from the women. This was the first social revolution.

Consistent with their assumption that the living primitive peoples represented stages in the orderly growth of culture, the evolutionists thought that surviving matriarchal societies would be found, as residues of this past. Many such groups were indeed reported, and the Iroquois remained for years a prime example of a matriarchy. But there had been considerable confusion of descent and power, and the word *matriarchy*, or female power, was at times used interchangeably with *matriliny*, or descent through females, in part because it was assumed that authority would naturally rest with the sex that gave descent. There was indeed persuasive evidence that matriliny commonly preceded patriliny, and it would follow from this that matriarchy, or female dominance, must precede patriarchy, or male dominance. The evolutionists were also supported by the general truth, borne out by subsequent research, that women usually enjoy higher prestige in matrilineal societies than in patrilineal ones.

The primitive matriarchate seemed to be a quite acceptable proposition, given the fragmentary evidence that was available to nineteenth-century anthropologists, but it has run aground on the facts. The cardinal fact is that all of the far-ranging and intensive research that has been carried out by professional anthropologists in this century has failed to turn up a single instance of a society in which women are the dominant sex. Moreover, our rereading of the same sources used by the evolutionists indicates that their presuppositions colored their interpretations. Every last bit of evidence at our command shows that male dominance, in varying degree, is general today and, to the best of our knowledge, has been so in the past. The matriarchal theory has about the same validity as the Mundurucú myth of the sacred trumpets—and probably derives from the same masculine uneasiness.

How, then, do we explain this social superiority of men, and in what conceptual terms do we discuss it? This has been a book about the women of the Mundurucú, a tiny group in the Amazon basin, and we cannot expect to find a universally valid answer to the first question in our limited data. But we can use the perspective of the Mundurucú as a vantage point for looking at the sexes in our own society and others. As for the second question, which is a methodological one, we can only raise problems and point to pitfalls of logic and semantics. Status relations between the sexes are unlike other forms of social hierarchy in that they are always binary and are wholly relative. That is, when we talk about the position of the female, it is with reference only to men and only to the men of the group or subgroup to which the women belong. Thus, no matter how abject and oppressed the men may be, the status of women is measured only against that of their men, especially, of course, their husbands. Unlike class stratification, which is concerned with the positions, relative to control over resources, of entire segments of a population, the issue of men and women is commonly treated in dyadic terms, as interpersonal relationships, rather than as a group phenomenon; the Mundurucú are actually unusual in the extent to which they lend themselves to a study of the sexes as collectivities. The problem is further complicated in class-structured societies by the fact, following from the above, that female status is also a function of class position. When discussing the status of white upper middle-class American women, for example, we usually confine ourselves to a comparison of their roles with those of upper middle-class men, not to lower-class men or black men or women. Our musings on the sex hierarchy are, therefore, highly relativistic and inevitably infused with the problems of marriage—and just plain sex.

Simple ethnocentrism, our own and that of the people being studied, introduces another source of confusion in the study of sex statuses. Men, for example, are more far-ranging than women. They travel to hunt, trade, and make war—or to go to conventions or on sales trips—while their women tend the children and the home. Most anthropologists are inclined to look upon this as a plus for men and a minus for women, as another index of lower female status. But, stripped of our own cultural preconceptions, what indeed is so great about travel? Is going off to war a good and prestigious thing? Those who have had combat experience reliably report that it consists of short periods of intense danger, long periods of equally intense boredom, and continuous authoritarian discipline; they remember nothing good. And witness the traveling man. He is crammed into a hermetically sealed tube with a few hundred other "prestige seekers" and hurtled through the air to a dismal airport, after which he eats a bad meal and sleeps alone in one of those cold and faceless hotels, all of them exactly alike, which are found from New York to Des Moines to Lagos to Hong Kong. Is this a boon or a banality? Lacking any real standards of what is good or bad, we usually rely upon our own judgments and those of our informants. And we know that in most cases activities and occupations that are considered good, prestigious, and so forth, and which are the province of the male, are valued not because they are intrinsically worthwhile but because men do them. That is, male ascendancy does not wholly derive from masculine activities but is to a considerable degree prior to them.

Here then is the anthropologist's problem. We are confronting the question of the universality of the cultural superiority of the male without a set of absolute standards of what constitutes superiority. The problem of hierarchy, which is comparatively transparent in the case of the master–slave or ruling class–plebian relationship, becomes muddied and opaque in the complex and emotion-laden tie—or breach—between the sexes. To cap it all, the anthropologist is just as enmeshed in the false veneer of sexual ideology as are his informants, and he or she is additionally encumbered with that enormous and largely unconscious baggage of fears, frustrations, hatreds, and longings that characterize sex roles. There is no easy solution to the problem, and we can only suggest caution and skepticism in its discussion. As in all things, the first step toward wisdom is the awareness that we really do not know what we are talking about.

A number of quite obvious factors have been called forth by the legion of writers on women to explain the circumstances, if not the subordination, of the female. Among the most important of them have been the work of women, their place and mode of residence, child-bearing and child-rearing, the peculiar ideology of men (machismo, chauvinism, and so forth), and personality, whether inherent or inculcated. The effect of each factor will be reviewed in this chapter, first for whatever light they may throw on the situation of the Mundurucú women and subsequently for whatever clarity our Mundurucú findings may bring to the general problem of the sexes.

The biological differences between men and women intrude upon and shape their social roles most strongly in the spheres of work and, of course, reproduction, and child-rearing. Among the Mundurucú, certain tasks are allocated to the men on the basis of sheer physical prowess. The felling of forest areas for gardens requires great strength, and hunting similarly calls for a kind of athleticism that is usually not found among women. Fishing is not a very strenuous activity, but it involves familiarity with weapons, and it also requires absence, sometimes at great distances, from the village. The latter is a critical factor, for in times past, the forests and rivers far from the settlements could harbor enemy war parties, to which the women would have been easy prey. Beyond that, the women are commonly barred from the more intense and energetic forms of activity by pregnancy, and the need to nurse children keeps them close to home, long after the region has become pacified.

This basic division of labor has been perpetuated in the villages of the Cururú River, with one significant difference— the organization of the work has undergone modification. Whereas the sexes used to perform their respective tasks in substantial isolation from one another, they now work in active cooperation and association. The issue of the organization of labor is fundamental to an understanding of the position of the woman. Writers on the subject of women's work frequently concentrate upon the gross importance of female labor to the economy in the belief that the prestige of the woman will vary directly with her contribution. But this need not be at all true, and we could dredge up endless examples in which the reverse proposition is equally valid and in which women, and children, are held down and exploited exactly because their labor is vital. Certainly, the fact that Mundurucú women do most of the garden work places them at least on an economic par with the men, but their evident autonomy derives not so much from what they produce as from how they produce it and who controls the product.

The principal crop, bitter manioc, lends itself to cooperative work both in its growing and its preparation. This brings the women together in a joint effort and in a common place. Thus, just as the men join in hunting and associate in the men's house, the women make manioc flour together and find a common meeting ground in the farinha shed. There is a true collectivity of women in every traditional village which matches the collectivity of the men and must also be understood, in part, as a defensive reaction to it. The men, as an organized body, are unable to dominate females as isolated individuals, nor does the

lone male really find a situation in which he coerces the similarly
lone female. Rather, they confront each other as two entities,
each having internal organization and cohesion and a sense of
identity and common interest. Women's work among the Mundurucú is largely directed and
initiated by women, and the men do not intrude upon their area
of responsibility and authority. Farinha making may indeed be
the worst task in the society, and it is indeed a drudge job that is
relegated to the women, but it is still work that remains under
their exclusive jurisdiction and control and it is still central to
survival. Superficially, it would seem that grating tubers and
standing over a hot oven for long hours is a mark of inferiority,
and on one level it is, but to the extent that it draws women
together and isolates them from the immediate supervision and
control of the men, it is also a badge of independence.

In stratified societies, one must ask who works for whom and
who gets what? Among the Mundurucú, however, this is not a
real question. Except for rubber production and the sale of small
amounts of farinha to traders, production is for immediate consumption by the producers and their dependents. The natural
resources from which subsistence is derived, whether forest
lands, hunting areas, or fishing grounds, are not the property of
any individual or group. The instruments of production, tools
and weapons, are hardly a form of capital except in a technical
sense; they are accessible to everybody either through trade or
their own manufacture, and no individual or group, again save
for the traders, is able to exercise control over their availability.
These, of course, are the classic ingredients of the classless society, but they also inhibit the development of forms of economic
domination of men over women. Gardens are not owned, only
their use rights, and these belong to the women just as much as
to the men. Houses, we have said, are not real estate, but the

consensus of most Mundurucú is that women have primary rights in them. As for artifacts and tools, women have every bit as much right to these forms of private property as do men. And foods, whether produced by men or by women, are usually distributed by the females.

Curiously, it is only in rubber production—so strongly encouraged by the women—that the men are able to obtain sure economic leverage over the women. Men, not women, have rights to rubber trees, and men do the trading. Despite the growing importance of the trade economy, and the marginality of the females in it, wives have surprising success in getting their husbands to buy things for them, though, it must be noted, they now have to ask. It would seem that the essential communality of the household unit, a traditional and valued part of Mundurucú culture, has persisted as a bulwark of female status in a changed situation. What the future will bring, however, is uncertain. In the families that have left the savannah villages, the men now help the women in their labors and associate with them to an extent unimaginable in the past. This has the appearance of growing equality, but it is a situation in which the men really hold the cards, though they do not seem fully aware of it yet. When the men do recognize the implications of their control over property and commerce in rubber, the women may well discover that they have traded the symbolic domination of the men, as a group, over the women, as a group, for the very real domination of husbands over wives.

The degree and way in which women are involved in labor beyond the domestic realm is important to their status in every society. There is a common belief among Americans today that women have just emerged from the household during the past century into the larger workaday world, but in reality industrial society is unique in the extent to which women, until recently, have been freed, or excluded, from subsistence pursuits. Even our own agrarian past saw women take a substantial role in farming and the raising of small stock, and the literature of ethnography gives ample documentation of the significance of women's work beyond child-rearing, cooking, and so forth. They hoe gardens, they tend goats, sheep, and fowl, they gather wild vegetable products, and they even lend a hand in fishing. In a sense, what we are now experiencing in our own society is a reemergence of women into the broader economy after a period of confinement.

The reasons for this change are complex and beyond our scope, and we can point to only a few of the more interesting circumstances of it. First, the entire drift of our technology has diminished the significance of the physical differences between the sexes in production. One may have to be a male to be a hunter but not to be a computer operator, a pilot, an engineer, or a salesperson. Machines have largely replaced hard manual labor, and now machines are beginning to tend machines; there are few occupations left that cannot be held by women. Moreover, the percentage of the labor force engaged in farming and capital production has been decreasing for many years, while the proportion in the administrative and service sectors, which have used female labor most extensively, has increased. The technology of an advanced industrial society erases sex differences in work.

All of these considerations are self-evident, but latter-day industrial society has done more than open up an opportunity to females—it has discovered in women the last large and unused pool of labor. In one sense, the entry of women into the job market may be looked upon as the outcome of a struggle for equality, and so it is. But the increased absorption of women in occupations long predated the women's liberation movement and is a function of post–World War II industrial growth. Women have entered commerce and industry because jobs have expanded faster than the male labor supply. They have been cheap labor, to be sure, just as southern blacks are in this country and Turks in Germany, and the real struggle is to attain parity with men in salary and job advancement. This will indeed occur in time, for one of the tendencies of an industrial economy is to universalize the labor force, to reduce social relations, people, and their labor, to object commodities. The female status and female labor have traditionally been of an ascriptive and particularistic kind—that is, women have been treated in a highly specified way due to the simple fact of birth as a female—but this pattern is incongruent with the needs of an industrial society, which views people as things. Women will undoubtedly achieve much of the status of the male, but with it will come depersonalization of their selves and their work.

There has been, we are often told, a "revolution of expectations" in much of the world that is commonly expressed at the popular level in spiraling consumer demands. Despite gains in industrial productivity, the male worker is hard pressed to satisfy the heightened requirements of his family by his labors alone. The problem is exacerbated by endemic inflation, which is not so much a temporary economic dislocation as a regular concomitant of an expanding economy and increased consumer demand.

The answer to this crunch between increased wants and higher prices is for the European or American wife to go to work, a phenomenon that is more pronounced at the lower economic levels, where the women's movement has been least active. Most women are not so much engaged in finding themselves or escaping from stultifying households as in helping to pay off the mortgage and new car, to buy a summer home, or just to eat. There is a curious parallel here with the Mundurucú, whose desires for trade items and involvement in a credit system has also altered the division of labor. The Mundurucú woman, following her husband along his rubber avenue, carrying the latex cups, and helping collect them when they are full, shares a true sisterhood with her American counterpart at a typewriter. And both may well feel that doing these things has improved their status, as women. The Mundurucú woman has, however, lost in the process the strength that comes with unity with other women—the American woman never had such a unity but now seeks to find it in a society that offers no practical basis for it either in economic cooperation or in residence.

The Mundurucú pattern of residence is a bulwark of female status. Again, one has to distinguish between simple appearances and hard reality, for it would seem at first glance that the separation of the sexes, the relegation of women to large noisome households inhabited by squalling babies and nasty dogs, is their ultimate denigration. But the households, we saw, are the only true corporate units within Mundurucú society. Whereas the memberships of the men's houses tend to be diverse with regard both to kinship and place of origin, the households are more stable and cohesive. A woman's residence in a house outlasts her marriages; she may not pass her entire life in the household of her birth, for other contingencies than kinship affect where one lives, but her association with it is stronger and more lasting than any association of men.

The preference for matrilocality is the key to the solidarity of the Mundurucú women. The presence of strong kin ties among the residents of the men's house is adventitious, but among the women of the dwellings it is given within the norms. Mothers and daughters tend to reside together, as do sisters, and the preference is upheld by a strong value upon the integrity of ties between females; there is no such value upon close male kin ties except for the more diffuse attachments that are prescribed between fellow clansmen, and men in general. That this same group of female kinfolk should also be a commensal and productive unit, central in cooperation and sharing, heightens the dependencies between its members. They can do without one or another of their men, confident that he will ultimately be replaced by another, but a fellow woman is central to a work team and must be kept. The household, at the same time, does not become isolated from others, because much work requires a village-wide effort. Women cannot be divided from each other along lines of nuclear family or household and then conquered, for they have a very real and continuing need for one another. They have their rifts, of course, but these tend to be resealed by the exigencies of everyday life. The women present a united front to the men, but, it should be remembered, they do so at the expense of the strength of marriages.

Matrilocality brings us back to one of the issues raised by the notion of the "primitive matriarchy." It was stated that female status is generally higher in matrilineal societies than in those having patrilineal descent. This pattern is so, however, not as a matter of female dominance which somehow perpetuates itself in matrilineal descent, but as a result of the fact that many matrilineal societies are also matrilocal. Descent through females may indeed have some effect upon the woman's public prestige, but far more critical is its association with a residence rule that holds together a core of related women. The Mundurucú are a remarkable illustration of this as they have one of the very few societies that combines patrilineality with matrilocality. As in many patrilineal societies, there is a series of rules and symbolic observances that supposedly guarantees the rights of the men over the sexuality and issue of their women, but these, we have seen, are largely illusory. Children do receive the clan names of their fathers, but they stay with their mothers. The men assert a strong show of dominance in sex relations, which has its principal expression in marriage. Otherwise, the women band together in such a way that men cannot intrude upon individual women; premarital love and postmarital philandery are the secure province of female strategy and planning. Mundurucú patrilineality shapes the symbolic expression of relations between the sexes, but it has little impact upon their day-to-day relations. These are molded instead by the presence in the dwellings, and in the village as a whole, of groups of women who are bound by ties of kinship and economic dependency. Under the firm leadership of their senior women, the households must be understood as political units.

Men do not supervise women or order them about, for this would bespeak a greater degree of association of the sexes. Judith Shapiro (1972), in her study of the women of the Yanomamö, a tribe of northern Brazil and southern Venezuela, notes that the kind of sexual division of work and residence that characterizes the Mundurucú is absent. Yanomamö husbands exercise continuing control over their wives, and the very fact that the women are imported through patrilocality leaves them vulnerable, without a close circle of supporting relatives. Mundurucú women experience no such isolation, and their husbands treat them with a deference and caution that is in sharp contrast to the ritual expression of sex relations. Shapiro concludes that although it may indeed be best to be integrated and equal, it is better to be separate and unequal than integrated and unequal. In much the same way, most black Americans find it more palatable to live in a northern urban ghetto than in a southern white man's back alley. The Mundurucú woman, too, has her "turf."

The Mundurucú female stays home, and the male leaves. The woman works in the village or close to it, but the man ranges out in hunting, fishing, trading, and, at one time, warfare. The woman remains in her household when she marries, but the man leaves his to join the village of his wife. The preadolescent girl stays close to her mother, helping care for the babies, and the boy wanders around the savannahs and forests, moving into the men's house as soon as the adults will accept him. This is, in one sense, a severe limitation for the woman, but, in another, it makes her the stable figure in the emotional economy of the society. The men may be the controlling political figures, for whatever that is worth in a classless and rankless society, but the women are the repositories of affective relations. They not only control the attachments of their sons, but they keep their daughters. And despite all the cohesion of the men, the women are bound together by stronger emotional ties.

The very fact that the men are public figures and minor political actors gives a peculiar coloration to their show of solidarity. It results in a characteristic reserve and a careful maintenance of personal distance between them. There is a veneer of fellowship, but one senses that it is maintained by the potential for social disruption if feelings were to be expressed. The women are under no such constraints. They are more open and outgoing, they laugh more easily, they express their hostilities more quickly. The latter fact might lead one to assume that the lives of the women are more invaded with divisiveness, but this is not the case at all. Rather, the strength of their attachments, unlike those of the men, is sufficiently strong to survive easily transient jealousies and disagreements. The men are really far more estranged from each other than are the women.

The women of the Cururú River have moved from this social setting into one that is closer to that of the American female.

They are still prisoners of the household, but, to a degree, so also are their husbands. Unlike most American families, the Cururú River couple spends much time together. The American husband may well leave for work at 7:30 in the morning and return at 6:30 in the evening, whereas the Mundurucú man will return in early afternoon from rubber collection, spend some time fishing and while away the rest of his day near the household. On many days, he will not bother going to his rubber avenue at all, and most of his day will be passed in the company of his wife—there is really nowhere else to go. This, and the fact that a small village necessarily places one in continual association with others, has undoubtedly protected the woman from the sting of isolation that might be expected with the move from the savannahs. The American woman, on the other hand, suffers acutely from sheer loneliness and boredom. This was brought home to us vividly one day when a woman asked Yolanda where she went to draw water in her village in America. Yolanda explained that we do not go to a stream, but bring water through a hollow tube, like a long piece of bamboo, right into our houses. The women were not impressed, only dismayed. "But if you don't go with the other women to get water and to bathe, aren't you lonely?" Yolanda thought about it a moment and answered, "Yes, we are."

The modern American woman often confesses to a feeling of entrapment and anomie. She is not only cut off from realizing some of the central values of the culture, such as they are, but she is also cut off from the association of others. Caught in a nuclear family household and in the constant company of small and demanding children, by the time the growth of the young gives her free time, her abilities are irrelevant to the changing world. And she finds not freedom but abandonment in the departure of the children. The family has been her special province, a jurisdiction that she herself may have carved out and jealously preserved, and the husband has long since found other forms of identification and interest. He has a job, he may hunt or fish, he may dabble in politics, or do any of the countless things that American men do; these are the ways they lose, not find, themselves. The culmination of the long and, for the woman, isolating child-rearing process is that the couple discovers suddenly that they have each other, and only each other, on their hands. This is one reason why so many American marriages break up after twenty or twenty-five years. The American family is self-destructing; it preserves little continuity and it has few extensions.

Unlike the Mundurucú woman, her American counterpart has few bases for structuring relations with other women. The middle-class woman may join clubs or become active in one or another form of community service, but these are of a wholly voluntary nature. She may find pleasant company and quite useful work, but it has none of the strong and compelling economic qualities of Mundurucú female cooperation. The American woman's relations with the opposite sex are usually confined to the one-to-one tie with her husband, except for casual business contacts or family friends and neighbors. And in her interaction with the husband, she has little support from others. Her family of origin is scattered and preoccupied with its own concerns; besides, it shares the American view that such problems are best left to the principals. As for other women, she may find a bit of sympathy or counsel, but little in the way of active and practical help. They, too, are locked into their own little worlds of house, husband, and children.

Certainly, nothing even remotely comparable to the unity of Mundurucú women exists to sustain the American woman. For all the low official status of the Mundurucú woman, there is far less wife beating among them than in the average American suburb, and, indeed, there is far less direct domination and coercion of wives by husbands. The Mundurucú females are protected by their unity, while ours are, at best, separate or, at worst, pitted against one another.

This sense of separation, coupled with increasing awareness of the problems of the female role, has been, of course, one of the forces behind the women's movement. Involvement in the cause, or in consciousness-raising sessions and so forth, may produce short-term results, but there is room for doubt that it will be an effective means, in the long run, of unifying women. In this day and age of mass media and instant communications, such movements exhaust themselves with astounding rapidity. They tend to spin out into ideological realms that, as they depart from the normative centers of the society, repel converts and alienate followers, ending in involuted disputes between leaders of empty phalanxes. We cannot even guess what the resolution will be. Mundurucú women find a cohesive core in work, residence, and the opposing unity of their men. American women do not have even the latter rallying point, for the men are as fragmented, confused, and dissatisfied as they are. Most work at jobs they loathe, and if they are tyrants at home, as so many are, their assertiveness can be understood in good part as a result of their marginality in the life of the family.

The American woman, to an even greater extent than the Mundurucú, holds a firm rein on the distribution of love within the family. She is, in the sociological terms of Talcott Parsons, the "expressive leader" of the family, whereas the husband is the "instrumental leader" (Parsons and Bales, 1955, pp., 35–131). This, however, is too simple a dichotomy, for the woman actually has very important and real instrumental, or practical and administrative, functions in the family. She has a good deal to say about the entire pattern of consumption and expenditures, and much of the discipline and direction of the children is within her sphere. Whatever may be the governing power of the female within the family, we should not place affective ascendancy as secondary in significance. In actuality, governmental agencies, as well as wives, have preempted many of the areas of family decision-making through educational laws, social legislation, and the statutes governing family life; the role of *paterfamilias* is no longer a very awesome one. What is left in our society is the hard core of the family, which, as David Schneider tells us (Schneider 1968), is based on enduring, diffuse, and intense attachments—or love.

One characteristic of public life, as opposed to family life, in industrial societies is that social relations are modeled on the bureaucracy. They tend to be narrow and highly specific in content, to involve only small segments of individual identities, and to be emotionally neutral. We like to say, using a sociological term that has entered the vernacular, that we are "alienated." People, especially younger people, express a yearning for deep, "meaningful," complete, undivided, and broad-based attachments with others. What are the models for such ties? The family, of course, with the single difference that many of the young apparently want attachment without designated objects and love without ambivalence—this will be hard to find. But getting back to women, the economic forces that are pushing them out of the house and into the market place are forcing them into the very kinds of ties that we are finding to be depersonalizing, even dehumanizing. And to the extent that the escape from the house is successful, the position of the woman at the affective center of the family will be weakened. Will the woman want to give up this focal and emotionally rich position? Most working women seem to find enormous role conflict between their jobs and their responsibilities as mothers and wives because they attempt to maintain the latter roles intact. To a certain extent they are forced into this bind by the unwillingness of their husbands to modify the traditional male role, but one may well suspect that they are also clinging to their old prerogatives. Like the Mundurucú woman, they want the men to "help" them, but they do not want them to enter deeply into their traditional sphere. Still, the Mundurucú woman is again in the better position, for her work in the public sector reinforces her kinship roles, and her economic contribution leaves her life undivided.

Mundurucú family life has an organic continuity that spans the generations, submerging the ephemeral nuclear unit in the household, and the household in a web of kin affiliations that links the entire membership of the society. The American family lacks this depth and scope; its life course, which requires that the young leave it definitively and permanently, brings inevitable personal tragedy. One would think that, faced with the sharp attenuation of these close ties, the American woman would invest less in them and, given the opposite situation, the Mundurucú woman more, but the reverse is closer to the truth. The circumstances of the tight and isolated nuclear family throw the American mother into a form of intense, and mutual, emotional interdependence with her children in which she alone is the nurturant and loving female. By the same reasoning, she is also the center of ambivalence, and the maturation and separation of the children from her is often traumatic. The Mundurucú woman, however, shares her child-raising obligations with her female housemates after the young have passed early infancy, and by the time they are five or six years old, they require little immediate and continual care.

It is worth stressing that child care among the Mundurucú and most other primitive peoples is quite different than in our own society, a fact that should be self-evident but really does not readily occur to people, even to anthropologists. Mundurucú women, quite simply, do not spend as much time looking after children as American women do, nor are they as preoccupied with their welfare. The reasons for this have less to do with devotion than with the circumstances of life. Mundurucú mothers do not have to prepare their children for school and supervise their studies because there are no schools. Mothers do not watch while their children cross streets or caution them against traffic because there are neither streets nor cars. Women do not warn the young about "strange men" because there are no strangers. They are not obsessed by the life chances of their children because the course of life is predetermined. Piano lessons, orthodonture, Little League, and all the other means by which the modern mother bedevils both herself and her children are absent. By the time the child is six or so, the burden of its protection and socialization shifts to the household, the peer group, and to the community-at-large. Mundurucú women are not "eaten up" by their young, as are American women, and child rearing is less work. Moreover, those children they do tend are often not their own.

This collective responsibility would seem the ideal resolution to the American dilemma of the working mother, having the additional advantage of spreading the child's dependencies and affections. The problem is, however, that the Mundurucú children raised under this regime do not really gain greater emotional security through the presence of a number of surrogate figures. The response to the partial loss of the mother is not compensated by young girls or other women, who have an understandably weaker attachment to the child, and the child responds with every sign of distress. In time, they learn to repress their frustrations, but they also learn that one should not invest too deeply in others. This aspect of the general Oedipal episode is especially acute for the boys, following Freud, for their attachment to the mother is more intense and their loss of her is more permanent and irreversible. The extended family child-caring arrangements do teach a child to spread its affect, but these arrangements also teach them to spread it thinly. There is an air of constraint and reserve that shelters every Mundurucú, especially the men, and a kind of personal disinvolvement and distance that permeates their relations with others.

This is a lesson for modern society, for the fuller incorporation of women into the labor force will inevitably produce an earlier and more abrupt interruption of the mother–child bond—something, of course, that is happening already. It also requires various substitute child-care arrangements, ranging from servants to nurseries and day-care centers, which, however necessary, have a potential for affecting the child's capacity to establish emotionally deep and enduring relationships. This benumbing of love and trust could go far beyond the Mundurucú situation. After all, among the Mundurucú, the mother is never far away, and her surrogates are not strangers.

The status of the Mundurucú woman is quite high when compared with women in other societies. What she lacks in public prestige and respect is more than balanced by autonomy and collective strength. She accepts a secondary role in life, but she defends her integrity with a consciousness that she is not alone. What, then, do we make of the men's house, gang rapes, the ritual instruments of masculine power, and all the other apparatus of male dominance? In 1971, Robert Murphy published a book entitled *The Dialectics of Social Life*, which systematically explored the thesis that there are massive discontinuities and even complete inversions between the ideal norms of societies and the concrete social activities that make up their lives. Though the contrast of Mundurucú female roles and male ideology was not cited as an example, it conforms nicely to the theory. If the men's house symbolism has any function at all in Mundurucú society, it is to conceal from the men the fragility of their own superiority; it perpetuates an illusion. Their position is a vulnerable one. They are transients in their houses and their communities, their own sense of unity is uneasily maintained, and their collegiality has begotten an even stronger unity among the women. Perhaps Margaret Mead (1972) summed it up best when she said, in a passing remark: "If the men really were all that powerful, they wouldn't need such rigmarole."

The sources of male weakness are manifold, many being specific to the social and economic conditions of Mundurucú society. There is one flaw in the male role, however, that is universal and existential. This is that they are born of women, nurtured and loved by women, protected and dominated by women, yet must become men. The male child's relationship to the mother is charged with diffuse sexuality, but beyond that it is the child's earliest mode of identification and sociation, his first breakthrough from his primary narcissism. It is a terrible bond, in the old and literal sense of the word, and it is not easily broken.

In order to understand the male, it is necessary to understand first that the Oedipal transition is never a complete success. He comes through on the other side as a young male, but the achievement is tenuous, and powerful psychic forces continually press to reverse his advance. The reversal threatens much more than a reversion to passivity, for the mother figure is sensed, ambivalently, as a negater and destroyer, as well as a giver, of life. Regression poses the ultimate goal of a return to warm amniotic oblivion. There is, then, in every male a struggle between his maturation and his status as a man, on one hand, and his return to passivity and then to nothingness on the other. The male protects himself against these fears by a number of devices. First, he bands with other males in a self-conscious assertion of independence and strength. The Mundurucú are an extreme example of this, and the extent of the division of the sexes in this particular society can be understood in part as a result of the processes of economic production, specifically hunting and farinha making. But this is hardly the total explanation, for other societies hunt and make farinha without a comparable display of internal solidarity of the sexes and mutual antagonism between them. The residence rule must also be considered, for the resultant unity of the matrilocally linked women contributes to the sex opposition, and the opposition, in turn, feeds back into the division of labor and exacerbates the breach. In this sense, ideology and activity reinforce each other and feed upon each other, even though the ideology actually misrepresents the reality of social action. And to the extent that the solidarity of the males arouses an equal solidarity among the females, it undercuts the very roots of male dominance. It is in this way that human actions undercut human ideas, leaving them as bare forms that find no referents in real life, serving only to endow it with false meanings—the Mundurucú men really believe in their absolute dominance, and this is one resolution to the problem posed by their birth from women.

It would be tempting to speculate that the strong theme of male dominance in Mundurucú culture derives, at least in part, from their warlike past, with its emphasis on valor and ferocity, but the thesis is rather facile. After all, the Mundurucú men are not at all bellicose toward their women in actual fact, and their chauvinism is confined to the ideational realm. Then, too, the equation of male strength in war and at home does not hold up when we consider other societies. The Iroquois woman, for example, had a particularly high status, but their men were among the more intrepid warriors of North America. And in few of the world's societies does the female enjoy such high public esteem as among the Tuareg of sub-Saharan Africa, whom we studied from 1959 to 1960. The Tuareg are camel and goat breeders and caravaneers with a reputation for being among the more warlike of nomadic populations. One of the bases of female prestige in this group is the fact that clusters of sisters and their daughters hold common estates of camels. These estates are originally endowed by the father to his daughters to be held in collectivity with and inherited in turn by their daughters; males do not share in the estates, though they may borrow stock from them, and only male animals may be sold from the herds. In time, the estates build up into very respectable holdings, allowing a female's wealth to frequently be greater than her husband's. Lest this be taken as a quick and easy materialistic explanation, one must ask why do the Tuareg fathers make such bequests? The men answered: "This is how a man shows his respect for his daughters." But, they were queried, why does a man wish to show such respect? "Because we are nobles," they replied. A valiant man shows his self-esteem through his respect for women; there may be a general lesson here.

The Mundurucú men's house and its ideology survived the end of warfare, and we may assume that they are in part a response to the needs of hunting and in part a reaction to female threat; phrased somewhat differently, the need for cooperation in hunting utilizes general human fears in shaping the institution of the men's house. When part of the population shifted over to fishing as the principal protein resource, the men's house organization collapsed. The fears and antagonisms are still there, but they are no longer socially useful and either lie latent or work themselves out in fantasy or interpersonal tensions. To this extent, the Mundurucú of the Cururú River have become a bit like Americans.

The anthropologist Lionel Tiger (1969), in his book *Men in Groups*, maintains that males have an inherent drive toward bonding together, a legacy, supposedly hereditary, of hundreds of thousands of years during which humanity survived by cooperative hunting. This, he believes, explains the greater "clubbiness" of men, whether expressed in the men's houses of primitive people or the propensity of men to dominate modern organizational politics. Our Mundurucú data suggest that Tiger may well be right in pointing to hunting as a source of strong male ties, but they entirely refute his thesis that this is somehow part of the inherited male makeup. Quite to the contrary, the deemphasis of hunting helped bring about the end of male solidarity in a single generation, and, of even greater significance, the cohesiveness of the women is stronger than that of the men. Although the women do not make a display of their unity, as do the men with their own house, their myth, and their rites, it is there in subdued and concrete form. It is present in substance, not in shadow, and the aggressive bravado of the Mundurucú men, like that of men in most places, must be understood as a form of overprotest. Tiger has missed most of the subtle social adjustments by which people love and work, and the result is a thesis that has the distinction of being among the most untenable in the behavioral sciences. To make matters worse, there is no genetic evidence at all to support his view. This recalls the words of our favorite sociologist, Georg Simmel: "We think we actually understand things only when we have traced them back to what we do not understand and cannot understand—to causality, to axioms, to God, to character." (Simmel, 1950, p. xxi)

That the men's house is just as much an expression of

weakness as of superiority has been demonstrated by its symbolism. The women of the myth of the sacred trumpets were once dominant, just as the mother once dominated the male child in individual experience. And just as the individual male must continually assert his masculinity to keep his hard-won status, so also must the men, as a collectivity, guard themselves against the women. The men are equipped by nature with penises and by culture with the secret instruments. Women used to have the latter, and by their sexual dominance, the former as well. Male defensiveness against the women is in good part an expression of castration anxiety. The emasculation theme appears in other myths and even in humor—the residue of permanent damage, albeit a very human one. Mundurucú men are, in a way, the overlords of the women, but it is a suzerainty born of overcompensation for weakness and fear.

The message of these observations for our own society is patent and open. American men do not express themselves or organize their activities in the same way as do Mundurucú men, of course, but they share their basic experience in life. They, too, have vagina dentata jokes and, in more serious moods, they express the same theme to psychoanalysts with regularity. Their antagonisms toward women do not become manifest as group conflict but in husband–wife relations, though their objections to the entry of women into former all-male preserves such as jobs, clubs, and schools do take on a collective character at times. And if they identify with their work and the broader world beyond the household, it is in part because they sense their role in the family to be secondary.

Children, after all, belong in the first place to their mothers; in all but a few societies, the only way that a man can become a father in the sociological sense is by marrying. Women, to the contrary, become legal mothers simply by bearing children.

One may debate the bases of legal parenthood, but women do indeed control the economy of love and they do command the primary loyalty and devotion of their children—the male is just as much a deportee from the house as a refugee from its annoyances. And, just as among the Mundurucú, the show of aggressive masculinity is a means of maintaining the male role, a defense against childhood fears still unconsciously apprehended. There is more at stake than a simple defense of the social superiority of the male, for total concession is a threat, not just to a role, but to the entire evolution of the ego.

One of the more remarkable aspects of the study of the sexes is that we are just beginning to develop an understanding of the biology and neurology of sex differentiation; the so-called "soft" social sciences are far ahead of the "hard" sciences in their analysis of the behavioral differences between males and females. The need for more physiological and genetic research is urgent, for there are universal differences between the sexes that cannot be understood by the study of cultures and social systems. Anthropology does tell us how the inherent characteristics of men and women are shaped and utilized by society, as in Margaret Mead's (1949) classic work, *Male and Female*, but it is essential to understand the raw material on which cultures work. We know that there is great malleability of sex roles, but we also know that the range of variation is limited. It must be remembered, no matter how hackneyed it sounds, that men and women are very, very different. To be more specific, let us state the case in a paradigm: Mundurucú women are different from American women; Mundurucú men are different from American men; both Mundurucú women and American women are different from their respective men; *but* Mundurucú women are, in essence, more similar to American women than to Mundurucú men, as are, also, the men to the men. Just as all mankind shares a common humanity, so also are there both a sisterhood and a brotherhood of humankind.

These universal, and elusive, differences may not, however, be wholly genetic and hereditary in origin, for heredity and culture do not monopolize the field of explanation. There are, we have stressed, fundamental ontological differences between the sexes—conditions of simple *being*—based in the first instance on anatomical distinctions but not immediately a part of them. One of these is the quandary of the child forced into maleness, an experience that is as universal as the Oedipal syndrome. The other is a point so obvious that we have barely mentioned it—this is that only women can bear and suckle children. The child is the prisoner of this experience, but so also is the woman the prisoner of the child. The male escapes from his shackles in part by a domination of the symbolic realm of culture—a sort of collective fetishism—but the woman remains the custodian and perpetuator of life itself. Those who would question the worth of this trust must first ask if there is anything else in human existence that has an ultimate meaning.

Bibliography

Agassiz, Louis. 1868. *A Journey in Brazil*. Boston: Ticknor and Fields.

Boyer, Ruth M. 1962. *Social Structure and Socialization Among the Apaches of the Mescalero Indian Reservation*. Unpublished Ph.D. dissertation, University of California, Berkeley.

Burkhalter, Brian. 1983. *Amazon Gold Rush: Markets and the Mundurucú*. Unpublished Ph.D. dissertation, Columbia University.

Gluckman, Max. 1963. "Gossip and Scandal." *Current Anthropology*, Vol. 4, No. 3, pp. 307–16.

Lowie, Robert H. 1920. *Primitive Society*. New York: Liveright.

Mead, Margaret. 1949. *Male and Female*. New York: Morrow.

—— 1972. Verbal communication.

Murphy, Robert F. 1956. "Matrilocality and Patrilineality in Mundurucú Society." *American Anthropologist*, Vol. 50, pp. 414–34.

—— 1957. "Intergroup Hostility and Social Cohesion." *American Anthropologist*, Vol. 59, pp. 1018–35.

—— 1958. "Mundurucú Religion." *University of California Publications in American Archaeology and Ethnology*, Vol. 49, No. 1. Berkeley and Los Angeles: University of California Press.

—— 1959. "Social Structure and Sex Antagonism." *Southwestern Journal of Anthropology*, Vol. 15, No. 1, pp. 89–98.

—— 1960. *Headhunter's Heritage: Social and Economic Change Among the Mundurucú Indians*. Berkeley and Los Angeles: University of California Press.

—— 1971. *The Dialectics of Social Life: Alarms and Excursions in Anthropological Theory*. New York: Basic Books.

Murphy, Yolanda. 1972. *The Mundurucú Women of the Village of Cabruá*. Unpublished M.A. thesis, Columbia University.

Parsons, Talcott, and Robert F. Bales. 1955. *Family, Socialization and Interaction Process*. Glencoe, Ill.: The Free Press.

Schneider, David M. 1968. *American Kinship: A Cultural Account.* Englewood Cliffs, N.J.: Prentice-Hall.

Shapiro, Judith. 1972. *Sex Roles and Social Structure Among the Yanamamo Indians of Northern Brazil.* Unpublished Ph.D. dissertation, Columbia University.

Simmel, Georg. 1964. *The Sociology of Georg Simmel* (translated and edited by Kurt Wolff.) New York: The Free Press of Glencoe.

Steward, Julian H. 1955. *Theory of Culture Change.* Urbana: University of Illinois Press.

Tiger, Lionel. 1969. *Men in Groups.* New York: Random House.

Index